The New Imperialists

The New Imperialists

IDEOLOGIES OF EMPIRE

Edited by Colin Mooers

ONEWORLD

OXFORD

THE NEW IMPERIALISTS: IDEOLOGIES OF EMPIRE

Oneworld Publications
(Sales and Editorial)
185 Banbury Road
Oxford OX2 7AR
England
http://www.oneworld-publications.com

ISBN-10: 1–85168–462–X
ISBN-13: 978–1–85168–462–5

Cover design by Mungo Designs
Typeset by Forewords, Oxford
Printed and bound by The Maple-Vail Book Manufacturing
Group, Braintree, MA, USA

CONTENTS

Contributors   vii

Acknowledgements   xi

Introduction: The New Watchdogs   1
Colin Mooers

1   Democracy as Ideology of Empire   9
    Ellen Meiksins Wood

2   After the Fact:
    Reading Tocqueville in Baghdad   25
    Aziz Al-Azmeh

3   Tortured Civilizations: Islam and the West   45
    Tariq Ali

4   Gender, Political Islam, and Imperialism   61
    Shahrzad Mojab

5   Imperial Narcissism: Michael Ignatieff's Apologies for Empire   87
    David McNally

6   Nostalgia for Empire: Revising Imperial History for
    American Power   111
    Colin Mooers

7 When Might is Right: Ancient Lamentations, Straussian
   Ministrations, and American Dispensations   137
   Thom Workman

8 Praising Empire: Neoliberalism under Pax Americana   167
   Adam Hanieh

9 American Soft Power, or, American Cultural Imperialism? 199
   Tanner Mirrlees

10 U.N. Imperialism: Unleashing Entrepreneurship in the
   Developing World   229
   Paul Cammack

   Index   261

CONTRIBUTORS

Tariq Ali is a novelist, historian, and playwright and commentator on the current situation in the Middle East. He has written over a dozen books on world history and politics including the recent bestsellers *Clash of Fundamentalisms: Crusades, Jihads and Modernity*, *Bush in Babylon: The Recolonisation of Iraq*, and *Rough Music: Blair/Bombs/Baghdad/Terror*. He is also the author of five novels and scripts for both stage and screen. The first novel of the Islam Quintet, *Shadows of the Pomegranate Tree*, was awarded the Archbishop San Clemente del Instituto Rosalia de Castro Prize for Best Foreign Language Fiction published in Spain in 1994 and, like the *Book of Saladin*, has been translated into several languages. He is an editor of the *New Left Review* and writes regularly for the *London Review of Books*.

Aziz Al-Azmeh is a Distinguished Visiting Professor, Humanities Center, Central European University, Budapest and Fellow at the Institute for Advanced Study, Budapest. He has taught and published widely in both Arabic and English on Arab history and culture, Islamic political thought, Middle East studies, and the work of Ibn Khaldun. His published works in English include *Arabic Thought and Islamic Societies*, *Muslim Kingship: Power and the Sacred in Muslim, Christian and Pagan Polities*, and *Islams and Modernities* as well as numerous articles in scholarly journals, edited collections, and newspapers.

Paul Cammack is Professor of Politics and Head of the Department of Politics and Philosophy at Manchester Metropolitan University, and author of *Capitalism and Democracy in the Third World*. He has written widely on Latin American and Third World politics and the politics of governance, most recently in *New Left Review, Historical Materialism,* the *Socialist Register,* and *New Political Economy.*

Adam Hanieh is a graduate student in the Department of Political Science, York University, Toronto. His research interests include political economy, Middle East and Palestinian politics, and the theory and practice of imperialism. He is co-author of *Stolen Youth: The Politics of Israel's Detention of Palestinian Children* (Pluto Press, 2004).

David McNally is currently Chair of the Department of Political Science at York University in Toronto, Canada. His research interests include globalization and global justice movements; concepts of freedom and democracy in political thought; radical theories of language and culture; Marxism, feminism and anti-racism; and radical political economy. His published works include *Another World Is Possible: Globalization and Anti-Capitalism, Bodies of Meaning: Essays on Language, Labor and Liberation, Against the Market: Political Economy, Market Socialism and the Marxist Critique,* and *Political Economy and the Rise of Capitalism.* He has published widely in *Historical Materialism, Studies in Political Economy, New Politics,* and the *History of Political Thought.*

Tanner Mirrlees is at York and Ryerson University's Joint Program of Communication and Culture, where he is working on the history, present, ideologies, and effects of U.S. foreign cultural policy and American cultural imperialism.

Shahrzad Mojab teaches in the Department of Adult Education and Counselling Psychology at OISE/UT and is the Director of Women and Gender Studies Institute, University of Toronto. Her areas of research and teaching are critical and feminist pedagogy; immigrant women and skilling; women, state, globalization and citizenship; women, war, violence and learning; and comparative analysis of lifelong learning theory and practice. She is the editor of *Women of a Non-State Nation: The Kurds* (2001, repr. 2003); co-editor with Himani Bannerji and Judy Whitehead of *Of Property and Propriety: The Role of Gender and Class in Imperialism and Nationalism;* and co-editor with Nahla Abdo of *Violence in the Name of Honour: Theoretical and Political Challenges* (2004). She is currently conducting research on women, war, diaspora, and learning;

women political prisoners in the Middle East; and war and transnational women's organizations (Women, War, Diaspora, and Learning: Research Resources: www.utoronto.ca/wwdl).

Colin Mooers is Chair of the Department of Politics and School of Public Administration at Ryerson University, Toronto. He is also affiliated to the York-Ryerson Graduate Programme in Communication and Culture. His has written on the public sphere; the politics of social movements; and capitalism and citizenship. He is the author of *The Making of Bourgeois Europe: Absolutism, Revolution and the Rise of Capitalism in England, France and Germany* (Verso, 1991) and a contributing editor of *Restructuring and Resistance: Canadian Public Policy in the Age of Global Capitalism* (Fernwood 2000).

Ellen Meiksins Wood was for many years Professor of Political Science at York University, Toronto. She has published widely on the nature and history of capitalism, ancient Greek democracy, and the history of political thought, ancient and modern. Among her books are *The Pristine Culture of Capitalism, Peasant-Citizen and Slave, Democracy Against Capitalism, The Origin of Capitalism: A Longer View*, and most recently, *Empire of Capital*.

Thom Workman writes and teaches in the area of critical political economy and political philosophy at the University of New Brunswick, Fredericton, New Brunswick, Canada. He is currently preparing a manuscript on the distinctly modern reading of the ancient Greek historian Thucydides, a study that forms part of a wider research project that explores the relationship between the intellectual foundation of modernity and contemporary forms of political irrationalism.

ACKNOWLEDGEMENTS

In a time of universal deceit, telling the truth is a revolutionary act.
(George Orwell, *Nineteen Eighty-Four*)

Driving to a university event one evening in early 2003, I listened on the radio with mounting frustration as the Canadian liberal intellectual Michael Ignatieff calmly spun yet another of his equivocal rationalizations for the impending invasion of Iraq. On my arrival, I complained to colleagues that such apologias for war and empire seemed to be receiving so little public challenge. To my (probably naïve) surprise, I was asked: what was the alternative? Hadn't Saddam Hussein terrorized the Iraqi people for decades? Wasn't the spread of democracy and human rights worth defending? Wouldn't women be better off in a liberated Iraq? Liberal imperialism, it seemed, had struck a chord far beyond what I had imagined. From this encounter, the idea for this book was born.

However, I also knew that on my own I could not marshal the necessary resources to challenge the many books and articles which sought to rationalize and justify "the new imperialism." An edited collection seemed an obvious solution. Therefore, my first debt of gratitude is to the authors, many of whom put aside other pressing projects to work on their contributions for this volume. I would especially like to thank Victoria Roddam, the commissioning editor at Oneworld, who pressed me to submit the initial proposal and to David McNally for convincing me of the urgency and importance of such a book. I am grateful to *The Walrus* magazine for allowing me to publish a revised version of Tariq Ali's "Tortured Civilizations" which appeared in their September 2004 edition and to the Central European University, Budapest, for allowing me to print a revised version Aziz Al-Azmeh's "After the Fact: Reading

Tocqueville in Baghdad" which appeared in their occasional paper series in 2004.

My greatest debt of thanks must go to Kate Zieman. Without her superb research and editorial skills this book could not have been completed in the timely manner which it has been. And finally, thanks to Marnie Fleming for her patience and friendly criticism of my own contributions. This volume is dedicated to her.

INTRODUCTION: THE NEW WATCHDOGS

Colin Mooers

> In this atmosphere of sickness, thoughtful men – members of the ruling stratum – are struggling to recapture that old sense of well-being and that peace of mind and that old certitude regarding the future of Western Civilization. They write books and reports, they give sermons, they conduct conferences and symposia, and they attribute almost everything that is happening in the world to diverse forms of temporary insanity (all curable) and diverse false opinions (all easily corrected). . . . The advent of disorder has shattered the serenity and the security of the powers that be. These powers are now seeking to regain their lost paradise.
>
> (Paul Nizan, *The Watchdogs*[1])

Nizan wrote *Les Chiens de garde*, his philosophical tirade against the complacency of the French intellectual establishment, shortly before he was killed at Dunkirk in 1940. In Nizan's view, the retreat of the philosophical elite into idealist obscurantism had disarmed an entire generation against the catastrophe that was about to envelope it. First published in 1960 at the height of France's bitter colonial war in Algeria (which claimed the lives of 1.5 million Algerians, 27,000 French soldiers and 4,000 French colonials), Nizan's book was incendiary. Its implicit target was a new generation of French intellectuals: those who constructed baroque apologies for colonialism or rationalized the murderous methods used by French forces during the eight-year-long Algerian war of independence.[2]

Times have changed, but not nearly enough. The old colonial imperialism, of which Algeria was a remnant, had its roots in the nineteenth century. Its apologists could still employ a language redolent of the racial and cultural superiority of the time; the "civilizing mission" of the Christianized West was still thought by many to constitute the "white man's burden" in the non-European world. Although a similar "civilizational" rhetoric exists today, it is no longer as easy to justify imperial conquest by resort to the overtly racist pieties of the past. If American generals still study French counter-insurgency methods in Algeria for pointers on how to combat the Iraqi insurgency,[3] they have had to find new methods to vie for the hearts and minds of those they wish to subdue. This is largely an achievement of the anti-colonial struggles of the second half of the last century. One of the many advantages of living in a "postcolonial" world is that the collective memory of the anti-colonial struggle is deeply ingrained in the consciousness of millions throughout the world.

Because of this fact, contemporary imperialism has had to drape itself in new ideological clothes; its defenders must now speak the language of democracy and human rights; of freedom and dignity; of inclusiveness and respect for difference; of gender equality and the alleviation of poverty; of good governance and sustainable development. Alongside these decidedly modernist tropes, others have appealed to the timeless verities of human nature or culture to justify the inevitability of war and empire. Still others have touted the supposedly beneficent legacy of older imperialisms. Such juxtapositions are in keeping with "a deep and perplexing doubleness" of the new imperialism: a primal military atavism reminiscent of older forms of empire combined with the "spectacular" deployment of up-to-the-minute technologies of mass deception and distraction.[4] Taken as a whole, the new ideologies of empire express the same contradictory combination of the retrogressive and the modern: of civilizational clashes and democratic ideals; of virulent racism and postmodern multiculturalism; of gender equality and religious oppression; of old-fashioned propaganda and newfangled forms of "soft power"; of torture and human rights.

Against this backdrop, it would be easy to lose sight of the difference between ideologies and lies. However, ideologies are different from lies even if they are sometimes (as in the case of Iraq) bolstered by lies. For ideologies to work, they must speak to some genuine longing on the part of those who believe in them, however distorted these desires have become by the realities of exploitation and domination. Hence the talk of democracy and freedom. But, like lies, ideologies often involve a good deal of self-delusion on the part of those who traffic in them – how else to explain the debacle of post-invasion Iraq? The *systematic* character of imperial self-delusion is perhaps best captured in U.S. Secretary of Defense Donald Rumsfeld's tortured explication of military ignorance:

> As we know, there are known knowns. There are things we know we know. We also know there are known unknowns. That is to say, we know there are some things we do not know. But there are also the unknown unknowns, the ones we don't know we don't know.[5]

As Slavoj Zizek observes, the one category that Rumsfeld failed to mention were the "unknown knowns": beliefs or practices – like the horrors of Abu Ghraib – which must be quickly repressed since their knowledge is too much for consciousness to bear. Zizek contends that the real danger for the American empire lies not in the threats which lie undiscovered, but "in the disavowed beliefs, suppositions and obscene practices we pretend not to know about."[6]

Be that as it may, a good deal of *conscious* effort has been expended to justify and normalize the "new imperialism." It is a mark of the times in which we live that the discourse of empire and imperialism – not so long ago considered an antique preoccupation of the Left – has been embraced by mainstream intellectuals from across the political spectrum. But, before examining these apologias in detail in the essays that follow, we need to ask: what has prompted this sudden desire to reclaim the language of empire? What changes in the global balance of forces account for this momentous ideological shift?

To answer these questions we must begin with what is "new" about the "new imperialism." First, it would be a mistake to view the recent U.S. turn to "preemptive" military action solely in terms of a reaction to the events of September 11th, or, more sinisterly, as the pre-planned goal of bellicose neoconservatives. That the Bush administration is more willing to resort to large-scale military intervention than previous administrations is undoubtedly true. However, to see this as a fundamental change in the nature of U.S. imperialism would be an exaggeration. The U.S.A. has a long and unbroken history of imperial conquest stretching back more than two centuries. It would be equally one-sided to see the invasion of Iraq as *only* about oil. Control of Middle Eastern oil reserves would give the U.S.A. an indisputable advantage over potential rivals, notably the fast rising powers of Asia. But if oil is a crucial part of the equation, the Iraq war is also part of a much wider "radical, punitive, 'extra-economic' restructuring of the conditions necessary for expanded profitability – paving the way, in short, for new rounds of American-led dispossession and capital accumulation ... a new form of military neoliberalism."[7] But, while America is still the preeminent military power on the planet, its superiority in firepower vastly exceeds its economic supremacy.[8] It is this imbalance between its economic and its military might that helps account for the shift to a more aggressive military posture. Thus, the drive of neoconservatives toward a more coercive orientation in international relations is intended to send a message not only to so-called "rogue" regimes and "failed" states, but also to its major economic competitors. In other words, while proximate causes are important in accounting for the emergence of the new imperialism, we need to situate these changes within the deep structural shifts in global capitalism that have occurred over the past two decades.

The neoliberal revolution that began in the 1980s represents an attempt to address a persistent problem for capitalism, namely its tendency toward overcapacity and overaccumulation – an issue which is particularly acute for the U.S. economy. Driving this process was the need to locate new sites of capital accumulation and new markets for commodities. In the 1990s the search for new sources of accumulation was highly uneven and regionally specific, hardly captured by the market utopianism of the term "globalization." In the advanced Western and Asian economies, it involved an intensification of commodification as new areas of private and public life were colonized by market forces while parts of the Keynesian welfare state were privatized or downsized. In the former "communist" countries, the advent of the free market meant the wholesale privatization of state assets and the erection of a kind of gangster-capitalism often abetted by former "communist" apparatchiks and their new allies in Western financial institutions. In the global South, the imposition of neoliberalism combined the privatization of state-run enterprises left over from the *dirigisme* of the 1960s and 1970s with a virulent new process of primitive accumulation or "accumulation through dispossession."[9]

For Marx, the "secret" of the primitive accumulation of capital lay in the fact that it was, above all, a *social* process through which the direct producers were (often forcibly) separated from access to the means of production and thus pushed into the ranks of wage labor. During the rise of English capitalism, this involved the enclosure of what had been formerly common lands accessible to peasant communities and their conversion into private property concentrated in the hands of a new class of capitalist farmers. "And this history," Marx writes, "the history of their expropriation, is written in the annals of mankind in letters of blood and fire."[10] David Harvey has shown that primitive accumulation is not a once and for all process restricted to the origins of capitalism, but an ongoing imperative made necessary by the need to find new sources and sites of capital accumulation. Accumulation through dispossession involves the colonization, expropriation, and enclosure of preexisting societal and cultural forms. Predation, fraud, and force are still commonly used to privatize such things as water resources or to enforce proletarianization. To these, over the past two decades, have been added an array of financial instruments of dispossession such as hedge funds, currency devaluations, asset stripping, and credit and stock manipulations. In conjunction with these changes, a new set of global institutions have been established to regulate and fortify market relations between states and regional trade blocs. Whatever the means, the outcome has been to unleash a new wave of "enclosing the commons."[11]

The current round of imperialism, therefore, has as its goal the export and entrenchment of capitalist social-property relations throughout the world; it is about the universalization of capitalism. And just as in earlier phases of capitalism, state military power has been central to the imposition of this new stage of primitive accumulation and enclosure. However, if state military power is still essential for the imposition of capitalism in some parts of the world, and if its spectacular display remains vital to U.S. global hegemony, there is an important sense in which the dynamics of imperialism have changed markedly. Unlike its earlier forms, imperialism today no longer relies on direct colonization. Nor does military rivalry between states over resources and territory exist on the scale that it did in the time of Lenin and Bukharin. But if imperialism is no longer defined by formal empire and military competition, how have militarism and capitalist imperatives become so closely linked in the new imperialism? The simple answer is that in a world comprised of limited territorial states and the global reach of capital, the use of overwhelming military might becomes the only way of policing capitalist interests. When terrorist violence beyond the state is thrown into the mix, the problem becomes even more intractable. For these reasons, a more or less *permanent* state of warfare – war without end – has become definitive of twenty-first-century capitalism: "Boundless domination of a global economy, and of the multiple states that administer it, requires military action without end, in purpose or time."[12]

If a state of permanent war has become the "new normal" of our time, it is clear why the discourse of empire has become so vital to those who defend this new order of things: the domestication of war and imperial conquest has become an urgent ideological imperative.

The essays compiled here are intended as a challenge to these new ideologies of empire; their goal is to engage a broad range of the apologies for the new imperialism that have appeared in recent years.

In the opening chapter, Ellen Meiksins Wood discusses why the new imperialism also requires a new concept of democracy, one that further removes the economic interests of capital from popular control and places the state more firmly than ever in the service of capital. Through a contemporary reading of Tocqueville's views on American democracy, Aziz Al-Azmeh explores the irrational and illiberal roots of American political culture and their contemporary expression in U.S. attitudes toward the Arab world. Al-Azmeh warns of a deep compatibility between the Puritan communalism and libertarian multiculturalism that informs American thinking and the religious and communal sectarianism now being entrenched in the political and constitutional structures of the "new" Iraq. In chapter 3, Tariq Ali challenges the rhetoric of "civilizational clashes" put forward by Samuel Huntington and others, and its long-term consequences for the Middle East. Shahrzad Mojab debunks the claim that Western imperialism can end the religious and social oppression of women, arguing that the twin realities of imperialist war and religious fundamentalism threaten to worsen dramatically the situation of women in the Middle East. David McNally, in chapter 5, deconstructs Michael Ignatieff's concept of "imperialism lite," revealing its fetishistic foundations. Ignatieff's imperialist narcissism, McNally argues, blinds him to the contradictions of a philosophical "ethics" which excuses torture and tolerates systematic human rights violations as "lesser evils." Chapter 6 critiques the rehabilitation of British imperial history by the conservative historian Niall Ferguson and his call for a return to formal empire as the only viable imperialist solution in a world order of limited states and the unlimited reach of capital. In chapter 7, Thom Workman traces the philosophical lineage of the neoconservatives who dominate the Bush administration, many of whom studied with the philosopher Leo Strauss. Strauss's tendentious interpretation of ancient texts, Workman contends, is key to understanding the justification for war and empire that informs American foreign policy. Adam Hanieh examines the influence of the neoliberal economist Deepak Lal's *In Praise of Empires*. Hanieh demonstrates that Lal's ideas about empire should be understood in the context of the material and social forces now shaping global capitalism. In chapter 9, Tanner Mirrlees exposes the new discourse of U.S. "soft power" as a disguise for a renovated, high-tech form of cultural imperialism. In the final chapter, Paul Cammack argues that over the last five years the U.N.-sponsored Millennium Development Goals have been transformed into a vehicle for a new imperialist project involving the export of capitalism to the developing world.

As these essays make clear, the rationalizations on offer for the new imperialism, like the system they seek to defend, are riven by deep contradictions. That such contradictions should exist is inscribed in the nature of ideology. It is the task of ideological critique – and therefore of this volume – to help lay bare these antinomies and to make visible that which the apologists for imperialism – the new watchdogs of our time – would prefer to leave in the shadows.

NOTES

1. Paul Nizan, *The Watchdogs: Philosophers and the Established Order*, trans. Paul Fitingoff (New York: Monthly Review Press, 1972), p. 117.

2. Among this group was the then French interior minister and future socialist president François Mitterand, whose response to the National Liberation Front's (F.L.N.) offer of talks was, "the only possible negotiation is war." The Algerian-born philosopher and novelist Albert Camus, although troubled by the French use of torture, ultimately supported the war against the Algerian rebels. Ahmed Ben Bella, one of the leaders of the Algerian liberation struggle, now in his late eighties, is still actively involved in the Middle Eastern anti-war movement against the U.S. occupation in Iraq.

3. Gillo Pontecorvo's brilliant anti-colonial film *The Battle of Algiers* is required viewing by American counter-insurgency experts in the U.S. Defense Department. See John Cherian, "Remembering a Revolution," *Frontline*, 21:24 (20 November–3 December,

2004), p. 4. http://www.flonet.com/fl2124/stories/20041203000806300.htm (accessed 25 July 2005).

4. Ian Boal, T. J. Clarke, Joseph Mathews, and Michael Watts, *Afflicted Powers: Capital and Spectacle in a New Age of War* (London: Verso, 2005), p. 14.

5. Donald Rumsfeld, Department of Defense news briefing, 12 February 2002, quoted in Hart Seeley, "The Poetry of D. H. Rumsfeld," http://slate.msn.com/id/2081042/ (accessed 16 August 2005).

6. Slavoj Zizek, *Iraq: The Borrowed Kettle* (London: Verso, 2004), p. 10.

7. Retort: Boal et al., *Afflicted Powers*, p. 72.

8. Whether or not this imbalance signals an actual decline in U.S. economic power is a complicated and still unresolved question.

9. David Harvey, *The New Imperialism* (Oxford: Oxford University Press, 2003), pp. 137–182.

10. Karl Marx, *Capital*, Vol. 1 (New York: Vintage Books, 1977), p. 875.

11. Harvey, *New Imperialism*, p. 148.

12. Ellen Meiksins Wood, *Empire of Capital* (London: Verso, 2003), p. 144.

1

DEMOCRACY AS IDEOLOGY OF EMPIRE*

Ellen Meiksins Wood

In his second inaugural address, George W. Bush told the world that the U.S. mission – a divinely inspired mission – was to bring freedom and democracy to the darkest corners of the earth and to abolish tyranny. Many people find something deeply incongruous between that mission statement and the realities on the ground. But the association of democracy with imperialist aggression is not just the madness of George W. Bush. George Junior is certainly not the first U.S. president to justify imperialist interventions on the grounds of a mission to defend and spread democracy. The association of imperialism and democracy seems to be a deeply rooted American idea, and many Americans firmly believe that this represents their country's manifest destiny.

FREEDOM, EQUALITY, IMPERIALISM

In the wake of 9/11, at the time of the war in Afghanistan, sixty U.S. academics issued a statement called "What We're Fighting For: A Letter from America." The signatories included some of the usual suspects, like Samuel Huntington and Francis Fukuyama, but also others whom we do not automatically think of as right-wing ideologues – such as the social democrat Michael Walzer. It is probably fair to say that their statement represented the views of a reasonably wide intellectual and political spectrum – at least by U.S. standards – from mildly left liberal to more-

---

* This chapter is based on a talk given at New York University in April 2005.

or-less respectable conservatism; and it is probably as civilized a defense of U.S. military intervention as we are likely to find.

The letter opens with a statement of the fundamental values that, according to the signatories, represent the best of the United States, the values for which they went to war:

> We affirm five fundamental truths that pertain to all people without distinction:
>
> 1. *All human beings are born free and equal in dignity and rights.*
>
> 2. *The basic subject of society is the human person, and the legitimate role of government is to protect and help to foster the conditions for human flourishing.*
>
> 3. *Human beings naturally desire to seek the truth about life's purposes and ultimate ends.*
>
> 4. *Freedom of conscience and religious freedom are inviolable rights of the human person.*
>
> 5. *Killing in the name of God is contrary to faith in God and is the greatest betrayal of the universality of religious faith.*
>
> We fight to defend ourselves and to defend these universal principles.

Most of us would find nothing objectionable in this list. We might even find it thoroughly admirable. The question is how we can square it with U.S. military adventures. We may subscribe to the values in that list and for that very reason regard the war in Afghanistan, to say nothing of the war in Iraq, as clearly imperialist. We might find it hard to understand how these values could be grounds for an essentially imperialist war, especially the first principle about the freedom and equality of human beings. It is especially puzzling when considered against the background of actual U.S. foreign policy, which has generally shown little inclination to support democratic regimes in its dependencies, to say nothing of the Bush regime's assaults on democracy in its own backyard and at home. It becomes even more confusing when the letter goes on to argue that this war – and what its signatories say applies to the whole so-called war against terrorism – meets the conditions of "just war." It is, they say, a just war first and foremost because it meets the condition that "wars of aggression and aggrandizement are never acceptable."

This may seem more than a little tasteless, under the circumstances, with the Bush regime hardly disguising its intentions of maintaining U.S. hegemony in the region by acquiring strategic positions in Afghanistan and Iraq. But however incongruous it may be, it is worth asking why such incongruities seem plausible to decent and intelligent people. How is it that freedom, equality, and universal human dignity can seem a convincing justification for imperialism and war?

The answer begins with capitalism. This is a system of appropriation that does not depend on legal inequalities or the inequality of political rights. Appropriating and producing classes can be free and equal under the law; the relation between them is supposed to be a contractual agreement between free and equal individuals; and even universal suffrage is possible without fundamentally affecting the economic powers of capital. In fact, capital benefits from the disappearance of the old formal differences among human beings, because it thrives on reducing all types of people to interchangeable units of labour. (I should add here that this has had some paradoxical consequences, one of which is the emergence in the nineteenth century of a uniquely rabid form of racism, which made it possible to exclude some people from the natural universe of human freedom and equality by marking them out as something less than fully human.)

Capital's ability to dispense with non-economic powers means that its exploitative powers can coexist with liberal democracy, which would have been impossible in any system where exploitation depended on a monopoly of political rights. And the reason this is possible is that capitalism has created new, purely economic compulsions: the propertylessness of workers, which compels them to sell their labour power in exchange for a wage, and the compulsions of the market, which regulate the economy. Both capital and labour can have democratic rights in the political sphere without completely transforming the relation between them in a separate economic sphere; and much of human life is determined in that economic sphere, outside the reach of democratic accountability. Capitalism can, therefore, coexist with the ideology of freedom and equality in a way that no other system of domination can. In fact, the idea that capitalists and workers alike are free and equal has become the most important ideological support of capitalism. Formal democracy, with its ideology of freedom, equality, and classlessness, has become one of the most effective mechanisms in sustaining and repro-ducing capitalist class relations.

On the face of it, the separation of economic and political spheres should make class inequality more starkly visible by highlighting the tensions between formal equality in one sphere and substantive inequality in the other. But the disappearance of legally and politically defined class inequalities has actually made class relations in capitalism less rather than more transparent. In feudalism, for example, there was little chance of mistaking the exploitative relation between lords and their legally dependent serfs – not just because the serf was transparently giving his labour, its products, or rent directly to the lord, but because the inequality between them was explicit in law. In capitalism, not only does payment go from employer to worker, rather than the other way round, there is also no legal or political recognition of their inequality. In fact, there is a constant emphasis on their equality.

This is a real ideological advantage for capital, but it also creates its own distinctive problems. When capital finds itself having to justify exploitation and domination, it cannot really do it by invoking any principles of inequality, so it has to adopt some fairly complicated strategies. This is true of relations between capital and labour on the domestic front, but we are particularly interested here in what it means for imperialist ideology.

IDEOLOGIES OF CAPITALIST IMPERIALISM

In the early days of capitalist imperialism, when it was still mainly a question of outright colonial settlement, there was one particularly inter-esting theoretical development, namely justifying imperialism by means of a theory of property. At first, the idea was simply that when land was not already occupied, it was available to be claimed by colonists who would make it fruitful, even without the consent of local inhabitants. This idea appears, for instance, in Thomas More's *Utopia*. But soon the argument became more aggressive: even occupied land was not real property and it was available for expropriation if it was not being used fruitfully enough – which meant essentially that it was not being used to produce profitably in a context of well-developed commerce. Something like this argument already appears in the justification of English imperi-alism in Ireland in the early seventeenth century. But it gets its most systematic theorization in John Locke's political theory, where the right of property is based on the productive and profitable use of property, in other words, on the production of exchange value.

So now it was possible to defend colonization in an almost impersonal way, entirely bypassing the question of rule and domination. It was just a matter of applying the same principles to colonial territories as the English were applying to property in their own domestic economy, where the principles of productivity and profit were beginning to trump all other property rights. Colonial territory was just like common or waste land in England, available to be enclosed by those engaged in profitable commercial agriculture. This was an application of capitalist principles, the principles of competition, accumulation, and profit-maximization by means of increasing productivity. It expressed a wholly new morality, in which exchange value took priority over all other goods, making possible the justification of everything from exploitation and expropriation to ecological destruction – all in the name of freedom and equality.

But the justification of imperialism in the form of a theory of property represents a specific moment in the history of imperialism, and it would soon prove inadequate. Capitalism would eventually develop to a point where colonization was no longer necessary or desirable. The new imperialism – which really only emerged in the twentieth century, and really only in the second half – was, and is, a different story. There came a time when capitalism could impose its powerful economic pressures on the whole world, so that it had no need to impose direct colonial rule. It should be said that this took a long time. Even in the British Empire, the economic power of capital and market imperatives were never enough; and in India, the imperial power even had to return to something more like a pre-capitalist empire, a territorial empire ruled by a military dicta-torship. The fully developed capitalist empire, which depends above all on economic imperatives, is basically the story of U.S. imperialism.

On the whole, the U.S.A. has preferred to avoid colonial entangle-ments and instead has maintained a so-called informal empire, imposing market forces and manipulating them to the advantage of U.S. capital. We all know that this would have been impossible without the support of military power, but that power has not generally been used for the old imperial purpose of capturing and holding colonial territories. Its job has been more diffuse and open-ended than that: to police the global system to make it safe for the movements of capital.

I shall return to that point in a moment. The question here has to do with the ideological problems thrown up by this new kind of imperialism. How does one theorize and justify a non-colonial, non-territorial empire? How does one explain and defend exploitation of people and resources that requires no direct rule or territorial expansion, and where there is no need for personal rule or the seizure of property?

The objective of this new empire, first and foremost, is free access for capital, and U.S. capital in particular, to anywhere in the world – what is euphemistically called openness. This does not mean colonial occupation. It does not mean direct rule of colonial peoples. And, in spite of what we are repeatedly told by theorists of globalization, it does not mean the disappearance of more-or-less sovereign territorial states. On the contrary, it requires a stable global system of multiple states to maintain the kind of order and predictability that capitalism – more than any other social form – needs.

Open access for capital also does not mean a truly integrated global economy. It is true that the world's economies are interdependent, if that means that they are all subject to pressures imposed by global capital; but openness and so-called free trade are one-sided. Global capital actually benefits from the unevenness of national economies, which allows it to exploit cheap labour and resources, while at the same time blocking competition from those low-cost economies. It also benefits from controlling the movements of labour. What global capital needs is not a global state but an orderly global system of territorial states, which maintain economic and political order within territorial boundaries and at the same time permit and facilitate the penetration of those boundaries by global capital, without presenting any dangerous challenges or competition.

How, then, is this global empire described and justified by its proponents? The new imperialism is not easily amenable to any of the old imperialist justifications. For one thing, it depends not simply on justifying imperial domination but on denying its existence altogether. Up to a point, it achieves this effect in more or less the same way that capitalism disguises class domination. Class relations between capital and labour lack transparency, taking the form of consensual, contractual relations between formally free and equal individuals, mediated by the ostensibly impersonal forces of the market. Similarly, exploitation in the new imperialism lacks the transparency of colonial rule. But to say that capitalist imperialism is not imperialism because it does not involve direct colonial rule is like saying that exploitation of labour by capital is not class exploitation. With capitalist market imperatives at its disposal, global capital can impose its domination without direct rule. Instead of using state power to impose direct dominion, it thrives in a context of many sovereign states. There is an analogy here between citizens in a capitalist democracy and states in a global capitalist empire. The democratic polity is made up of formally free and equal civic individuals, just as the global order is made up of formally free and equal sovereign states. And just as citizenship tends to mask class domination in capitalism, legal state sovereignty tends to mask imperial domination.

But this is not quite enough to justify the new imperialism. Because it depends on the imposition and maintenance of capitalist economic imperatives, it also requires a justification of this economic order itself. Since economic imperialism in this sense only really came into its own in the latter part of the twentieth century, the ideological strategy is still in a process of development. But its general outlines are by now fairly clear. The main strategy in recent years has been to treat the global capitalist economy as an impersonal, natural phenomenon and a historical inevitability, an idea nicely conveyed by conventional notions of globalization. Globalization, in the current capitalist and even U.S.-dominated sense, is conceived as the result of two inevitable natural processes: the impersonal, natural laws of the market and technological determinism. We are given to understand that the laws of the market will inevitably embrace the whole world, so there is really no point in fighting them; and the new information technologies have not only enabled that process but may even be its principal cause.

And yet even this is not enough to make the case for the new imperialism. There is a deep contradiction at the very heart of the new empire which makes its ideological needs rather more complicated. No matter how strong purely economic imperatives may be, no matter how much the imperialist power may benefit from purely economic domination instead of more risky and less profitable colonial ventures – or precisely because it does not dominate the world by direct rule – this empire cannot do without a global system of states to organize the global economy. A truly global state that could sustain global capital the way national states have sustained their domestic capitals is all but inconceivable. So there is a real disjuncture between the economic reach of capital and the political force that sustains it.

A global system of multiple states presents problems of its own. It is not so simple to maintain order and a congenial environment for capital in the global state system. That requires political, military, and ideological supports that are not supplied by purely economic power. The irony is that it seems to require a military force more massive than any empire in history, despite the fact – or rather because of it – that its object is not territorial expansion or colonial rule. If it has any identifiable objective, it is something vague and all-embracing, like policing the world to make it safe for capital. In other words, its purpose is completely open-ended. So the new imperialism needs not only an ideology to help sustain the right political environment in the global state system but also a justification for massive military power. And it needs a justification of that military power not just for defence against real threats, or even for colonial expansion, but for open-ended objectives. To put it bluntly, it needs an ideology to justify what amounts to a state of permanent war.

At this point in history, more than ever, it is hard to invoke a discourse of inequality and hierarchy, so the available ideological strategies are more limited than ever. They are largely confined to ostensibly democratic and egalitarian ideologies – and, in any case, those ideologies do have real advantages for imperial capital. The concept of democracy covers a multitude of sins, and it has become especially useful now that the old postwar imperial strategies no longer work. For a while, it was possible to justify, or disguise, imperialism in the postwar projects of development and modernization, the idea that the so-called Third World would be lifted up to Western standards with help from the West. This would, of course, happen on Western terms, in accordance with imperial interests and demands; but at least this imperial strategy promised some positive advantage to "developing" countries.

But, as the long postwar boom in the advanced capitalist countries gave way to a long economic downturn, the development strategy gave way to neoliberalism, with its policies of "structural adjustment," privatization, and the complete vulnerability of subordinate economies to foreign capital and financial speculation. At least behind the scenes, some prominent neoliberals are even admitting, perhaps even boasting, that the future we are looking forward to is one in which 80 percent of the world's population will be more or less superfluous, that high-tech agriculture and agribusiness will displace millions from the land, who will flock to the cities to populate huge slums, and so on. That vision of the future holds out little hope for the welfare of the millions; and even a less rabid neoliberalism promises much less than old development strategies did. But talk of democracy is cheap and makes a useful rhetorical substitute, at least for home consumption in imperial capitals.

THE U.S. IDEA OF DEMOCRACY

Now, it may seem that democratic rhetoric rules out most of current U.S. foreign policy. It certainly seems to make nonsense out of U.S. support for various oppressive regimes, now as before. It certainly seems incompatible with Guantanamo Bay, to say nothing of assaults on civil liberties at home. And it is very hard to square with the state of permanent war. But let us, for the sake of argument, set aside all those realities and consider how the Bush regime can justify its mission on its own terms.

The first thing we have to understand is that the new imperialists have at their disposal something that was never available to earlier imperial ideologues. They have a far less threatening conception of democracy to work with, something very well suited to class domination and imperial expansion. This is an idea of democracy invented in the U.S.A. very early in its history. Its main purpose – and we should have no illusions about this – was not to strengthen democratic citizenship but, on the contrary, to preserve elite rule in the face of an unavoidable mass politics and popular sovereignty. The object was to depoliticize the citizenry and turn democracy into rule by propertied classes over a passive citizen body, and also to confine democracy to a limited, formal political sphere. The founding fathers adopted various strategies to achieve that end, but what is most interesting from our point of view here is that they did everything possible to make democratic citizenship compatible with, or rather subordinate to, a hierarchy of economic interests.

History had already provided for a separation of economic and political power, and it was now necessary to reinvent the political sphere to make it subordinate to economic power. Politics was explicitly defined as a way of managing class inequality and differences of economic interest. In the face of already strong popular forces which emerged from the American Revolution, the idea was to neutralize democracy as much as possible.

The constitutional founders wanted to ensure that democratic citizenship did not mean democratic state power, power really in the hands of the people. On the one hand, the power of the majority had to be disarmed by fragmenting and diluting the majority as much as possible, to prevent its coalescence into an overwhelming force. That was, as James Madison pointed out, one great advantage of a large republic. On the other hand, the power of the propertied elites had to be protected by filtering popular sovereignty through a representative system designed to favour large landowners and merchants and through powerful institutions not subject to direct election – the Senate and above all the presidency (a strong executive presidency, instead of a parliamentary system, was itself another safeguard against popular rule).

So here was a democracy whose essential purpose was to leave class domination intact, while maintaining democratic suffrage and other democratic forms. Capitalism, even at that early stage of development, had made it possible by creating a separate economy and exploitative powers that no longer depended on exclusive political rights. There already existed a separate economic sphere, with its own principles of order and domination. But it was U.S. democracy that created the political sphere to go with it, a political sphere to suit the capitalist division of labour between political and economic power. Today, the U.S.A. represents the model capitalist democracy. It combines, in ideological conception and in practical reality, the formal sovereignty of the people with the substantive rule of capital. In the U.S.A. it is possible to distribute citizenship democratically without automatically and directly affecting class power in any serious way. Capitalism allows "democracy" to be confined within a limited sphere of operation.

But – and this is a big "but" – the division of labour between the power of appropriation and the power of coercion that makes this possible also makes the state a vital organ for the capitalist class. Capitalist exploitation can certainly go on in the economic sphere without interference, even where all citizens are juridically equal and even in conditions of universal suffrage. But capitalism relies on the state to create the conditions of accumulation and enforcement that capital cannot create for itself. So state power in the wrong hands is still a dangerous thing. The U.S. idea of democracy, for all its undoubted benefits, especially in the constitutional protection of civil liberties (now more than ever under threat at the hands of the Bush regime), is designed to make politics subordinate to class inequality and differences of economic interest.

Up to now, U.S. democracy has served capital well by preserving the balance between "formal" democracy and capitalist class rule, both outside and inside the state. I shall suggest in a moment that the new world order may be threatening that balance. But first, just a few words about how the U.S. conception of democracy operates in support of imperialism.

DEMOCRACY AND IMPERIALISM

The essence of democracy as conceived in the U.S.A. is the coupling of formal democracy with substantive class rule, the class rule of capital. This involves a delicate conceptual balancing act between an assertion of popular sovereignty – government of, by, and for the people – and the dominance of capital, the subordination of politics to capitalist markets, and the imperatives of profit. Those of us who grew up in the United States are well primed to accept this tricky combination. We are well prepared to view class power as having nothing to do with either power or class. We are educated to see property as the most fundamental human right and the market as the true realm of freedom. We are taught to view the state as just a necessary evil to sustain the right of property and the free market. We are taught to accept that most social conditions are determined in an economic sphere outside the reach of democracy. We learn to think of "the people" not in social terms, as the common people, the working class, or anything to do with popular power, but as a purely political category; and we confine democracy to a limited, formal political sphere. As the founding fathers intended, we think of political rights as essentially passive, and citizenship as a passive, individual, even private identity, which may express itself by voting from time to time but which has no active, collective or social meaning.

So there is nothing immediately implausible to most Americans about applying this idea of democracy to imperialism. At the turn of the twentieth century, the U.S.A. pioneered a form of empire which has been called Open Door imperialism – with roots that go back to the foundation of the republic. The so-called Open Door policy was first explicitly stated in relation to China. This doctrine began by asserting the territorial integrity of China, in other words, its right to be free of foreign domination. Yet the territorial integrity of China was intended to serve the interests of U.S. capital by giving it free rein to penetrate the Chinese economy. On the face of it, this was meant to create a level playing field, so that the U.S. could do what other major powers were already doing. But the calculation was – not unreasonably – that a world in which various existing states would maintain their territorial integrity while opening their economies to foreign capital would, given U.S. economic power, generally work to the advantage of the United States and U.S. capital. There is an obvious connection between this conception of the international order and the U.S. idea of the democratic republic, where democratic citizenship is coupled with the rule of capital through the medium of economic imperatives.

The U.S.A. was from the outset prepared to open those doors by military means – all in the apparently anti-colonial name of fairness, equality, and the spread of democracy. What made this plausible was the formal separation of political and economic power, which permitted the U.S.A. to support, at least nominally, the territorial integrity and sovereignty of subordinate states. Even people ostensibly on the left seem to have been persuaded by this ideological strategy. Consider, for example, Antonio Negri and Michael Hardt's fashionable book *Empire*, which describes the U.S.-dominated empire in terms that would have been entirely congenial to the architects of Open Door imperialism – talking about a U.S.-dominated empire which, for all its unfortunate consequences, is, unlike other forms of empire, an extension of an essentially benign democracy, with open, expansive, and inclusive tendencies.

Nevertheless, for all its democratic rhetoric, the U.S.A. has generally tended to prop up friendly autocratic regimes. No reader of this volume will need reminding of all the occasions when the United States has intervened, by military and other means, to prevent the accession of a democratic regime or to overturn a democratic election. But that is not always possible, and obstructing democracy in the name of democracy is another option, which has become more important in recent years. In the Middle East, for instance, it has become more difficult to prop up old friends. Islamist movements, which are challenging autocratic friends of the U.S.A., have been threatening to become truly mass movements; and in these circumstances the best available strategy is to replace these autocratic regimes with some kind of congenial democracy in which enemies of the U.S.A., Islamist or otherwise, are somehow sidelined, while as many spheres of public life as possible are put out of reach of democratic accountability – for instance, by privatization.

The U.S.A. – reluctantly and belatedly – supported the election in Iraq. They had little choice. Bush says his mission is more of the same. But it goes without saying that his administration will not support any truly democratic transformation, a real transformation of class power. It will not support even the most limited democracy that endangers the interests of U.S. capital, and it is doing everything possible to prevent that in Iraq, as elsewhere. This can be achieved either by direct intervention, as in Iraq, or by supporting friendly regimes in their attempts to limit the damage of ostensibly democratic reforms, as in Egypt.

Here, the U.S. conception of democracy is particularly useful. It suggests two essential strategies. One is to find electoral processes and institutions that will thwart the majority in one way or another. The other – and this is ultimately the most important – is to empty democracy of as much social content as possible. On the first point, certain political groups can be excluded altogether – as the main opposition force, the Muslim Brotherhood, is excluded from the Egyptian electoral process. Or else it is possible to give an unfair advantage to a minority, to protect propertied, or pro-U.S., interests as much as possible. Consider, for instance, the confessional system of representation in Lebanon. Giving Christians an advantage incommensurate with their numbers also means giving an advantage to privileged middle classes over people from the Shia slums of Beirut and the impoverished south of the country. In Iraq, the U.S. occupation has meant much more direct interference with a truly democratic transformation, as the occupying power has limited the field of candidates as narrowly as possible and made every effort to ensure the continuation of the regime which it installed – even if its efforts to sustain a friendly regime and a suitable constitution in Iraq may finally be thwarted by internal opposition.

But when all is said and done the desocialization of democracy is the really crucial anti-democratic strategy, more important in the end than any electoral devices. The whole point of this strategy is to put formal political rights in place of any social rights, and to put as much of social life as possible out of reach of democratic accountability. That is exactly what has happened in Iraq, where the parameters of democratic politics were set long before the election by Paul Bremer's economic directives and privatization programme. More generally this is the effect, and to a large extent the purpose, of neoliberal globalization. If globalization is preparing the ground for democracy throughout the world, as leaders of the advanced capitalist states would have us believe, it is doing so by ensuring that much of economic and social life will be beyond the reach of democratic power, while becoming ever more vulnerable to the power of capital.

I want, however, to conclude with a different point. The conceptual balancing act in the ideology of empire and democracy has depended on a particular division of labour between political and economic spheres, and up to now it has worked fairly well. But the old relation between political and economic power that made it possible for capitalism to tolerate formal democracy is being disrupted. The division of labour between the state and capital is being undermined. I suggested earlier that the separation of political and economic power, which has allowed capital to extend its reach around the globe and across political boundaries, has also produced a growing gap between the economic powers of capital and the political powers it needs to sustain the global economy. The consequence of a globalized economy has been that states have become more, not less, involved in managing economic circuits through the medium of inter-state relations, and capital has become more, not less, dependent on organization of the economy by a system of many local states. This means that the division of labour between the economic and political is less clear-cut than it was. We may, then, be entering a new period in which global capital's need for a congenial state system makes democratic transformations even more threatening than they were before. It may turn out that democracy now threatens to have a more substantive meaning, as it did when it was first invented in ancient Greece, before the U.S. definition emptied it of social content.

To manage the global economy, capital needs local states not only in the imperial centre but throughout the global system. In this new world order, democracy, even in its limited form, is likely to be under growing attack. Bush's mission to spread democracy at best means trying to ensure compliant regimes and to prevent genuinely democratic transformations. At worst, it means war. And in a state of perpetual war, even the formal democracy of capitalist societies is under threat. That was true in the Cold War, and it is true in the so-called war on terror. There has already been an assault on liberal democracy, an attack on civil liberties in the U.S.A. and elsewhere.

That's the bad news. The good news is that local and national struggles are more important now than ever. Global capital's dependence on local states may be its greatest vulnerability; and nothing could be more threatening than real democratic struggles, in every state, everywhere, but especially in the imperial homeland.

2

AFTER THE FACT:
READING TOCQUEVILLE IN BAGHDAD*

Aziz Al-Azmeh

How and why might one conceivably read Tocqueville in Baghdad? I hope that those of you who wonder about this do not for some reason assume that Baghdad's inhabitants do not read – though under present conditions reading there is getting very hard indeed and requires extraordinary dedication. I would like to propose that you bear in mind my primary intention, that of looking at how our Frenchman of genius observed a new world in the making, and take this further to examine how the United States, now grown much older but still beholden to thoughts of perpetual newness, is today trying to make a new world in Iraq and beyond. And I hope that you will enter with me into some complicity with Tocqueville, and share the benefits of the unflinching nature of his arresting gaze upon democracy in America, a gaze at once of fascination and admiration for what he considered to be the strange and alluring manifestation of human society and polity that is the U.S.A.: boundless energy, a strong judiciary, and intense public participation in civic life – to which we might now add a unique blend of science, architecture, top-class universities, exemplary philanthropy, cinema, jazz, and much else. It is into this complicity with Tocqueville's intriguing interplay between head-on actuality and sceptical distance that I propose to enter, hopefully drawing at least a few of you into it with me.

* Revised and expanded version of a lecture delivered at the Harold Pratt House, New York, on 19 November 2003, in the series "Transatlantic Dialogues," organised by the Central European University and reprinted in its Occasional Papers series.

Tocqueville's is to my knowledge the only truly and integrally profound reflection on the nature of American polity, and this is so not only because it compares favourably with those of Professor Bloom or Michael Ignatieff, for instance, or even of Thomas Jefferson and George W. Bush. Tocqueville's celebration of democracy in America both lauds and estranges; his fascination with the country has edges that are decidedly discomfiting. Such discomfiture dampens the appetite for disquisitions on impeccability and on election, human or divine, and might help restore to the United States and its foreign policy, particularly in the Arab world, a certain poise, a sense of proportion and temperance, and the sense of the standardly human. Such a restoration of equilibrium would help the U.S.A. to go beyond the usual toing and froing between postures of the heroic and the semi-divine, which figure in the drama of "Manifest Destiny," on the one hand, and on the other, cultural exports of post-human mutant figures such as Michael Jackson or the Terminator, before his latest transmogrification.

Put differently, Tocqueville offers us an insight into the workings of U.S. democracy beyond the undoubted idealism of many Americans, indicating certain conditions under which this idealism operates – conditions often overlooked, and usually overlaid with references to Founding Fathers and foundational texts such as the Constitution.[1] Many Arabs are discomfited by the situation in the Arab world and call for multifaceted reforms. So do many Americans, not least in terms of official American stands on the Arab world. Yet for many Arabs who recognize this need as well as the need for engaging the U.S. sweep into the area, this does not imply countenancing U.S. dictates, but rather critical engagement. These Arabs would not accept the proposition that it is only the Arab world that requires repair and rehabilitation. Thus it is my aim to suggest the concept of a critical dialogue in which Americans cannot indefinitely sustain an attitude of superior complacency and hubristic swagger. I will make remarks on U.S. foreign policy which are not unknown to America, and which have been recently put in a most forthright way by Zbigniew Brzezinski, who, like me, is worried by "extremist demagoguery that emphasizes worst-case scenarios, stimulates fear and induces a very simple, dichotomous view of world reality" and which "theologizes" any challenge as "terrorism," and speaks against "political cowardice" with regard to the Arab–Israeli conflict.[2]

Now to reading Tocqueville. I am not proposing what might more properly take place in a university seminar, but suggesting you listen to reflections by a particular reader on the description of U.S. democracy by a Frenchman. A multiplicity of overlapping perspectives are possible for a reader such as myself who, being at once a Syrian Arab of European nationality and an Old European of Arab origin, might be able to conjoin two largely concordant Arab and European views of America, of its democracy, and of its foreign policy. "Reading Tocqueville" refers us to Europe and an older America, while the view from Baghdad updates him, and might stand here emblematically for looking at America from the Arab world, particularly "after the event" – this event being of course the dangerous drift in U.S. policy after 9/11, manifested in the Arab world at once by the invasion of Iraq, and by unlimited, tail-wags-the-dog support for the systematic Israeli destruction of all possible elements of Palestinian statehood. Israel has destroyed the Palestinian economy, housing, and agricultural land, as well as the administrative and educational infrastructure, and has also been responsible for the murder or incarceration of virtually the entire political elite of the Occupied Territories, the relentless dispossession of Palestinian land and water resources, and the implantation of colonies for immigrants from Cincinatti or Birobidjan. There has also been wide-scale murder of civilians (which adjusted to population figures would equate to a quarter of a million American deaths and to four million wounded).

This is a dangerous drift indeed. That there has so far been no catastrophic failure for the occupying coalition in Iraq is no evidence of impending "success," however sophistically this may be described, and the signs grow daily more ominous and are indeed tending towards a catastrophic outcome. It is unsurprising that America's credibility, once extraordinarily high in the Arab world, is at rock bottom. The recent report by distinguished diplomat Edward P. Djerejian on U.S. "public diplomacy" is evidence that many Americans have become aware of this, though it is not sufficiently realized that hostility to the United States in the region is only in very small measure the concern of Islamic political forces. I do not have time now to speak of such forces, and most saliently of the radical, nihilistic wing of bin Laden and his associates, until recently favoured allies of the U.S.A. But let it be said here, as a cautionary remark, that Arabs cannot, if one is to have any measure of realism, be described simply as Muslims – this commonplace is a fatal categorical and historical error made by Ambassador Djerijian and his team. Neither should Islam or Muslims be summarily assimilated to the more perverse interpretations of their religion, any more than Christianity be summarily reduced to the Inquisition or to evangelical fundamentalism, or indeed Judaism assimilated to the views and actions of the rabbinical ayatollahs in the Palestinian occupied territories. Be it coming from inside or outside, this view should be as little believed as the claim that all Americans are virtuous, or that all are cowboys, as the common Arab stereotype has it, much exercised as it is by vintage Hollywood westerns.

Hostility to U.S. policy has less to do with what America is than what it does, contrary to what one hears in the U.S. media and from the loftiest heights of American officialdom; less to do with a visceral or resentful anti-Americanism, which does indeed exist in a variety of forms and inflections[3] – as exist animosities towards other nations, countries, and collectivities – than with a perception of national and, indeed, universal danger, of what the United States does. It is unsurprising that a recent European Union poll has established that 53 percent of EU citizens regard the U.S.A. as a danger to world peace – six percentage points lower than the 59 percent scored by Israel.

This takes us to the second vantage point for reading Tocqueville, one that is less immediately political and more universal, relevant to the question of democracy, to the genuine or formulaic declamation of "American values," to their muscular proclamation as universal. It must be said at the outset that democracy is not an American, but a universal political concept (not really a value) that has taken many forms, one of which is peculiar to America. I will not for the moment beg the question of "American values," or enquire whether these might be those of the Revd. Al Sharpton, of wrestler-turned-governor Jesse Ventura, of the American Israel Public Affairs Committee (A.I.P.A.C.) or Enron, of Pat Robertson, of the late Timothy McVeigh, of the joggers and skaters at Venice Beach, of assorted hillbillies, of East Coast universities, or indeed those most interesting and eminently changeable combinations one encounters in speeches by U.S. politicians seeking election or re-election. For though the United States is a vast and diverse country, it does, like other countries, conduct itself formally and project itself to the outside by claiming that its complexity is for practical purposes suspended, superseded by an official discourse that bespeaks more self-image than reality. This is what is known as official, hegemonic ideology. The discomfiting Tocqueville is surely second to none as a guide to reflecting upon the interplay of reality and illusion in U.S. public life. And though I am a reader of Tocqueville who has the deepest possible aversion to anachronism, by general consensus this Frenchman produced an image of U.S. democracy as lasting as that of the founding fathers, and certainly far more reflective.

Reflective, among other things, upon the implications and assumptions of the statement from Arthur Miller's poignant play *The Crucible* (written under McCarthyism and redone in cinematic form during evangelical fundamentalism's recent move from the margins to the centre of the U.S. polity), spoken by Departmental Governor Danforth during the Salem witch trials at the end of the seventeenth century: "A person is either with this court or he must be counted against it, there is no road between." This is a statement not unlike a more recent one that still reverberates throughout the world, though it must be said that the former is somewhat more articulate. Like most Arabs, most Europeans – especially those disparaged by Donald Rumsfeld as belonging to "Old Europe" – have felt grievously bullied since 9/11. Certain ruling circles in eastern Europe in turn received the dubious Rumsfeldian compliment of being described as the "New Europe" – this "accolade" was bestowed on former communist countries turning their back to the east, and offering fawning and automatically complaisant support to the U.S.A. This has not been in keeping with East European sentiments and views at large, and aroused the European (and Arab) fear of the emergence of a bloc – led by the U.K. and Poland (and for a time Spain, until domestic politics forced its withdrawal) – within the E.U. more anachronistically Atlanticist than properly European in orientation. This situation would clearly be to the detriment of an emergent rational pan-European policy concerning the Middle East. Most Europeans and Arabs, moreover, feel bullied by a country that presents itself fully as a hyperpower, despite exception taken to this term by the U.S.A. itself, one that is seen at once as institutionalizing a state of permanent war on a planetary scale,[4] and casting this endemic condition as necessarily arising from the overriding primacy of local values, American values, clearly set above universal values expressed in, for instance, the Kyoto Protocol, the International Court of Justice, the A.B.M. Treaty, and, not least, the U.N. Security Council.[5]

It is this violently particularistic orientation and its extra-legal presumptions, premised on unparalleled economic and military capacity and served up in the name of universality, that is especially worrisome, and which requires explanation. For after all, as one "Old European" observer remarked,[6] the U.S.A. seems to be adopting a classic strategy of a rogue state, a strategy of intimidation by irresponsibility, which is ill-suited to a country of continental proportions. This strategy might indeed sway Europeans with regard to smaller but peculiarly aggressive countries like Israel, but was inappropriate for the dispassion that one would ordinarily associate with more mature empires which, when truly imperial, tend to be cosmopolitan rather than provincial in outlook. Such empires might be and are indeed often muscular, but are normally capable of managing ecumenical diversity without recourse to shrillness.

It is almost as if the U.S.A., as it appears officially, takes the world for its unruly hearth, the model of a Salem, Massachusetts, duly reconfigured from a folksy Thanksgiving remembrance[7] to one whose moral economy is ruled, according to Tocqueville, by unrestrained instincts and passions: passions with a puritanical expression implacably dividing Light from Darkness, friend from foe, fighting angels of virtuous retribution from demons, Good from Evil empires and axes. These passions are propelled by the sovereignty of received opinion and are beholden to a majoritarianism "fettered by numbers," to the tyranny of the majority,[8] served up as "consensus." The early Puritans had their own axis of evil, of course: Quakers, witches, and Indians. Later Americans were and still are susceptible to apparitions of uncanny outsiders and enemies within: Catholics, the Irish, Blacks, and others, including Native Americans. They hounded them mercilessly, by various acts of reservation and discrimination under the title of what we might call "social-political hygiene" including eugenics; by lynchings (4,742 recorded between 1882 and 1968 – festive occasions fit for the whole family, where spectators exchanged postcards[9]); by Prohibition; by the Committee on Un-American activities; by the continuous production of science-fiction films featuring preternatural and devious aliens, some dressed up as natives; by anti-Arab and anti-Muslim hate-mongering (even by one of Bush's generals who asserted "Our God is better than theirs," and by preachers who officiate at state occasions under Bush); and by official racial and religious profiling, and murderous private vigilantism. With respect to anti-Arab hysteria, though no one doubts the reality of international terrorist networks, Satan must be confined, as Bin Laden has been, to some cavernous abode in order to be properly tackled, rather than certain collectivities demonized after his image. Terrorism has no solution that is purely military, or purely imaginary.

Tocqueville alerts us to the dark, irrational, and highly illiberal and intolerant side of the way in which U.S. politics – U.S. democracy – functions, rendering it at times undemocratic in all but formal arrangements. This has been the subject of some excellent recent work by American and other scholars, on collective hysterias like some of those I mentioned, on various religious and secular forms of nativism, on the politics of sin[10] – on the fevered style in public expression generally, on precedents to the sanctimonious voyeurism of a Kenneth Starr or the present erosion of civil liberties under the Patriot Act (or its predecessor, the National Security Act of 1947).

Yet this is part and parcel of the American democratic order. This is a democratic order modelled in part, in its relation to the outside, on that of a small community, severely managing unwholesome outsiders, as reflected in the notorious U.S. penal regime based on principles of retributive justice, resulting in facts such as the State of California spending more on prisons than on state universities since 1994,[11] or the U.S. joining China and the Congo in accounting for 80 percent of executions worldwide[12] – while crime rates overall have been falling. The ostracism of miscreants benign or malign (those standing against Christ, against the American way of life, against American values), this communalist inflection of national selfhood, tends, according to Tocqueville, to sap the virtues of public life and is in his opinion admirably suited to human weakness, as "the power of the majority [or what presents itself as speaking for the majority] is so absolute and irresistible that one must give up one's qualities as a man if one intends to stray from the track which it prescribes," and public opinion, or what stands for it, becomes "a species of religion, and the majority its ministering prophet."[13] For such communalism tends to devalue liberty in favour of collective virtue, be this religious or liberal, and dissolves civility into community. It consequently configures the body-politic as a coalition of communities (Black, gay, Hispanic, and Jewish, gun lobbies, agricultural lobbies, church lobbies, the arms industry, A.I.P.A.C., and so forth), and tends to turn national politics into a space for special pleading. This is the basis of the strength of U.S. federalism, according to Tocqueville: America is a nation where towns were organized before counties, counties before states, states before the Union. This process combines, in his words, the advantages of both "the magnitude and littleness of nations," but is not necessarily appropriate elsewhere,[14] particularly when "littleness" prevails.

Of this model, of Puritan New England provenance in the remarkable continuity that marks U.S. political life, which has been noted by a long line of commentators from Tocqueville to Robert Bellah and others,[15] Tocqueville wrote: "The civilization of New England has been like a beacon on a hill which, after it has diffused its warmth immediately around it, also tinges the distant horizon with its glow,"[16] thus describing the continuity of a model of free individuals (and communities), more independent than equal, who confound equality with freedom, in the expression of Tocqueville,[17] each a *Mayflower* with some errant passengers. But this unique composite must manage diversity, and must manage the staggering inequalities and unevennesses of Third World proportions that exist in the U.S.A. today, so as to produce a serviceable platform for action inside and outside the country on behalf of this entire collectivity of collectivities. This is done by setting a ceiling for acceptable dissent from a central cluster of positions taken for self-evident consensus, beyond which ostracism or worse comes into play, both centrally and individually, as witnessed respectively by regimes of national and sectoral codes of political correctness and by the related phenomenon, unique to the U.S.A., of fierce and rampant litigiousness. Thus what Tocqueville characterized as the American moral world, in which "everything is classified, foreseen, and decided beforehand," is in contrast to U.S. politics, where "everything is agitated, disputed and uncertain."[18]

There are various ways and means of managing diversity, from informal vigilantism to formal police action to the manipulation of public opinion, which is the subject of so much negative comment on the United States (though with the U.K. and Italy not far behind) in both Europe and the Arab world, by mass media, generally but by no means exclusively alternating between tonalities of sheer frivolity and loftiness that address very basic unreflected clichés and sentiments, described by one European as "informing without being informed."[19] Tocqueville wrote: "The characteristics of the American journalist consist in an open and coarse appeal to the passions of his readers; he abandons principles to assail the characters of individuals, to track them into private life and disclose all their weaknesses and vices." Exorbitant generalization apart, one might well assent with Tocqueville's conclusion from this crude trait, which with some notable exceptions tends to characterize much contemporary U.S. written and televisual journalism, that this "extreme licence" tends indirectly to enhance the maintenance of public order.[20] This whole matter has attracted much public commentary on a theme cognate with Tocqueville's "tyranny of the majority," inside the U.S.A. by intellectuals such as Thornstein Veblen, C. Wright Mills, Herbert Marcuse (who spoke of "repressive tolerance"), Dean Acheson (the "conditioning of the public mind"), and Noam Chomsky (who speaks of "the manufacture of consent"), all of whom commented on the ultimately authoritarian dialectic of revelation and obscuration in American public life, and on other characteristics of national culture in the U.S.A.[21]

Public opinion is not the natural emergence of some public self: the ingathering of private concerns and sentiments, highly differentiated, fragmented, and dispersed, its uniformization and evening-out so as to create a smooth space of agreement over issues made common, is an elaborate and very costly process. It is a process that, for Tocqueville, makes much too plentiful use of benign and idealistic general terms, such as "freedom" and "equality," terms that are like "a box with a false bottom; you may put in it what ideas you please, and take them out again without being observed."[22] Ultimately, according to our Frenchman, powers in effective control cover the face of society with

> a network of small complicated rules, minute and uniform, through which the most original minds and the most energetic characters cannot penetrate. . . . The will of man is not shattered, but softened, bent, guided; men are seldom forced by it to act, but they are constantly restrained from acting. Such power . . . does not tyrannize, but it compresses, enervates, extinguishes and stupefies.

Further, such a system of controls, often invisible and imperceptible, allows citizens to "shake off their state of dependence just long enough to select their master and then relapse into it again."[23]

I must add, and this is a crucial point in my view, that this recursive model of communal cohesiveness, harking back to the much earlier America witnessed by Tocqueville, represents a regression from another America much admired, one whose universalism reached its apogee in the three decades following World War Two. It is a turn from open curiosity and a certain genuine globalism towards an introverted denial of the existence of the world "out there" except in so far as it is made to appear as a demonic un-American domain, excluding always reliable allies like Britain, Estonia, or the Federated States of Micronesia, and much like ancient Muslim law dividing the world between the Abode of Islam and the Abode of War. This strange world, in which the United States appears to be acting as a pyromaniac fire-fighter,[24] goes very much against another grain, another seam of U.S. polity, celebrated by Tocqueville. This is the one that calibrates the Declaration of Independence and the Constitution so as to manage the arithmetical simplicities of popular will through the stately minuet of the legislature, the executive, and the judiciary, beyond the cant of communalism and exclusivism, indeed beyond the pleasing grail of "Manifest Destiny." It is also the America out of which emerged the New Deal, desegregation, the Great Society, and the great universities. The two Americas had always coexisted, sometimes interpenetrated, sometimes conflicted, and neither of them is some prelapsarian utopia.

What seems to have occurred in recent years, particularly since the Reagan presidency, is the extension of the Monroe Doctrine from a strict geographical to an ideological interpretation, from an anti-colonialist to an imperialist reading and a global unilateralism – though this trend is not so much a derangement as a decided affirmation of very long-term trends in U.S. foreign policy. This had been done sixty or seventy years earlier by that canniest and most brilliant of political meta-strategists Carl Schmitt, in defence of the notion of a *Lebensraum*.[25] The muscular liberalism of contemporary U.S. neoconservatives, the most sophisticated of whom is perhaps Robert Kagan, is older than that particular group of strategists, and has very strong affinities to Schmitt who is again coming into fashion, most particularly with his fundamental idea that the most basic units of politics are friends and foes. And it seems to me that this group of the East Coast intelligentsia, which has not been particularly welcome in liberal universities, has consequently drifted into public service under Kissinger, and in later years[26] has had a decisive influence on the recession of universalism and the reclamation of other strands in U.S. foreign policy in a line associated with Morgenthau, Wohlstetter, the Rand Corporation, the American Enterprise Institute, the Hudson Institute, with fundamentalist inflections in the American Heritage Institute.

This last is perhaps not surprising in a country where three times as many people would rather believe biblical accounts of the virgin birth than Charles Darwin, where 39 percent of the 80 percent of Americans who are believers describe themselves as born-again Christians,[27] and one in which (according to Tocqueville) "religious insanity is very common."[28] Ideas of America as a "Christian Sparta," a covenanted nation embarking upon an Exodus towards a destiny manifest – first to the Wild West, then worldwide – expressed in religious and non-religious terms, are constant in local self-perception.[29] This yields the heady, militaristic ideological cocktail currently in place in Washington, in which are mixed, but not particularly well-shaken, Wolfowitz, Pearl and Cheney – the one element that solders them together and makes them act as one, apart from agreement on a natural theology of the market and the person of the president, seems to be the savage social-Darwinist suprematism they hold in common, and sharing uncritical and unlimited support for Israel far in excess of what may be perceived as being in the national interest of the U.S.A.[30]

This seems to be the right point at which to move on to Baghdad, carried along by the swell of anti-Arab animosity complementary to uncritical support to Israel, eschatological and communalist, and propelled by the sub-Schmittian strategic pastiche of Spengler produced by Professor Huntington. At the confluence of these trends lies the demonization of Islam in much public discourse, though I do not for one moment believe, as many Arabs do, that the U.S.A. is engaged in a neo-crusade in the Arab world, despite what is said by U.S. fundamentalists and some members of the intelligentsia, or in an ungainly statement by President Bush. The whole enterprise is carried forward with an air of strident small-town ostracism that characterizes mass paranoias in the U.S.A. and elsewhere. Yet the United States, after the fact, is offering the Iraqis freedom and democracy, it being noted that pronouncements on the Arab world are not in the habit of including "justice" to the list of gifts proffered, which might highlight the crucial question of Palestine, but also a profound racism that implicitly regards Arabs as subhuman.

Which freedom, and which democracy, are Iraqis and other Arabs supposed to be believe they are receiving under U.S. patronage? How might they, after the fact, recompose their minds and wills, and think of themselves not as victims of collateral damage, military and political, left in the wake of U.S. policies in the area, but as recipients of collateral advantage from the removal of the Baathist regime? The collateral damage has over the years been very considerable: not only the chaotic conditions in Iraq after the invasion and the calamitous devastations of the embargo before, not only the consequences of Israeli depredations, or support for repressive and retrogressive Arab regimes, but also until quite recently sustained U.S. patronage for Islamic political movements.

This is a story not unlike that of Dr. Frankenstein, starting with what we might call the cultural plank of the Truman Doctrine, with the use of Islamist political forces as bulwarks against what, without the requisite very large pinch of salt, was taken for communism in the Middle East, and dealt massive blows to secular and progressive forces in the Arab world. It culminated in the U.S.–Saudi enterprise of setting up the Organization of the Islamic Conference in 1969 (helping ultraconservative Islamic propaganda subsequently to spread worldwide), and in U.S. support for the very godly regime of Zia-ul-Haq in Pakistan and for fundamentalist forces in Afghanistan, together with Pakistan, Saudi Arabia, and, to some extent, Sadat's Egypt – all favoured allies of the U.S.A. The consequences are well known and need no repetition here, except to recall that the anti-Soviet Afghan engagement of the U.S. (and now the occupation of Iraq) produced thousands of transnational, murderous cavemen who have plagued countries like Algeria and Egypt, and more recently Morocco and Saudi Arabia. The subversion in the same context of Arab (and Iranian) democratic regimes in the 1940s and 1950s by the C.I.A. and its predecessors is well known and well remembered.

Now for possible collateral advantage, and I do not need here to go into talismanic prescriptions of democracy as a cure for all ills, for I prefer to be concrete. The Puritan communalist model of democracy, today wedded to a libertarian model of multiculturalism (the two for practical purposes yielding the same results), is the one on offer. It is much in keeping with what, while reading Tocqueville, I tried to disengage a short while ago: the nation as a community of communities rather than a political assembly of citizens – a model of democracy which, along with many other matters already mentioned, is often cited by European authors wary of U.S. self-ascriptions of universal political values, and eager to distinguish Europe from America.[31] The model on offer is clearly at variance with Arab and European notions, traditions, and experiences of democracy, in short of democratic "values" outside America, more attuned to citizenship than to the communalization of individuals, though this is not absent, and more inspired by models of French republicanism than the federalist communalism of communities of birth and pressure groups. This notion, now being offered as exemplary, was reflected in the communalist composition of the Iraqi Provisional Ruling Council (P.R.C.) set up by Paul Bremer and which, according to a benign reading of the American multiculturalist Shangri-La, fosters diversity, equality, and so forth. The P.R.C. was composed as an oligarchy of communal – sectarian and ethnic – worthies, in the most part long-resident abroad, who find their party-political affiliations smothered by their affiliations of blood. Thus the surreal spectacle of a communist figuring on the Council as a Shiite, or a secular liberal figuring as a Sunni, and so forth, as if the country were being politically and socially engineered along a model of internal fragmentation which will lead, at best, to a cold civil peace, at worst to civil war, in the image of Balkanization or Lebanization, which is clearly not a formula appropriate for nation-building. This holds true despite Bremer's praise – fanciful, implausible, but most unfortunately probably genuine – for the Lebanese model, clearly heedless of Tocqueville's preference for a power "so constituted as to represent the majority without necessarily being a slave of its passions."[32] The electoral arrangements in 2005 and the resulting transitional government were based on similar principles. As one U.N. official commented after the election, "The election was not an election but a referendum on ethnic and religious identity. For the Kurds, voting was about self-determination. For the Shiites, voting was about a fatwa issued by Sistani."[33] More real an indicator of the consequences of such communalization is the spectacle of mobile telephone contracts for Iraq having been awarded by the occupation authority to three separate companies, not competing with each other but rather each covering the territory of a potentially independent political entity.

There is no denying the diverse composition of Iraq, as of any other country, nor the fact, now harnessed to its own purposes by U.S. policy, that in his last years Saddam Hussein did encourage the retribalization of politics, starting with his own community of blood, his sons, and maternal cousins. It is worth reminding you here that sectarianism – the

transformation of religious or ethnic communities into political parties –
is a new political phenomenon, and that the Iraqi polity like most Arab
polities had been engaged for decades in a largely successful process of
forming citizens, of neutralizing social groups of blood as political actors,
and that Jacobin methods have historically been part of all such processes. Nor can one belie the surge of some of the most primitive and
retrogressive social forces and ties amidst the predictable chaos resulting
from deliberate state collapse that accompanied the advent of the
occupation forces, whose presence is to most Iraqis inflammatory, not
least because of a natural patriotism which Americans generally prize so
much in themselves, but also because they brought with them conditions
of unemployment, of infrastructural dysfunction, along with trigger-
happy and nervous troops who have sometimes resorted to collective
punishment like the uprooting of trees and destroying the houses and
rendering homeless the families of suspected enemies (like Saddam
Hussein before, and Israel before and since).[34] They also brought
insecurity and lawlessness (except for U.S. military and oil installations,
and even then not very successfully – insecurity of which Mr. Wolfowitz
had personal experience, and which clearly cannot be ameliorated by the
U.S. expeditionary force, which is using private security companies[35]);
the same insecurity that constrained President Bush to visit his troops in
Iraq almost furtively, flying in the dead of night, in November 2003. The
plight of Iraqi women who have to obscure themselves in these circumstances after decades of progress should also be noted here. The situation
is such that the U.N. and the Red Cross have had to suspend operations,
and most Europeans and many others are unwilling to bring aid, investments, and other forms of participation and stabilization.

But emergency action is no excuse for the perverse notion of representation adopted, for dissolving civility into community, for eliminating
the civic in favour of blood, not even if this appears in the heat of the
moment as a way of cutting corners and losses, as had been done by
Saddam Hussein before. This communalization of Iraq, this casting of
Baghdad after the image of Salem and of Harlem, had long been in some
derisory measure premeditated, not only with the American communalist model in mind, but also according to half-baked ideas about Arabs
being primitive and exotic tribals and religious fanatics (hitherto
preferred allies of the U.S.A.), sublimated as "communities": ideas of
sheer nonsense, misleadingly abetted by the Iraqi National Council

hovering in antechambers of the Pentagon, in concert with some academics, prior to the invasion and thereafter, pandering to uninformed prejudices in Washington, and placed in the trusty hands of a person (Mr. Khalilzad, presently U.S. ambassador in Baghdad) whose experience, apart from neoconservative milieux in Chicago and Washington, is confined to tribes and pipelines in Afghanistan.[36] Afghanistan and Iraq are in no way comparable, though among ruling circles in Washington they might well be thought to be indistinguishable, both being "out there."

Such ideas appeared all the more credible in an administration whose State Department, marginalized for the occasion, counted until recently a mere fifty-four competent Arabists,[37] experienced ones having been pushed aside in favour of pro-Israeli personnel. Yet I am not sure that State Department intervention would have made a significant difference apart from one of nuances. Be that as it may, it is clear that the communalization of Iraq as reflected in the constitution of its new polity and the draft of its constitution is directly in keeping with such ideas as are being propounded, with various nuances, by tired triumphalist scholars and eager, untried younger ones, who concur on the communalization of the country on the assumption that an "Islamic" polity would be the appropriate one in this war against modernity and modernism waged under the title of the Greater Middle East.[38] Hence the predilection of the occupation authorities in Iraq for more than flirtatious relations with the conservative Shiite clergy, including foreign, Persian clerics, and their acquiescence to the abolition of the fairly modernist Law of Personal Status and its replacement by a bundle of communalist laws run by clergymen, Muslim and Christian.

The idea that the Middle East is a "mosaic" is a resilient one, one that marries the supposedly anachronistic social forms of the Middle East to external political wills while fragmenting their national polities. Israel is a good model here of a nation of blood and atavistic notions of identity. This, of course, invites the thought, incongruous to those not wishing to reflect clearly, that it is thereby an anachronistic historical phenomenon, as was shown recently with eloquence by Tony Judt.[39] Hankering after the revival of the Ottoman millet system of communal self-government is not only anachronistic. It ignores the fact that memories of the millet system as might persist in the Middle East, including Iraq, and as celebrated by outside commentators and policy-makers, are of its terminal phase of degeneration in the nineteenth century, when it became dysfunctional, but was kept deliberately alive by foreign powers seeking footholds in the area and seeking to prevent its national integration, and by reactionary clerical circles, now again engineered back into life in Iraq. The only remnant of it in the course of the twentieth century was Lebanon, where communalism led to a devastating civil war of proportions that were, in relative terms, greater than that of Spain before the triumph of General Franco, and which now faces an uncertain future.

That the occupation authorities in Iraq were systematically unprepared, sometimes running around like headless chickens, is common knowledge. One German newspaper has referred to the preference in Washington for thinking in terms of "complexity-reduction,"[40] to which one might more concretely add the private and public use and abuse of intelligence already politicized, ignoring inconvenient advice and information, with barely a thought given to the political aspects of the war and its consequences. In the spaces of this disorientation enter more focused, rapacious operators. I do not wish to speak of well-known matters such as Halliburton subsidiaries, ultimately needing to subcontract to local operators, including some connected to members and families of the new ruling circles,[41] and two examples will suffice here. The first is the insidious confiscation of Iraq's national culture – and I mean national, not tribal culture – with the plunder of its antiquities and libraries under the noses of U.S. tanks parked outside museums and of U.S. bases adjacent to archaeological sites – this quite apart from the barbarous vandalism of Babylon's pavements and antiquities by U.S. and Polish tanks and soldiers stationed there. All indices signal that amidst generalized chaos and random vandalism, plunder took place to order by persons who knew what they were looking for. There may indeed have been some internal involvement, but the world market in antiquities is not run from Baghdad, but from London and New York. And though it would be unwise to point fingers in murky waters such as this, much has been said in this connection about the American Council for Cultural Policy. This is a conglomerate of former museum directors, lawyers with chequered careers, and art dealers, who had lobbied the Pentagon against what they call "retentionist" antiquity policies in Iraq, Egypt, and elsewhere, high-mindedly pleading conservationist expertise (certainty not lacking in Iraq or in Egypt), and seeking to change relevant U.S. and international legislation such that looted objects might be legitimately imported if a U.S. court chose not to recognize Iraqi or other legislation.[42]

Unedifying stuff, indeed, not least because this takes place in the wake of the Enron affair and of attempts to tighten up controls over business dealings and to ensure a greater degree of fairness and transparency. It is very much hoped that Iraq Revenue Watch, set up by the Open Society Institute, or recent work by the Center for Public Integrity, will help render what is fit for the U.S.A., apart from democracy, fit for others, and that an eye be kept on the second example that might be mentioned in this regard. This is the lobbying and consultancy group for Iraq business called New Bridge Strategies, whose boss, President Bush's former campaign director in 1988 and in 2000, says of himself in advertising his firm that "being affiliated with the President for nine years of my life, I know a lot of people who are part of the administration."[43]

Such facts and, inevitably, tales of buccaneering under the flag, of patriotism and profit, of the marriage of God and Mammon, unedifying as they may be, yet leave unscathed the sense of American mission, and do not much encourage Iraqis to read Tocqueville's *laudatio*. One Arab admirer of the U.S.A., who describes himself privately as "something of a neoconservative," has recently urged America, whose democracy he says is a "universal programme," to enracinate her civilization of law and science the world over. But he almost despairingly repeats his worry that Americans are not truly aware of this universality.[44] My concern is that the disjunction between self-proclamation and policies in place, occupied as it is with disorientation and greed, might make the image projected of the U.S.A. a favoured argument against democracy. Iraq does not need messiahs, but professionals; Iraqi, European, and inevitably after the fact, American. For this to be possible the U.S.A. must realize that it is very exceptional, not the norm. A long line from Tocqueville through Seymour Martin Lipset and Daniel Bell to the ultra-atlanticist London weekly *The Economist*,[45] have emphasized the peculiarity of the U.S.A. Clearly, a certain sense of reality, and a certain maturity of spirit are required, large enough to have the wisdom to think multilaterally, as many senior U.S. politicians and public figures have recently been urging, including Dr. Brzezinski and Diane Feinstein: what I have in mind is meaningful multilateralism, beyond such pious statements or "coalitions of the willing" as exist, beyond the bandwagon jingle of grateful clients embedded in the expeditionary force, like the British or the Poles. Such multilateralism requires that the U.S.A. be prepared to cede unilateral control of Iraq – cede control, not only the de facto sovereignty acquired by conquest, as nominally acquired after the handover of power in July 2004. Only then might collateral advantage be realized. And this presupposes a real willingness to consider what might be appropriate or inappropriate to a situation outside the U.S.A. in their own terms, thus rendering unthinkable matters such as peremptorily nominating to the presidency of the U.S. Institute for Peace a fevered anti-Arab and anti-Muslim person, or to the U.S. ambassadorship at U.N.E.S.C.O. a person whose background is in political advocacy, voter mobilization, and the training of candidates for the Republican Party,[46] or indeed the pesident himself habitually addressing the world, which differs in values and political vocabularies from the desiderata of American public discourses, as if he were addressing a local audience.

This is the kind of determined and glib removal from reality which gives the impression of autism, and the fear that 9/11 might have caused a derangement of terrifying proportions. What is being enjoined upon the Americans is not pure reason and enlightenment, but an invitation to eschew irrationality and to acquire a sense of impending catastrophe if the U.S.A. persists in unilateralism and in flaunting international legality. 120,000 military personnel in Iraq and $89 billion alone cannot do the job. Long gone are the days when, as Tocqueville said in a remarkable passage, Native Americans had the misfortune of receiving at once knowledge and oppression from the same hand.[47] The world cannot be recast according to this eschatological self-image, reiterated in Tocqueville's expression as "perpetual . . . self-applause," commenting on which he said there were certain truths the Americans could learn only from strangers or from experience.[48] The whole world cannot be made exceptional, and most of us non-Americans, Europeans and Arabs alike, would rather settle for humbler aspirations.

NOTES

1. A contrastive reading of the Founding Fathers and of the course of US policies at home and abroad is offered by Gore Vidal, *Inventing the Nation: Washington, Adams, Jefferson* (New Haven: Yale University Press, 2003).
2. Z. Brzezinski, in *International Herald Tribune*, 15–16 November 2003.
3. As an example: *Philippe Roger, L'ennemi américain. Généalogie de l'antiaméricanisme français* (Paris: Seuil, 2002).
4. Emmanuel Todd, *Après l'empire* (Paris: Gallimard, 2002), p. 17.
5. The extent to which this power is unlimited, and the proposition that the resort to

militarism in fact obscures a serious weakness, are made by Todd, *Après l'empire*, and I. Wallerstein, *The Decline of American Power* (New York and London: New Press, 2003).

6. Todd, *Après l'empire*, p. 10. See also C. Prestowitz, *Rogue Nation: American Unilateralism and the Failure of Good Intentions* (New York: Basic Books, 2003).

7. See Richard T. Hughes, *Myths America Lives By* (Urbana and Chicago, Ill.: University of Chicago Press, 2003), for a discussion of the abiding motifs that idealise the U.S.A.

8. Alexis de Tocqueville, *Democracy in America*, trans. H. Reeve, rev. F. Bowen, ed. P. Bradley (New York: Vintage Books, 1990), I: pp.14, 53, 301; II: pp. 10, 11.

9. A. Chaon, *Le Monde Diplomatique*, 24 June 2000.

10. For instance: J. Monroe, *Hellfire Nation: The Politics of Sin in American History* (New Haven: Yale University Press, 2003); S. M. Lipset and E. Raab, *The Politics of Unreason: Right-wing Extremism in America, 1790–1970* (New York: Harper & Row,1970); D. Bennett, *The Party of Fear: From Nativist Movements to the New Right in American History* (Chapel Hill: University of North Carolina Press, 1988); R. Bellah, *The Broken Covenant* (Chicago: Seabury Press, 1988); M. Gardell, *Gods of the Blood: The Pagan Revival and White Separatism* (Durham, NC: Duke University Press, 2003).

11. See in general D. Garland, *The Culture of Control* (Chicago: University of Chicago Press, 2003).

12. S. Mallat, *al-Dimuqratiyya fi Amerika* (Beirut: Dar al-Nahar, 2001), p. 76.

13. Tocqueville, *Democracy in America*, I: pp. 98, 123, 267, II: pp. 11, 123.

14. Ibid., I: pp. 40, 163.

15. Bellah, *Broken Covenant*, pp. 48ff. and passim; Tocqueville, *Democracy in America*, passim.

16. Tocqueville, *Democracy in America*, I: p. 31.

17. Ibid., I: p. 301, II: p. 95.

18. Ibid., I: pp. 43–44.

19. E. Balibar, *L'Europe, l'Amerique et la guerre* (Paris: La Decouverte, 2003), p. 140.

20. Tocqueville, *Democracy in America*, I: p. 187.

21. Ibid., II: chs. 10–18.

22. Ibid., II: p. 70.

23. Ibid., II: p. 319.

24. Todd, *Après l'empire*, pp. 143, 156, and ch. 5, passim.

25. G. Salamé, *Quant l'Amerique refait le monde* (Paris: Flammarion, 2005). See C. Schmitt, "Volkerrechtliche Foemen des modernen Imperialismus," in idem, *Positionen und Begriffe im Kampf mit Weimar-Genf-Versailles* (Berlin: Duncker und Humblot, 1994), pp. 184ff.; Balibar, *L'Europe, l'Amerique et la guerre*, pp. 107ff.; G. Balakrishnan, *The Enemy. An Intellectual Portrait of Carl Schmitt* (London: Verso, 2000), ch. 18.

26. See the excellent article by A. Frachon and D. Vernet, *Le Monde*, 16 April 2003.

27. "A Survey of America," *The Economist*, 8 November 2003, p. 9.

28. Tocqueville, *Democracy in America*, II: p. 134.

29. Bellah, *The Broken Covenant*, pp. 24ff., ch. II, and passim; Tocqueville, *Democracy in America*, I: pp. 300–318.

30. See A. Callinicos, *The New Mandarins and American Power: The Bush Administration's Plans for the World* (Cambridge: Polity Press, 2004). For a particularly savage scenario: R. Perle and D. Frum, *The End of Evil. How to Win the War on Terror* (New York: Random House, 2004).

31. One might cite, almost at random, S. Kauffmann and T. de Montbrial, both in *Le Monde*, respectively 6 and 14 June, 2003.

32. Tocqueville, *Democracy in America*, I: p. 261.

33. Quoted in Seymour M. Hersh, "Get Out The Vote," *New Yorker*, 25 July 2005.

34. S. Antoon in *Al-Ahram Weekly*, 6–12 November 2003.

35. T. Catan and S. Filder, "The Military Can't Provide Security," http://amsterdam.nettime.org/Lists-Archives/nettime-1-0309/msg00169.html

36. *Washington Report on Middle East Affairs*, 17 April 2003, http://www.wrmea.com.

37. E. Djerijian et al., *Changing Minds, Winning Peace* (Report of the Advisory Group on Public Diplomacy for the Arab and Muslim World submitted to the Committee on Appropriations, Washington D.C., 2003), p. 27.

38. See P. Waldman, "A Historian's Take on Islam Steers U.S. in Terrorism Fight," *Wall Street Journal*, 3 February 2004; N. Feldman, *After Jihad: America and the Struggle for Islamic Democracy* (New York: Farar, Strauss & Giroux, 2003).

39. Tony Judt, "Israel: The Alternative," *New York Review of Books*, 23 October 2003.

40. M. Siemons, "Prisma 11.9," *Frankfurter Allgemeine Zeitung*, 14 July 2003.

41. *al-Sharq al-awsat*, 9 November 2003.

42. Ann Talbot, "The Looting of Baghdad's Museum," http://www.wsws.org/articles/2003/apr2003/loot-a19_prn.shtml; Walter Sommerfeld, *Süddeutsche Zeitung*, 8 May 2003, English translation at http://www.informationclearinghouse.info/articles3311.htm; Liam McDougall, "US Accused," at http://www.sundayherald.com/32895; *The Economist*, 24 May 2003, pp. 43–44

43. *Fortune*, October 27 2003, p. 28.

44. Mallat, *al-Dimuqratiyya fi Amerika*, pp. 26, 109, 175–177, 179.

45. *The Economist*, 8 November 2003.

46. E. Sciolino, *International Herald Tribune*, 30 September 2003.

47. Tocqueville, *Democracy in America*, I: pp. 343ff.

48. Ibid., I: p. 265.

3

TORTURED CIVILIZATIONS:

ISLAM AND THE WEST

Tariq Ali

On a visit to London in 1931 for a conference on the future of India –
then still occupied by the British – Mahatma Gandhi was asked by a
journalist, "What do you think of Western civilization?" The old fox
smiled. "It would be a good idea,"' he replied. Seventy-five years later,
Iraqis suffering the abuses of an oppressive two years under the U.S.
occupation would probably endorse Gandhi's sentiment.

To sell the Iraq instalment of the war against terrorism, the U.S.A. had
justified the war as necessary to free the good and common people from
a tyrant. Once removed, and with the benefit not of foreign nation-
builders but of bureaucrats to ease the transition, the path would clear;
swords could be turned into ploughshares, and the desert would bloom
in a transformed and democratized Middle East. If at home President
Bush and his cadre of acolytes were merchants of fear, on the road, to
justify foreign adventures, Donald Rumsfeld et al. were merchants of
hope.

Some in the West hoped that the U.S. intervention in Iraq would lead
to democracy. Few in Iraq suffered such illusions. They were only too
well aware that at the height of the repression in Iraq, Saddam Hussein
had been a favoured Western ally, barely criticized in the U.S. media. And
what has happened has confirmed Iraqi doubts. At a single nod from the
conquerors, time-servers such as Ahmed Chalabi (aptly described in
the *New Yorker* as the man "who sold the war") are reduced to primitive
obscurity. Saddam's former ally (whom Saddam later tried to have

killed), the ex-Baathist Iyad Allawi, was appointed new puppet prime minister before the fixed elections which allowed Shia groups to become the government. And all this is welcomed by the "international community," showing once again that it is the wealth and military strength of the U.S.A. that enables it to buy the services of poorer and weaker states.

In any case, with the revelations of the abuses at prisons in Iraq, Afghanistan, and Cuba, the U.S.A. has lost whatever moral authority it purported to have, and the result is a genuine clash of civilizations – one that could have been easily avoided.

In the spring of 1917, when the British entered Iraq, the statement of purpose was similarly virtuous: the generals and their battalions came not as conquerors but as liberators. To allow that controlling Iraq back then was part of a grander design to secure the Middle East as a European access route to Asia would have divested the occupying force of the moral authority necessary for success. The occupier always requires a mask: the benign bestower of a better life, a better "civilization."

The British, of course, had assets the U.S.A. lacks. One was a long and storied colonial legacy rooted in a commitment to settlement. Legions decamped from the British Isles to populate the globe. In so doing, they – at home, the marginalized, the impoverished, the outcasts; away, the pioneers, the entrepreneurs, the pirates – contributed mightily to another great asset: through the ingenious workings of mercantilism, they filled the treasury of Westminster with ever-ballooning capital and established Britain as the world's banker. Most importantly, the British embraced their empire as righteous, utilitarian, and a civilizing force.

In contrast, latter-day Americans suffer from intellectual and historical amnesia, and a sense of denial bordering on the delusional. Despite U.S. insistence to the contrary, we have, for the first time in human history, the existence of a single empire, and it is the American Empire at the beginning of the "New American Century." The U.S. military is stationed in 138 countries, and in key geopolitical regions, such as the Middle East, it secures strategic partnerships through the provision of defence services, military hardware, and corporate investment. This is especially true in Israel and Saudi Arabia, the Middle Eastern bêtes noires for Muslim fundamentalists. Israel is a false economy, more and more dependent on Western capital inflows and by the day losing its claim to being the region's only democracy. In Saudi Arabia, U.S. corporate investments exceed $400 million a year, and U.S. companies have more than 200 joint ventures (principally in the petrochemical and energy sectors) with Saudi Arabian companies. Certainly support for Israel opens the doors to Islamic and Arab charges that the West aids and abets the unlawful occupation and confinement of Palestinians. But, post-Iraq, all indications now suggest that the long-standing reciprocity between the U.S.A. and the House of Saud – to Islamic critics, oil in exchange for military bases in the home of Mecca and Medina – will result in Saudi Arabia becoming the new hotbed and target of Islamic militancy.

There is no system whereby the financial benefits of foreign investment accrue directly to the U.S. Treasury, which must bear the costs of maintaining and expanding the American empire. And notwithstanding America's status as the world's largest debtor nation, the present administration appears committed to military budgets in excess of the next largest fifteen nations combined. What, after all, is this global overreach putting at risk? If the economists are correct, how can social security cheques, state medical insurance, the welfare state, and so on, be sustained in the face of a balance sheet that reads "$45 trillion in the hole"? But, given the administration's refusal to use the "E" word, President Bush's beliefs in divine guidance and "might is right," and only faint challenges from American liberals to U.S. imperial aspirations, it is hard to imagine a change of course.

The most recent evidence of historical amnesia and a messiah complex lies in the lack of a measured exit strategy following "Operation Iraqi Freedom," a war whose short-term result could have been guessed at by schoolchildren. (Tony Blair knew that this war would be a long haul, and the complicity in this charade of the British prime minister, whose country's occupation of Iraq lurched on until 1955, proves that the diseases of blind faith and hubris have spread across the Atlantic.) But there is more to it. The absence of planning bespeaks a collective mind existing in a permanent present, and an adolescent insistence that "history begins with us."

Contributing to this permanent present are television and the Internet – two "assets" the British were free of when they occupied Iraq – and it is these tools of communication that have caused the U.S.A. to lose both the propaganda war and its moral authority. (Embedding journalists was a brilliant strategic ploy, which, with rare exceptions, successfully contained the story for the homeland audience. In hindsight, this may have been the only "mission accomplished.") In the interregnum between President Bush's proclamation of victory and the day of uneasy transition to a dubious Iraqi self-rule, the bombs and body counts continued to soar, and the negative news became a daily headline. The image is more powerful than the word, and matters reached their nadir when the torture photographs from the Abu Ghraib prison were broadcast on Arab television and released over the Internet. The damage could not be controlled; the mask was off. On the ground, the liberators suddenly looked no better than the Baathist thugs of Saddam Hussein's security militias.

The Taguba Inquiry confirmed independent reports that U.S. soldiers had raped women prisoners. Some of them were forced to bare their breasts for the camera. The women detainees sent messages to the resistance, pleading with them to bomb and destroy the prison and obliterate their shame and suffering. As far back as November 2003, word was getting out. *The Guardian* reported a woman prisoner pleading, "We have daughters and husbands. For God's sake don't tell anyone about this."[1] Another Iraqi prisoner, a male, was more forthright: "The Americans brought electricity to my arse before they brought it to my house!"[2] This was Western civilization at its rawest, and reprisals were inevitable.

Circulating on the streets of Baghdad is a photograph of a U.S. soldier having sex with an Iraqi woman. War as pornography. In the West, this and similar images have been suppressed. (Was it out of deference to John Ashcroft, then U.S. Attorney General, a fanatical evangelist who blushed each day when he saw the stone breasts of the gorgeous Spirit of Justice in the hallway outside his office and so had them covered?) Was the Pentagon fearful of the reaction from the world at large? And what about the women of Afghanistan, who, we were informed only a few years ago by the White House women – Hillary Clinton and Laura Bush – would be liberated by invasion and occupation? The women are still waiting, while rapes and tortures in that country go unreported.

Into this amoral terrain, the other side responded with eye-for-an-eye justice. The Iraqi resistance responded to the U.S. rapes and torture with kidnappings, car bombings targeting U.S. military and civilians alike, and, in Saudi Arabia (because, to the resistance, this war is borderless), ritualized beheadings of Western hostages. At first, the images of rape and torture trickled out (shame seemingly keeping their reproduction in check), but the opportunity to exploit these hideous transgressions was too ripe, too available, and the slow seepage became a flood. Newly equipped, local mullahs, clerics from neighbouring states, and others demanding the immediate evacuation of the "Western infidels" busily recast the short history of the war: since Gulf War I the West has been bombing Iraq; economic sanctions, not the Baathist regime, crippled its opportunity; and only we can protect the proud face of Islam against the Christian hordes. You can hear the chant: "I ask you, which civilization, Islam or the West, is collapsing?"

I was in Egypt and Lebanon when news of the Abu Ghraib torture broke. I did not meet a single person (not even among Europeans and North Americans who work there) who was surprised. Outside the U.S.A., the echoes of history have never ceased to resonate. The tortures in Iraq revived memories of Aden and Algeria, Vietnam and, yes, Palestine. But what can explain the shock evinced by so many in the West when the torture was made public? One can excuse forgetting the Inquisition or the Ordeal by Fire or the heresy-hunters of Christianity who tortured and killed Cathars and Albigensians, or, later, the majestic polemic by Voltaire against the cruelty of torture. But have the citizens of North America forgotten what happened in South and Central America, Asia, and Africa less than fifty years ago? When dead Iraqis are not even counted, why the surprise that the live ones are mistreated? To understand this collective amnesia we must, against the strongest impulses of a U.S. administration intoxicated by the future, straddle the present while stepping back in time.

On 8 June 2004, the *Financial Times* reported that U.S. lawyers said, "American interrogators can legally violate a U.S. ban on the use of torture abroad," and "legal statutes against torture could not override Mr. Bush's inherent powers." From leaked administration documents, it is now clear that the U.S. justification for torture at Abu Ghraib (and at Guantanamo Bay) was predicated on the notion that Al-Qaeda "irregulars" do not observe, and therefore cannot be covered by, the laws of war. In the battle against these anarchic warriors – this asymmetric devil intent on destruction – the U.S.A. sought to circumvent not only the Geneva Conventions, but its own 1996 U.S. War Crimes Act. It is pointless to pretend that the soldiers implicated were indulging in spontaneous fun. These men and women were wrong to obey orders, but who will punish their leaders?

Collective memory loss in the West could be the result of a superiority complex. We won. We defeated the "Evil Empire." Our culture, our civilization is infinitely more advanced than anything else, which might explain the shock waves created by the torture revelations at Abu Ghraib. One of the features of domination is that those who do not identify with it are categorized as the enemy. George W. Bush's post 9/11 injunction, "Either you are with us, or you are with the terrorists," was, for a while, accepted without question throughout the Western world and by elites everywhere. It was merely an adaptation of the New Testament's "He who is not with me is against me." The notion that he might not be against you but in favour of something more constructive was/is regarded as impermissible.

It was Carl Schmitt, a gifted legal theorist of the Third Reich, who insisted that the totality of politics was encompassed by the essential categories of "friend" and "enemy." This view suited most empires and Schmitt's writings were influential in the United States after the Second World War. Conservative thinkers such as Leo Strauss acknowledged his influence. The message – studied, learned, and adopted by the "Straussians" now surrounding President Bush – was straightforward: if your country does not serve the interests of our empire, it is an enemy state. It must be occupied, its leaders removed, and more pliant satraps placed on the throne. In time, they hoped, the presence of a Roman legion would become unnecessary. However, soon after the legion withdraws, the satrapy begins to crumble. Occupation, withdrawal, rebellion, another occupation, and, sometimes, self-emancipation, is a pattern in world history.

To justify their excesses, imperial regimes require intellectual legitimizers, and, in the U.S.A., the torch was passed from Leo Strauss and the Chicago School to Samuel Huntington and Francis Fukuyama. Huntington was a senior counter-insurgency expert in the Johnson administration at the time of the Vietnam War. His fertile imagination contributed to the scheme of "strategic hamlets," after studying the insurgent texts of the enemy – Mao Zedong, Che Guevara, Fidel Castro, Vo Nguyen Giap – on guerilla warfare in which all four practitioners explained that success was impossible without the support of the population. Failing to understand what motivated the guerilla fighters or the causes of the war, and believing the main problem was the links of the resistance to the people ("fish in water," according to Mao), Huntington conceived of separating the two. The scheme envisaged herding poor peasants into "strategic hamlets," which were glorified rural concentration camps surrounded by barbed wire and guarded day and night by soldiers. The U.S. military decided to give it a try. What Huntington and his superiors had failed to grasp was that many of "the people" were, in fact, members or supporters of the Vietnamese resistance. Soon they began to organize inside the strategic hamlets. The weaknesses of each hamlet were mapped and dispatched to the guerillas, and the scheme came to an ignominious end.

Fukuyama did not engage in anything as dramatic, but as a State Department employee he wrote a policy paper on Pakistan during the years of General Zia's brutal dictatorship suggesting that Pakistan turn its back on India and concentrate on its links with the Islamic world, that is, the Gulf States and Saudi Arabia. The generals were grateful for this advice, which suited their material and strategic needs, and were very admiring of Fukuyama's démarche. When the Berlin Wall came down, a new version of an old idea, the triumph of liberal democracy, began to agitate Fukuyama.

Then came the total collapse of the Soviet Union and the restoration of a peculiar form of gangster capitalism in the world. Did the triumph of capitalism and the defeat of an enemy ideology mean we were in a world without conflict or enemies? Both Fukuyama and Huntington produced important books as a response to the new situation. Fukuyama, obsessed with Hegel, saw liberal democracy/capitalism as the only embodiment of the "world-spirit" that now marked the "end of history," a phrase that became the title of his book.[3] The long war was over and the restless world-spirit could now relax and buy a condo in Miami. Fukuyama insisted that there were no longer any available alternatives to the American way of life. The philosophy, politics, and economics of the Other – each and every variety of socialism/Marxism – had disappeared under the ocean, a submerged continent of ideas that could never rise again. The victory of capital was irreversible. It was a universal triumph.

Huntington was unconvinced, and warned against complacency. From his Harvard base, he challenged Fukuyama with a set of theses first published in *Foreign Affairs* ("The Clash of Civilizations?" – a phrase originally coined by Bernard Lewis, another favourite of the current administration). Subsequently these papers became a book, *The Clash of Civilizations and the Remaking of the World Order.* The question mark had now disappeared. Huntington agreed that no ideological alternatives to capitalism existed, but this did not mean the "end of history." Other antagonisms remained. "The great divisions among humankind and the dominating source of conflict will be cultural. . . . The clash of civilizations will dominate global politics."[4] In particular, Huntington emphasized the continued importance of religion in the modern world, and it was this that propelled the book onto the bestseller lists after 9/11.

What did he mean by the word civilization? Early in the last century, Oswald Spengler, the German grandson of a miner, had abandoned his vocation as a teacher, turned to philosophy and to history, and produced a master-text. In *The Decline of the West*, Spengler counterposed culture (a word philologically tied to nature, the countryside, and peasant life) with civilization, which is urban and would become the site of industrial anarchy, dooming both capitalist and worker to a life of slavery to the machine-master. For Spengler, civilization reeked of death and destruction and imperialism. Democracy was the dictatorship of money and "money is overthrown and abolished only by blood."[5] The advent of "Caesarism" would drown it in "blood" and become the final episode in the history of the West. Had the Third Reich not been defeated in Europe, principally by the Red Army (the spinal cord of the Wehrmacht was broken in Stalingrad and Kursk, and the majority of the unfortunate German soldiers who perished are buried on the Russian steppes, not on the beaches of Normandy or in the Ardennes), Spengler's prediction might have come close to realization.

He was among the first and fiercest critics of Eurocentrism, and his vivid worldview, postmodern in its intensity though not its language, can be sighted in this lyrical passage:

> I see, in place of that empty figment of one linear history, the drama of a number of mighty cultures, each springing with primitive strength from the soil of a mother-region to which it remains firmly bound throughout its whole life-cycle; each stamping its material, its mankind, in its own image; each having its own idea, its own passions, its own life, will and feeling, its own death. Here indeed are colours, lights, movements, that no intellectual eye has yet discovered. Here the Cultures, peoples, languages, truths, gods, landscapes bloom and age as the oaks and stonepines, the blossoms, twigs and leaves. Each Culture has its own new possibilities of self-expression, which arise, ripen, decay and never return.[6]

In contrast to this, he argued, lay the destructive cycle of civilization:

Civilizations are the most external and artificial states of which a species of developed humanity is capable. They are a conclusion, death following life, rigidity following expansion, intellectual age and the stone-built petrifying world city following mother-earth . . . they are an end, irrevocable, yet by inward necessity reached again and again. . . . Imperialism is civilization unadulterated. In this phenomenal form the destiny of the West is now irrevocably set. . . . Expansionism is a doom, something daemonic and intense, which grips forces into service and uses up the late humanity of the world-city stage.[7]

Three-quarters of a century later, Huntington returned to Spenglerian themes, but inverted their message. He amalgamated culture and civilization. For him a civilization is a meta-culture, "the highest cultural grouping of people and the broadest level of cultural identity people have short of that which distinguishes humans from other species."[8] Huntington's chart of the top eight cultures/civilizations consists of Western, Sinic/Confucian, Japanese, Islamic, Hindu, Slavic-orthodox, Latin American, and, reluctantly, African. (The reluctance is due to an inner voice that injects doubt as to whether Africa really qualifies as a civilization.) And religion is "perhaps the central force that motivates and mobilizes people."[9] The gulf is between "the West and the Rest."[10] The West is the only civilization that defends freedom, democracy, and the free market, while the rest resist Western efforts to advance these noble values. The West is at the height of its power and, argues Huntington, utilizes the United Nations and the International Monetary Fund to impose its will globally. He discards the notion of a real difference between unilateralism and multilateralism because "the very phrase the 'world community' has become the euphemistic collective noun to give global legitimacy to actions reflecting the interests of the United States and other Western powers."[11] He is correct on this, if not on religion.

I do not believe that faith is the main determinant of global mass mobilizations. It plays a part, the extent of which is variable. The West is certainly divided on this: Europe is not deeply religious, whereas in the U.S.A. the situation is frightening. According to the latest surveys, 95 percent of Americans believe in God, including 91 percent of those who define themselves as liberals. (Only 70 percent believe in angels. This always disturbs me. I wish the angels had the majority since it would provide belief with a slightly surreal edge. More satisfying is a Gallup briefing [25 February 2003] that reveals a bipartisan belief in the horned one: the Democrats are so pious that 67 percent of them actually believe in the Devil, only 12 percentage points below the Republicans. Why more satisfying? "Who believes in the Devil," wrote Thomas Mann in *Doctor Faustus*, "already belongs to him.") Neither in China nor Russia does religion play a similar role, and I am convinced there are more un-believers in the house of Islam than can ever be counted in public, but this is a theme to which I shall return below.

In Huntington's world, the most dangerous combination would be the unity of Confucian and Islamic civilizations, neither of which shares the West's attachment to human rights. And both of which, he might have added, could hold the West to ransom. (Wary of China, the U.S.A. is pushing to open it up for business, and hoping that the steamroller of American culture and product-selling will take hold. Masses, it is hoped, will be satiated by shopping.) The U.S. global strategy necessitates con-trol of the world's oil reserves, while domestically its economy is heavily dependent on cheap imports from China.

Soon after Huntington's book appeared others joined the fray and stressed the importance of cultural differences in understanding politics, economics, demography, and so on. Much of this was sidelined after 9/11 focused the debate on "the threat of radical Islam" and the "war against terror." Instead of the West against the Rest, the new turn made it the Rest versus Islam. Huntington, to his credit, was not tempted by the neoconservative arguments dominating White House ideology before the debacle in Iraq. He modified his own views and argued that it was a clash within Islam that was the main problem and not one of civiliza-tions, which was not the case either, but certainly made one wonder how this could be squared with his view that "faith and family, blood and belief, are what people identify with and what they will fight and die for."[12]

And what is this Islam, this new bogeyman used to frighten the children? The very idea of Islam as an institutional matrix that organizes terror and resistance to the West throughout the globe is a travesty of past and present. For most of the twentieth century, organized or political Islam was, more often than not, supportive of the British Empire, and later, its American successor. It was a conservative social force, rattling the chains of superstition and fanaticism to stifle even the most fragile tremors of radical revolution. Throughout the Cold War, the Wahhabi preachers of Saudi Arabia (currently viewed as Enemy No. 1) were dispatched across the Muslim world to preach the virtues of religion and counter-revolution, and where divine truth would not prevail over reason, there were always purses pregnant with petrodollars to help win new recruits. When neither worked, the U.S.A. organized a military coup. One such case was Indonesia.

At college in Pakistan during the early sixties, Muslim socialists like me were in a permanent debate with the Islamists, who would declare that religion and the state were indivisible because "Islam is a complete code of life." We used to laugh when we heard this sentence and often pre-empt them by mouthing it to ourselves in parrot fashion. Sometimes, when debates became heated, we would ask: "Which is the largest Muslim country in the world?" Back would come the reply: "Indonesia!" Another question would be hurled back by our side: "Which is the largest Communist Party in the non-communist world?" Silence. We would chant in unison: "The Communist Party of Indonesia." These youthful exchanges were not pure banter. We were arguing that it was perfectly possible to be part of Muslim culture, appreciate its finer points, without being a believer. The Indonesian left (more than a million and a half strong) was wiped out in 1965 by General Suharto. It was one of the worst massacres of the Cold War, fully backed by the U.S.A. The vacuum in Indonesia created by the massacres of thirty-nine years ago left the field clear for the army and the Islamists. The same pattern, if not on the same scale, occurred elsewhere.

I remember well the mood that gripped Pakistan during 1969–70. A three-month-long rebellion against a pro-U.S. military dictator by students, workers, and peasants had triggered a societal upsurge. Lawyers took to the streets one day, prostitutes the next. The dictatorship crumbled and the country's first-ever general election took place. Throughout the campaign secular, socialist currents dominated politics. The religious groups were totally marginalized and often resorted to violence. As a visiting academic, when I arrived in Multan to address a rally of nearly 50,000 workers and peasants, the student wing of the Jamaat-i-Islami physically attacked the group of students who had come to meet me at the airport and escort me to the meeting. They stoned us as the police stood by and watched. This was a common occurrence in those days, but the intimidation did not work.

The 1970 Pakistani elections saw the Islamists wiped out as a political force. When, in 1972, Prime Minister Zulfikar Ali Bhutto was addressing a rally in Lahore, a group of mullahs started abusing him. Bhutto, who often spoke at several meetings a day, had an attendant who carried a tiny whisky flask and when the prime-ministerial voice became too hoarse, a glass containing amber liquid would appear and relieve the prime minister's exhaustion. At the Lahore rally there were half a million people present as well as diplomats, foreign journalists, and so on. As Bhutto sipped from the glass, a bearded man stood up, pointed at him, and shouted: "Look, people. See what he is drinking." Bhutto, who loved repartee, held up the glass and declared, "Yes, look. It's sherbet." The crowed roared with laughter. The well-placed mullahs stood up in different places and replied: "It's *sharab* [alcohol]." Finally Bhutto lost his temper and shouted: "Fine. Yes, you motherfuckers, it is *sharab*. Unlike you, I don't drink the blood of the people." The crowd was ecstatic. A spontaneous chant arose and rent the air: "Long may our Bhutto live! Long may our Bhutto drink!"

Times are different now, but not just in the Islamic world. I emphasize these very different events in Indonesia and Pakistan to show that the two largest Muslim states were subjected to the same political storms and influences as the non-Muslim world. I am no apologist for radical Islam, the widespread corruption of Islamic kingdoms, the atavistic mullahs and Qur'anic literalists, the utter venality of the House of Saud, and so on. But if Muslim civilization has become a spent force (see Bernard Lewis' *What Went Wrong? Western Impact and Middle Eastern Response*[13]) in need of top-down reform, one must eschew political agendas and deconstruct what actually happened. We require a social vision that transcends religious conservatism in the Islamic world, and the U.S. model simply will not work. It has proven itself an unviable alternative. In Indonesia and Pakistan there was an internal dynamism demanding reform. Those deemed "communists" or "socialists" by successive U.S. administrations were, in fact, moderates committed to democratization. These were the reformers in need of foreign support. Over and over again, U.S. Cold War myopia resulted in backing the wrong side. Today, in the Middle East there will be no transformation until the West answers the simple questions being asked on the street: why Iraq and not Saudi

Arabia? Why blanket support for Israel and blindness to Palestinian suffering?

This is why I reject the civilizational theses of Huntington and the Islamist ideologues who also believe that the difference of religion and blood is the determining divide in the modern world. And I reject the deracinated house Muslims in the North American and European diasporas, so desperate to please, so eager to be integrated – and on any basis – that they sink to their knees and join the sickly chorus, winning the earthly rewards of media attention and tenure. At the top of this heap lies Ahmed Chalabi, the Iraqi handmaiden to the White House operatives.

A point repeatedly made by professors of human rights on U.S. campuses and "civil society" groups to justify Western interventions, including the invasion and occupation of Iraq, is that it is democracy and the plurality of institutions independent of the state, but rooted in capitalism, that defines the culture of the West. In 1919, an anti-imperialist wind arose in Afghanistan and the tribal confederacy accepted Amanullah as the king. He was a modernizer and admirer of Kemal Atatürk. His wife Soraya was a proto-feminist. The nationalist intellectuals in Amanullah's circle prepared a draft constitution. It included universal adult franchise. If it had been implemented, women in Afghanistan would have obtained the vote before their sisters in Britain and the West. The reason it was not implemented was that the British, via an experienced agent – T. E. Lawrence – stoked up a few tribes, paid them, and told them that women were being encouraged to become prostitutes. The British themselves then intervened to topple Amanullah.

Ironically, as the culture of democratic life deteriorates in the West, there is a growing demand for self-expression in much of the Muslim world. The citizens of Egypt and Saudi Arabia, not to mention Syria and the Gulf statelets, are desperate to choose their own governments, but there is a problem. It is what Huntington has referred to as "the democracy paradox."[14] Or in plain language: democracy might produce elected governments hostile to the U.S.A. This is true. It might. That is why Washington prefers the kleptocratic Saudi dynasty and the moth-eaten military regime in Egypt.

And Iraq? The demand for an elected constituent assembly (first put forward by Ayatollah Sistani) is straight out of the French Revolution. But it would probably produce a government that would unite the country on the basis of two clear-cut aims: the withdrawal of all foreign troops and Iraqi control of Iraqi oil. To have occupied a country and then watch it flout the Washington consensus would be too painful. So puppets are appointed and the resistance continues. The war has been a tremendous help to Al-Qaeda, enabling them to recruit hundreds of new supporters.

Meanwhile, in neighbouring Iran, a decrepit clerical regime is increasingly isolated from the population. Sixty-three percent of the people are under thirty years of age. All they have known is the rule of the clerics. They want something different. Despite the clerics, Iran has a vibrant semi-clandestine culture. The Iranian new-wave cinema is flourishing and, as enthusiastic exploiters of the Internet, Iran's dissident bloggers dominate cyberspace. While the clerics continue to suppress free speech (closing down dissident newspapers such as *Neshat*), such reprisals are addressed in courts of law. Iran offers hope. When the clerics are defeated, the people of this country who accepted the leadership of the mullahs to get rid of the Shah might inaugurate a reformation with far-reaching effects. I would not be surprised if mosque and state were divided forever after another upheaval in Iran. In the current climate, Iranian self-emancipation would be seriously delayed or halted by foreign intervention. The recent election of a hard-line president was a desperate throw by the clerics, which is unlikely to succeed.

In 1995, an Afghan-American ideologue Zalmay Khalilzad (formerly the proconsul in Kabul who busily negotiated deals with Taliban factions to preserve his puppet protégé and now proconsul in Iraq) published an essay in which he suggested that U.S. hegemony had to be preserved at all costs – if necessary, by force! September 11 provided the opportunity to try out the theory. For President George W. Bush, Ahmed Chalabi provided a perfect bookend to this history, but Iraq is proof that the use of force can provoke a mighty resistance.

Cultures and civilizations are now, and have always been, hybrids. To suggest otherwise is to fall prey to the twin devils of ideology and chauvinism. The tragedy of the abuses at Abu Ghraib is that they created a clash of civilizations where no such clash had existed. Through its own myopia, the West has given radical Islam the ammunition it was thirsting for. In the short term, President Bush will insist that his hands are clean and that the forces of darkness are behind every door. If this blindness and these lies persist, the long-term prospects are too desperate to contemplate.

NOTES

1. Luke Harding, "G2: Women: The Other Prisoners: Most of the Coverage of Abuse at Abu Ghraib Has Focused on Male Detainees. But What of the Five Women Held in the Jail, and Elsewhere in Iraq?," *The Guardian*, 20 May 2004, p. 10.

2. Dahr Jamail, *Asia Times Online*, 11 January 2005. http://atimes01.atimes.com/atimes/middle_east/ga11ak01.html (accessed 27 September 2005).

3. Francis Fukuyama, *The End of History and the Last Man* (New York: Free Press, 1992).

4. Samuel Huntington, "The Clash of Civilizations?," *Foreign Affairs*, 72(3), Summer 1993, p. 22.

5. Oswald Spengler, *The Decline of the West: Complete in One Volume*, trans. Charles Francis Atkinson (New York: A. A. Knopf, 1932), p. 507.

6. Ibid., p. 21.

7. Ibid., p. 31.

8. Samuel Huntington, *The Clash of Civilizations and the Remaking of World Order* (New York: Simon & Schuster, 1996), p. 43.

9. Ibid., p. 66.

10. Ibid., p. 33.

11. Ibid., p. 184.

12. Samuel Huntington, "If Not Civilizations, What? Samuel Huntington Responds to His Critics," *Foreign Affairs*, 72(5), November/December 1993. Article available at: http://www.foreignaffairs.org/19931201faresponse5213/samuel-p-huntington/if-not-civilizations-what-samuel-huntington-responds-to-his-critics.html (accessed 19 September 2005).

13. Bernard Lewis, *What Went Wrong? Western Impact and Middle Eastern Response* (Oxford: Oxford University Press, 2002).

14. Huntington, *Clash of Civilizations*, p. 94.

4

GENDER, POLITICAL ISLAM,
AND IMPERIALISM

Shahrzad Mojab

Challenging imperialism and fundamentalism with the aim of replacing the status quo with better and more viable alternatives is a major challenge. It is not surprising, therefore, that anti-imperialist literature presents a diverse range of intellectual, theoretical, and political positions. Other chapters in this book offer a critique of positions that vindicate or rationalize the new imperialist order; here, I examine an intellectual trend that is opposed to all forms of domination and oppression, but is held back by its own theoretical and methodological commitments. This is post-structuralism, which rejects concepts such as imperialism, capitalism, and patriarchy as "essentialisms" or "grand narratives," and fails to confront them politically. I will focus on the war waged on the women of the Middle East by the U.S. and by Islamic "fundamentalists" in Iran, Iraq, and Afghanistan.

THE CONTEXT

There is a bloody war being waged between imperialists led by the Bush administration and "fundamentalists," especially in Afghanistan and Iraq. The war is over the control of resources, human and natural, in the Middle East. This war is fought on many fronts. While the brutal physical war appears in sanitized form on Western television screens, the pro-imperialist intellectual establishment is engaged in a bitter war on the ideological and cultural fronts. This war, by no means less intensive or aggressive than the McCarthyist propaganda of the early 1950s, is aimed at winning the hearts and minds of the public; its target is anyone opposed to imperialism.

In the U.S.A., for instance, the extreme right expects specialists on the Middle East to be anti-Islamist, anti-Arab, pro-American, and pro-Israel. The neoconservative line was outlined by President Bush after 9/11: "Either you are with us, or you are with the terrorists." In this political environment, academic freedom, like all civil liberties, is readily violated.[1] There seems to be no end to this war. The unprecedented spread of the capitalist market in the last two decades has been associated with unceasing wars, genocide, poverty, hunger, violence against women, homelessness, violence against children, and destruction of the environment. It would not be far-fetched to claim that the new imperialism has the cultural and physical potential to drag the world into world wars and genocide just as the older form did.

Preventing new imperialist disasters is by no means easy. It demands a large-scale mobilization of the peoples of the world, something like the worldwide anti-war protest of 15 February 2003, although in the form of active, unceasing, and global social movements. It also requires considerable struggle amongst those opposed to war. We need to find the best ways to overcome imperialism, fascism, and their never-ending wars.

Post-structuralists have created an important body of knowledge about modes of oppression often ignored by other theoretical positions. This consciousness is, no doubt, a step forward for those who struggle to build an alternative to imperialist domination. I contend, however, that post-structuralism, especially its critique of essentialism and binary thinking, undermines its ability to offer an adequate explanation of the desperate situation in which we live, let alone map any alternatives. I just used the word "explanation"; that many post-structuralists reject the concept of explanation but may consent to alternatives such as "understanding" or "interpretation" anticipates some of my criticism.

My approach here follows the lines that Karl Marx charted 160 years ago. My position is Marxist-feminist, and I engage in radical criticism that is not "afraid of the results it arrives at," and is "just as little afraid of conflict with the powers that be."[2]

Today's anti-Islamism demonizes a billion Muslims into potential terrorists, zealots, fanatics, violent patriarchs, or hate-mongers. This totalization of Muslims into enemies of the West is as dangerous as the anti-Semitism of the 1930s. Is it such a great leap of imagination to see mass round-ups and internment of Muslims in Western countries being undertaken in the name of the war on terror? We need knowledge, theoretical perspectives, and education aimed at overcoming imperialist racism. Cultural relativism, which was a powerful intellectual tool in the struggle against the eugenic strand of early twentieth-century racism, fails to contribute to the struggle today. I will argue that post-structuralism, too, is in a weak position to offer alternatives.

POLITICAL ISLAM AND THE PRODUCTION OF KNOWLEDGE

With the foundation of Iran's theocracy in 1979, Islam became a major site of political and intellectual conflict throughout the world. Ayatollah Khomeini created this theocracy in the wake of a very popular revolution, which overthrew the half-century rule of a Westernizing, "modernizing," and secularist monarchy. He inspired Muslims throughout the world to fight not for Islam-friendly regimes, as he himself did until the early 1970s, but for the creation of Islamic states. Some fifteen years later, the absolutist theocracy of the Taliban assumed power in neighboring Afghanistan in the wake of a highly destructive war between a pro-Soviet secular regime and Muslim groups supported by the U.S.A. and the region's conservative states.

When the Shah of Iran (labeled the "U.S. policeman" by American media) was on the verge of falling, Western powers, especially Washington, opted for Khomeini's takeover of Iran in order to thwart a potential communist takeover in a strategically vital part of the world. There was nothing unusual in this policy, especially during the Cold War era. Back in the 1940s and early 1950s, the U.S.A. had advised the Shah to use Islam against growing social movements. In 1953, Washington planned and executed a *coup d'état*, which overthrew the democratically elected government of the nationalist leader, Dr. Mossadeq. Similar plans to support Islam against "communists" were on the agendas of other Middle Eastern countries (for example, Turkey, Israel, Saudi Arabia).

The imperialist interests of the United States and other Western powers acted as a brake on the struggle for the separation of state and religion, which had begun in the late nineteenth century. Western states consistently encouraged the suppression of civil liberties, nascent civil societies, and public spheres, which they considered to favor communism.[3] As a result, instead of securing the separation of state and mosque, the region is now in the grip of theocratic politics. If pre-1979 social movements led by secular nationalists and communists had the upper hand in the oppositional politics of the Middle East, today Islamist fundamentalists pose as anti-colonial, anti-imperialist forces. Although the two theocracies and the Islamist movements that they inspired or supported have now declared war on the U.S.A. and the West, their main targets are the peoples of the region, especially women. Their anti-Westernism and anti-modernism serve the politics of enslaving women and the working people of the region.

NEW GROUND IN UNDERSTANDING ISLAM?

Since 1979, we have learned a great deal about the Middle East, especially Islam. At the same time, the empowerment of neoconservatives in the U.S.A., and the implementation of their post-9/11 policies, has unleashed a new phase of Islamophobia. Today, Islam occupies a visible place in films, talk shows, journals, encyclopedias, video games, news reports, and new research and teaching programs devoted to Islamic studies.

In spite of the quantitative leap in the study of Islam, there has been no breakthrough in our understanding of contemporary conflicts involving Islam and Islamist movements. This is the case in spite of the fact that the new round of conflict over Islam has coincided with major shifts in Western knowledge, namely the turn away from structuralism and towards post-structuralism, along with its many offshoots carrying the prefix *post-*. This shift involved the critique of all previous knowledge systems, especially modernist thought and its theoretical, methodological, and political claims. The shift involved, among other things, the critique of linear, binary thinking, and essentialism. In this context, the work of Edward Said, especially his critique of Orientalism (published in 1978), highlighted the intellectual and political biases of Western knowledge about Islam, and contributed to the formation of post-colonial studies.

The two major non-Marxist modes of interpretation – structuralism and post-structuralism – fail to provide complex, contextual, and historical understandings of these conflicts. Taking a dialectical approach, this chapter claims that post-structuralism, much like structuralism, engages in linear, dualistic, and binary modes of interpretation.

THEORETICAL FRAMEWORKS

Post-structuralist Critique of Binarism and Essentialism

Post-structuralism identifies "binary thinking" (also either/or logic, dualistic, dichotomous, and linear thinking) as a major obstacle to critical understanding. Feminists have contributed to the critique of Western binary thought by emphasizing its androcentric and patriarchal order.[4] In order to state briefly the limitations of binarist thinking from a feminist perspective, I quote the short article on "binaries/bipolarity" from the *Encyclopedia of Feminist Theories*:

> Binary oppositions, and bipolarity, refer to a practice that runs through western thought of arranging conceptual/theoretical systems in opposed, contrasting pairs. The idea is that *good*, for example, can be understood only in contrast with *bad, light* by contrast with *dark.* Characterizing these contrasts as *bipolar* represents the opposed terms as radically separate from one another, not as points on a continuum. The arrangement might appear to be a perfectly neutral way of classifying attributes of the world, both physical and human. But feminist critiques contest the neutrality, showing that the pairs mark not merely descriptive but also evaluative contrasts, which are enlisted to condemn one "side" while promoting and celebrating the other. The male/female polity is no exception.[5]

Another article on "dichotomies," based on the work of Nancy Jay, identifies the problems of dichotomizing:

> A dichotomy is a conceptual division into two mutually exclusive kinds: male is radically distinct from female, reason from emotion. Nancy Jay traces the gendered significance of dichotomous thinking to Aristotelian logic, where everything must be A or Not-A; A and Not-A exhaust all possible characteristics. Continuity or overlap between them is logically impossible, for Not-A is the privation or absence of A. In the principal dichotomies constitutive of western philosophy – mind/body; objective/subjective; reason/emotion; universal/particular; active/passive – the terms are hierarchically ordered with the first representing the positive, valued attribute, the second, the negative, devalued one. Feminists

have demonstrated parallels with the male/female and public/ private dichotomies to show how dichotomous thinking functions to denigrate everything aligned with the female, containing it within private, controlled social spaces.[6]

Thus, the post-structuralist alternative to binary thinking is not to treat contrasts as "radically separate" but as "points on a continuum," and not as "mutually exclusive" but, rather, as continuous and overlapping. In its popular and, perhaps, dominant form, this approach discards binarisms such as man/woman or male/female, and questions the usefulness of crucial concepts such as "patriarchy" or "woman" even if they do not appear in dichotomous relations with other concepts. According to Code, for example,

> Despite patriarchy's heuristic value for theorizing hierarchical social structures, for feminists its usefulness is diminished by its essentialism, according to which male dominance of women is an inevitable response to natural differences. Such assumptions sustain ahistorical conceptions of "woman" and "man" as universal categories, ignoring racial, class, and other differences. Patriarchy's usefulness as a theoretical concept is contested around these issues.[7]

I argue, however, that "patriarchy" cannot be branded as an essentialism just because some interpreters treat male dominance as "an inevitable response to natural differences," as Code states above. Indeed, there has long been considerable consensus that such interpretations are not valid for reasons other than essentialism: very simply, there is nothing natural in gender or human relations. Moreover, just because some feminists do not account for racial, class, ethnic, national, or religious differences, the concept "woman" does not turn into an ahistorical, universal category. This post-structuralist claim is itself rooted in binary thinking in so far as it treats essentialism and belief in difference as mutually exclusive. It is an either/or logic, which cannot see the coexistence of difference and essence in, for instance, the conceptualization of "woman." One may, for instance, believe in the diversity – ethnic, racial, class, language, sexuality, or disability – of women and still essentialize them as the inferior, evil, fair, or weak gender. While structuralism is, indeed, able to delve into the dynamics of opposites such as difference/sameness, post-structuralism lags behind it by universalizing difference into an ahistorical category, which has nothing to do with sameness or, at best, enters into a mutually exclusive relationship with it.

The fear of essentialism and binarism (and the failure of post-structuralists to offer an alternative to this way of thinking) has turned post-structuralist feminism into an intellectual enterprise that fails to challenge patriarchy. Post-structuralists have noticed that their theoretical commitment is in conflict with their ideas of emancipation:

> But by identifying with the category of "women" and attributing any positive elements to it, feminists risk becoming essentialists. That means not only denying differences among women, but also taking part in the reification of the category. Thus feminism is placed in a paradoxical situation in which it is both dependent on the idea of "woman" and has to refuse it.[8]

This "paradox" is so debilitating that some advocates of post-structuralism have had to recall essentialism from the back door. Gayatri Chakravorty Spivak, for instance, has retrieved essentialism, but on a "temporary" basis and in the guise of "strategic essentialism."[9] Inspired by Spivak, Ryan has proposed strategic and temporary alliances with "relativism."[10]

Such paradoxes also emerge when dealing with "imperialism" and "capitalism," to mention only two "essentialisms" or "grand narratives." If imperialism is an essentialism that defies or distorts understanding, it would be appropriate, I agree, to abandon it theoretically; politically, it would be honest to ignore it. However, imperialism, much like patriarchy, does not leave anyone alone, and post-structuralists have only a few choices – compliance, silence, or resistance. Resistance to imperialism does, however, invite conflicts between their theory and politics.

Post-structuralists find it difficult to resolve the conflict between their theoretical and political commitments. This is, in part, due to the fact that their anti-essentialism is part of a theoretical package, which privileges uncertainty and relativism and challenges foundationalism, universalism, and binary thinking.

In order to resolve the problem of binary thought, post-structuralism adopts a strategy of eliminating binary constructs by eliminating only one of its components. For instance, by eliminating binarisms such as man/woman, male/female, masculine/feminine, mind/body, determinism/ contingency, reason/emotion, universal/particular, or necessity/freedom, post-structuralists ignore one side, and universalize the other side. Thus, "reason," "determination," and "universal" are discarded and their opposites, "emotion," "contingency," and "particular" are privileged as the modus vivendi of a new intellectual world.

If post-structuralism makes compromises with binary thinking, it still cannot reconcile with the most serious alternative, that is, dialectics. While the rejection of dialectics is primarily political and ideological, it is done by conflating it with binarism.

The Dialectic Alternative to Binary Thinking

Dialectical ways of thinking can be traced back to ancient philosophical struggles from China to Greece. However, dialectics is primarily associated with the names of Heraclitus, Hegel, and Marx. Heraclitus (*c.* 535–475 B.C.), for example, suggested that everything flows and changes; change alone is unchanging; no one can step into the same river twice; and all phenomena are composed of the unity (or identity) of opposites. Reality for him was always in a state of flux, movement, and change. Hegel and Marx adopted and refined the idea of universal flux and unity of opposites.[11]

Even in its earliest Heraclitian beginnings, dialectics provides a methodology for understanding the world that shares little with post-structuralism and its preoccupation with eroding conflicts, oppositions, and contradictions. The main problem for Marxist dialectics, as for all dialectical thinking, is to explain change or motion. If structuralism is interested in opposites as explanatory framework, and post-structuralism reduces such opposites to binarisms and dichotomies, dialectics is, according to Lenin, "the doctrine of the unity of opposites."[12] Opposites in a dialectical contradiction coexist in unity and conflict. According to Lenin, "the identity [that is, unity] of opposites . . . is the recognition (discovery) of the contradictory, mutually exclusive, opposite tendencies in all phenomena and processes of nature (including mind and society)."[13] Opposites not only coexist but also transform into one another, and this coexistence is, at the same time, a process of mutual transformation. Contradictions, internal and external, are the sources of change. There is nothing static; motion/change is absolute and rest/ stability is relative.

IMPERIALISM, SECULARISM, AND GENDER RELATIONS

It is well known, especially after Edward Said's critique of Orientalism, that colonialist constructions of societies practicing Islam have treated this religion as essentially different from Christianity or other religions. Islam is the source of all backwardness and the main obstacle to change; it is by its very nature fundamentalist, tyrannical, and obscurantist, and not compatible with democracy and other Western values. This interpretation of Islam not only helps Western states and colonialists in presenting their societies as the ideal or superior ones, but also serves the purpose of imperialist domination. Anti-Islamism and Anti-Arabism in post-9/11 times find a firm ground in the old Orientalist knowledge.

If imperialist constructions of Muslims treat the West and Islamic East as inherently different entities, many Muslim intellectuals and politicians do the same, though for different reasons. For instance, they treat feminism, modernity, secularism, liberalism, and socialism as inherently Western, and incompatible with Islamic traditions.

Post-strucuralists reject Islamophobia (there is no essential, fixed, monolithic Islam or Muslim) as an essentialization of the religion and its practitioners. They also undermine this form of racism by criticizing its binarist and us/them frameworks. This theoretical framework, useful as it may be, converges with Islamist and colonialist claims that Muslims are Muslims, and the West is the West, and, to borrow from Rudyard Kipling, "never the twain shall meet." No doubt, these groups – Islamists, Orientalists, and post-structuralists – do not advocate a single policy. However, their politics often conflict with the interests of the social movements in the region, especially women's movements. I try to demonstrate this convergence of interest by looking at the struggle over secularism in the Middle East.

The Struggle over Secularism

I mentioned earlier that, after World War Two, U.S. imperialist interests promoted Islam against secular social movements in the Middle East. In the midst of the Cold War, Saudi Arabia (a staunch U.S. ally) used fundamentalist Wahhabism against Arab nationalist movements, the revolutionary movement in Oman in the late 1960s and early 1970s, communist movements, women's movements, and secular and leftist Palestinian resistance. Washington relied on Saudi Arabia as the major headquarters for a religious war against democracy, secularism, and socialism. The U.S.A. and the U.K. made close alliances with Afghan and foreign fundamentalists against Afghanistan's pro-Soviet regime, and for more than a decade provided the most sophisticated arms, training, and leadership in order to force the Soviet Union out of Afghanistan. Some of these fundamentalists later turned against the U.S.A. before and on 9/11. The conflict between the U.S.A. and its former allies led to two major wars, in Afghanistan and Iraq, which continue to this day.

The second U.S. war against Iraq aimed at overthrowing the Baathist regime of Saddam Hussein, and replacing it with a client state. This war brought Shiite leaders into alliance with the warring and occupying power. The Shiite leadership advocated a theocratic state while others (including the Kurds) called for the separation of state and religion. As a result of the ongoing war, women in the Arab regions of Iraq have been subjected to unprecedented violence, including abduction and rape; they are unable to leave home without male protection.

Less than two years after the fall of Saddam, Women for Women International, an U.S. aid group working in Iraq, concluded in a report that "Iraqi women have been marginalized and excluded by both the U.S.-led Transitional Governing Authority and its successor, the Iraqi Governing Council."[14] Very few women were invited to participate in the April 2003 meetings, which planned the creation of an interim government. And only three women were nominated to the Interim Governing Council. No women were included in the nine-member rotating presidential council or the twenty-four-member committee which drafted the interim constitution. If women were excluded from the nation-building process, tribal and feudal lords, religious patriarchs, exiled nationalists, former Bathist dissidents, aristocrats, pro-U.S. technocrats and bureaucrats, and U.S. advisors worked as architects of the new state.

After the fall of Saddam, an ultraconservative U.S. organization, the Independent Women's Forum (I.W.F.), received a $10 million grant from the Department of State as part of its Iraqi Women's Democracy Initiative, in order to train Iraqi women for democracy.[15] The I.W.F., in partnership with American Islamic Congress and the Foundation for the Defense of Democracies, offer leadership training and "democracy education" for Iraqi women.[16]

The 2005 draft of the Iraqi Constitution has all the ingredients to act as a theocratic state. According to Article (2):

1st – Islam is the official religion of the state and is a basic source of legislation: (a) No law can be passed that contradicts the undisputed rules of Islam. (b) No law can be passed that contradicts the principles of democracy. (c) No law can be passed that contradicts the rights and basic freedoms outlined in this constitution. 2nd – This constitution guarantees the Islamic identity of the majority of the Iraqi people and the full religious rights for all individuals and the freedom of creed and religious practices.[17]

The U.S.A. has installed a similar, though more openly theocratic, structure in Afghanistan. According to the 2004 draft constitution, "the religion of Afghanistan is the sacred religion of Islam . . . no law can be contrary to the sacred religion of Islam and the values of this Constitution."[18] According to Amnesty International, religion, tradition, and the state combine to perpetrate the harshest forms of male violence:

[V]iolence against women and girls in Afghanistan is pervasive; few women are exempt from the reality or threat of violence. Afghan women and girls live with the risk of: abduction and rape by armed individuals; forced marriage; being traded for settling disputes and debts; and face daily discrimination from all segments of society as well as by state officials. Strict societal codes, invoked in the name of tradition and religion, are used as justification for denying women the ability to enjoy their fundamental rights, and have led to the imprisonment of some women, and even to killings. Should they protest by running away, the authorities may imprison them.[19]

While Islamists in Iraq and Afghanistan have been busy constructing new theocracies, in Iran we have seen a widespread revolt against theocratic rule over the last twenty-seven years (this includes resistance by "religious intellectuals," who call for the separation of state and religion; see below). Women in Iran have violated Islamic codes of dress, often at the risk of repression. How do we account for these experiences?

The group of theories prefixed with *post-* constitute a diverse body of interpretation. However, they share considerable ground, which distinguishes them from Marxism. For instance, Sayyid's interpretation of Islamism (the term he uses instead of fundamentalism) is based on ideas of the decentering, breaking down of boundaries and meta-narratives, leading to the decentering of the West and the end of "the Age of Europe."[20] Islam is, as in Orientalist literature, the engine of history. In this genre of literature, produced by Muslim and non-Muslim post-structuralism, secularism is considered a Western project that is in conflict with Islam. These interpretations remain, however, within the framework of binarist thinking (Islam vs West), and fail to explain the ongoing revolt against theocracy in Iran, and growing Islamist activism in Turkey and Iraq where secular regimes have been in power for a long time.

The Marxist approach is radically different from post-structuralism. Like most theoretical positions, it differentiates religion from other social formations such as nation, state, family, patriarchy, ethnicity, economy, or culture. However, unlike other positions, which confer on religion an independent, usually determining, role, it emphasizes interconnections between religion and other institutions. For instance, while religion and state can be distinguished even in theocratic political orders such as Iran or Taliban Afghanistan, Marxist dialectics unravels their coexistence even in secular democratic regimes such as Canada, France, and the U.S.A., where the separation of state and church is a credo of these "civic nations." Thus, dialectically speaking, the autonomous status of religion is not the negation of its dependence. In other words, independence and dependence, far from being a binarist opposition, form a dialectical contradiction in which opposites exist in unity and conflict, rather than in mutually exclusive relationships.

Islam, then, cannot be understood qua Islam. Put differently, Islam should be treated not simply as religion but at the same time as politics, culture, economy, ethnicity, nationality, and much more. This religion is as complex and diverse as the individuals, groups, and peoples who practice it. Although it has a universally accepted "divine" scripture, that is, the Qur'an, there is no single interpretation or understanding of it.

The multiple interpretations of the Qur'an are not simply a question of the "polysemic" nature of the text. This book does not, for instance, prescribe the death penalty for adultery, *zina*, but patriarchal practitioners of this religion, both "fundamentalist" and nonfundamentalist, disregard their most fundamental text, and practice the death penalty, including stoning married adulterers to death. Thus, sharia, developed by human beings after the Qur'an, violates the verdicts of Allah. Sharia texts provide legitimation for the brutal violence against women throughout the region. To give another example, while the Qur'an allows for the inheritance of property by females, the feudal class has generally ignored this "divine" verdict, and denied women inheritance of agrarian land because it is not compatible with the dictates of the patrilineal feudal order. In these cases, the requirements of patriarchy and feudalism have rewritten the holy script.

From a dialectical perspective, religious claims should be assessed in the context in which they are expressed. First and foremost, the claim of a religious group to return to fundamentals or origins is a statement about the present. All such claims express contemporary interests in this world.[21] It is worldly concerns rather than "divinity" that drive some Muslims to create an Islamic state. Some students of Islamist politics question the validity of the term, and use "political Islam" instead of fundamentalism.[22]

Western imperialism, now in conflict with its former Islamist allies, uses both fire and water in order to defeat its enemy. While resources are focused on war, including perpetration of war crimes against prisoners in Abu Ghraib and many other locations, there is considerable effort to promote "moderate" or "reformist" Islam as an alternative to fundamentalism. While the U.S.A. violates domestic and international law regarding the laws of war, it also speaks the language of constitutions and the rule of law in Afghanistan and Iraq.

The European Union, too, promotes moderate Islam. For instance, the Norwegian Nobel Committee awarded the 2003 peace prize to an Iranian lawyer, Shirin Ebadi, in recognition of "her efforts for democracy and human rights." The Committee noted that she "favours enlightenment and dialogue as the best path to changing attitudes and resolving conflict. . . . Ebadi is a conscious Moslem. She sees no conflict between Islam and fundamental human rights." The Committee hoped that "the Prize will be an inspiration for all those who struggle for human rights and democracy in her country, in the Moslem world, and in all countries where the fight for human rights needs inspiration and support." It also emphasized that the awarding of prizes was aimed at speeding up the advance of democracy and human rights.[23]

From a Marxist-feminist perspective, the major contradiction in this web of contradictions is between Islamist movements and the peoples of each region. In other words, the main target of these groups is not the West, Western states, capitalism, or Western culture. Fundamentalists are fighting over the control of the natural and human resources of the oil-rich region. They have targeted women, workers, youth, peasants, and secular, democratic, and socialist individuals and institutions. Much of the post-structuralist and post-colonialist literature fails to see the seriousness of these contradictions, while it ignores the close ties between capitalist powers and Islamists. In order to illustrate this point, I return to the politics of granting the Nobel peace prize to a Muslim Iranian woman.

Shirin Ebadi is the typical "moderate" or "reformist" Muslim, also a woman and a lawyer, who has tried to reform the Islamic theocracy of Iran into a modern or moderate state. The Nobel award immediately created, or rather re-created, a web of contradictions. Conservative Islamists treated the award as an American-Zionist plot against genuine Islam; liberal Muslims hailed it as a recognition of Islam; and for some Iranian nationalists it was no less than a matter of national pride.[24] However, radical secular Iranians overcame the lure of national pride, and one of them, an Iranian poet in exile, wrote a poem in which he treated the Nobel Committee's decision as a "blind blow against secularism throughout the world." The poet, Yadollah Royai, resents the Committee's policy of treating theocracy as the fate of Iranians, and at the same time considers this policy not only against secularism in Iran but also "throughout the world."[25]

The conflict over Shirin Ebadi's Nobel peace prize highlights the mainstream and Orientalist perceptions of peoples who practice Islam. The dominant view is that all Muslims are eternally tied to a religion, which is incompatible with secularism, secular politics, and secular ways of life. This rather old Orientalist view is shared even by some who are opposed to Orientalism, for instance, advocates of politics of "difference." Since the late 1980s, "difference feminists" have insisted that Islam is the framework for the moderation of gender relations in the Islamic theocracy of Iran. They essentialize Iranian women as Muslims, and do not see any secular alternative to an Islamic model of womanhood. Much like the Islamists, they believe that Iranian women should be defined by their religion alone, and that they should engage in "woman-friendly" interpretations of the Qur'an and sharia in order to improve their lot.

The claim that patriarchal gender relations can be subverted through "woman-friendly" interpretations of Islam underestimates the seriousness of contradictions between patriarchy and women, which are reproduced with utmost male violence, including honor killing. It also denies the possibility of conflict between religion and secularism, and rejects this conflict as Western and non-Islamic. It fully ignores a century of struggle for separation of state and mosque in the region. This struggle is, from a "difference perspective," not part of the history of peoples whose religion is Islam.

It is not an accident of history that Michel Foucault, one of the major figures in the intellectual upheaval of the late 1970s, rushed to Iran to experience the "Islamic revolution" first hand.[26] If Khomeini was promoting his state-building project as "neither Eastern nor Western," many Western intellectuals such as Foucault were seeking in the Islamic project a new opening to the world they had failed to explain or to build. Much like the Islamists, they, too, were looking for a way out of the conflict between capitalism and socialism. Dissatisfied by capitalist modernity, they were also seeking a way out of Marxist or socialist alternatives such as "really existing socialism." In a recent study of Foucault's writing on the Iranian revolution, Afary and Anderson conclude that "Foucault's Orientalist impressions of the Muslim world, his selective reading and representation of Greco-Roman texts, and his hostility to modernity and its technologies of the body, led him to prefer the more traditional Islamic/Mediterranean culture to the modern culture of the West."[27]

Marxism and post-structuralism offer two diametrically different views of the relationship between religion and secularism. For post-structuralists this is only a binarism, while Marxist dialectics views it as a major contradiction. In Iran, for example, the state is built on the basis of Islamic principles, and a Council of Guardians ensures that the legislation passed in the parliament does not conflict with Islam. Even in countries where the separation of state and religion has already been enshrined in constitutions and legal documents, the contradiction is not resolved. As we can see from the current debates over same-sex marriage, the definition of family, or abortion rights in Canada, religion is still present inside and outside of the institution of the state.

The contradiction between religion and secularism, or patriarchy and women, is a product of a long history, and will take a long time to resolve. While gender relations are regulated by the state in a theocracy (to the extent feasible through law, courts, prisons, and so on), the oppression of women is also perpetrated every minute and every hour in the privacy of the home, on the streets, and in the workplace. Oppression is also reproduced in language, music, arts, literature, media, and education. To claim that "Muslim women" will achieve equality with woman-friendly readings of the Qur'an and sharia would at best amount to an under-rating of patriarchy as a social and political institution. Islam thrives on patriarchy and patriarchy is anchored in this religion. No woman-friendly reading of this system, even if it is rooted in mass "Islamic feminist" movements, can displace let alone replace it. In his dialectical approach to Reformation, Marx said that Martin Luther:

> shattered faith in authority because he restored the authority of faith. He turned priests into laymen because he turned laymen into priests. He freed man from outer religiosity because he made religiosity the inner man. He freed the body from chains because he enchained the heart.[28]

In other words, bourgeois democracy was interested only in driving religion out of the seat of state power. Marx noted that emancipation required continuing secularization, this time even more difficult than "pillaging the churches," because it has to be against the "priest inside."[29] In Iran, the struggle for separation of state and mosque has intensified due to more than two decades of theocratic tyranny. A number of "religious intellectuals" have called for the separation of religion and state based on theological arguments that are similar to those of the Enlightenment.[30] Some advocate an Islam without clerics (*rouhaniyat*).[31] However, postcolonial studies tends to deny that secularism is an integral part of the history of peoples in Islamic countries. If Orientalism treats the Islamic world as an exception to world history, if it treats secularism as a question of us/them or self/other (Muslims cannot be secular), post-structuralists appeal to the politics of difference to arrive at similar conclusions. This politics also converges with the Islamist claim that secularism is a product of capitalism and should be rejected by all religions.[32]

Islamists had to respond to the emergence of women as a new social force in the late nineteenth century. They had to meet the challenge of feminism, which like many components of modernity came from the West. Some rejected the idea of the emancipation of women, while others had to reconcile with it. The rejectionist front suffered major setbacks due to the hegemony of secular nationalist, democratic, and socialist politics. However, with the formation of the Islamic Republic of Iran, rejectionists launched the most ambitious project of constructing an Islamic model of womanhood. The ideal Muslim woman was to negate two centuries of achievements of feminism in the West by offering an Islamic alternative. However, if this was the most ambitious project backed by the authority of Khomeini and a popular revolution, women's resistance against it was equally prominent. Still, the project of Islamizing gender relations failed at its very inception. While many women resist the Islamic state by risking their safety and security in Iran, they put on the veil in countries such as Turkey and Egypt as a form of struggle against the state.

Islamists create a monolithic or essential entity called "Muslim woman." They argue that ideas of equality between women and men cannot apply to Muslim women because they are based on Western concepts of gender relations rooted in secularism and modernity. The claim to the particularism of "Muslim women" found a ready confirmation in the new intellectual environment. If some Islamists sell their patriarchal politics under the guise of particularism, Western academia provides them with the most rigorous theorization of their "exceptional" gender politics. If Muslim women constitute a unique phenomenon in the history of the world, Western social theory confirms it by claiming that difference is the essence of the universe.

The emergence of women as a new social force and their struggle for equal rights invited diverse responses from Islamist forces. In the course of these struggles, the concept of "Islamic feminism" was used in the 1990s. Although the merging of Islam and feminism dates back to the late nineteenth century, the concept "Islamic feminism" triggered considerable debate. The problem has been posed as one of "compatibility" between Islam and feminism. Two broad perspectives have emerged. Some Islamists reject feminism as a Western phenomenon and argue that Islam is a religion of equality and justice, and feminism is redundant, irrelevant, and, as a secular project, is non-emancipatory. Starting from very different positions, some secular feminists have argued that women's emancipation cannot be achieved within any religious framework, and that feminism and Islam constitute a contradiction in terms.[33]

Part of the post-structuralist theoretical baggage is branding universal women's rights as "grand narratives," and rejecting them as "totalitarianism." This is the best theoretical shielding of political Islam and Islamic patriarchy in Iran, Afghanistan, and Iraq. This line of argument is not useful, however. Let us accept that Islam and feminism, or Judaism and feminism, are compatible. Our task is to unravel the limitations of any feminist project based on any group identity such as religion, ethnicity, or nationality. This is the main question: why should the struggle against women's oppression be based on Islam, its sharia or its culture (if such a unified culture exists at all)? Whose interests does it serve if the demand for women's rights is shaped by sharia? An alternative position is the compatibility position, which, like its opposite, comes from both religious and secular quarters. Certain liberal Islamic groups argue that their religion, much like Christianity and Judaism, is flexible, and is able to advance women's rights, and develop Islamic gender relations based on equality and justice. Secular thinkers reject the incompatibility claim by arguing that Islam and feminism should not be constructed into a dichotomous pair, one essentialized as a project of subordination and the other as a project of emancipation. This secular claim is often rooted in post-structuralist critiques of essentialism and binarism.[34]

The post-structuralist critique of dichotomization does not, however, break new ground. This problematization of the conflict in terms of comparability is rooted in binary thinking in which Islam and feminism constitute two mutually exclusive poles, and Islam is independent of class and other social cleavages. Dialectics finds in Islam a religion practiced by human beings who are divided along different lines such as class, nation, race, and gender. While it is easy to highlight patriarchal relations in Islamic scriptures, it would be wrong to deduce from any text a unified behaviour for all Muslims or even for one person. Thus, instead of treating the abstract "Islam" as the agency of all Muslims, one should focus on the interconnections between this religion and other interests. Thus, one may argue that liberal practitioners of Islam are more likely to ally with liberal feminism, and adopt its legalistic approach to gender equality.

At the same time, dialectics does not reduce Islam, its scriptures, and its clerical hierarchy to a position of irrelevance or nothingness. For instance, it is not difficult to see how belief in Islam, personal attachments to the religion, and even single texts inform the politics of individuals and groups. This is not a problem of different readings or the polysemic nature of texts, because readings themselves depend on ideological attachments to class, gender, race, or sexuality. For instance, belief in divinity cannot but play a role in claiming that the Qur'an is a "revealed" text, and, as such, is egalitarian and anti-patriarchal, and "affirms the complete equality of the sexes."[35] To give another example, a female exegete, Haida Mubarak, has used methods of traditional exegesis to argue that a famous verse of the Qur'an does not mean what male exegetes have claimed it to mean: authorizing the "beating," "striking," or "scourging" of women.[36] The subtitle of the book *Gender Hierarchies in Islam and International Law: Equal Before Allah, Unequal Before Man?* also reflects belief in divinity and Islam, in so far as it takes the holy book out of this worldly context and exempts it from the patriarchal influence of the time and place into which it was born.[37]

In sum, the reduction of the conflicts in the Islamic world to the question of religion or "fundamentalism" serves the interests of different sources of power. The U.S.A. and other Western powers benefit from the simplistic construction of an enemy, which can be used to mobilize their citizens in support of imperialist domination. Islamists of diverse tendencies also benefit from promoting Islam as the only source of resistance against oppression and domination, thereby mobilizing people under the flag of religion.

A dialectical and historical materialist approach has a very different problematization. The starting point is not problems of identity, authenticity, space, or body. If such concepts or phenomena are pertinent they find their relevance in the context of the central issue: the oppression of the people of the region and the exploitation of women and men of the working class, peasants, and urban poor. Death and starvation in the midst of enormous wealth. Why after more than a century of struggle for freedom and democracy, and more than half a century of independence, do women, men, and children of the region continue to suffer, probably more than they did in the last century? Why are genocide and ethnic cleansing on the rise? Why has the destruction of mosques, churches, and synagogues reappeared? Why is stoning to death, once largely abandoned, now enshrined in state laws?

From a dialectical perspective, Islam is a partisan player in these struggles. The religion cannot be separated from its followers, and as such it assumes different and often conflicting positions. However, the conflict cannot be reduced to a question of identity. Indeed, if identity is a problem at all, it is itself a product of struggles to change the status quo. Nor can the current situation be explained in terms of "difference." From a dialectical perspective, difference presupposes sameness. In their struggles against despotism and colonialism, the people of the region have used religion and have also fought against it. Post-structuralist approaches fail to depict the complexity of this struggle through concepts such as difference, identity, and anti-essentialism, which thrive on binary thinking.

CONCLUSION

While working on this chapter, I traveled, in July–August 2005, to the Kurdish region of Iraq (a region under the reign of Saddam's dictatorship for about thirty-five years and under U.S. occupation for three years). The area, designated a "safe haven" and "no fly zone" after the 1991 war against Iraq, was protected by the U.S. and British air forces. In the absence of the Baathist state, the Kurds established their "regional government," and tried to create a "civil society" to be a model throughout the Middle East. In my first visit in 2000, surveying women's N.G.O.'s, I doubted the ideological and political capability of these organizations to address gender inequality.[38] The women I met seemed determined to feminize the nation-state that was being built, which was being subverted by various forces including Islamic fundamentalists.

Five years later, I found the "gender scene" desperate in Kurdistan. It is beyond the scope of these concluding remarks to elaborate further on the nature and cause of this march backward. Suffice to say that the N.G.O.-ization of the Kurdish women's struggle, made possible by U.S. control of the safe haven, has contributed to a passive feminist politics, which relies on donor agencies to set a plan of action. This financial and political dependency on outside sources has contributed to a culture of spontaneity, corruption, animosity, and masculine-like competitiveness amongst women activists. More significantly, it has depoliticized the women's movement to the extent that the struggle against feudal-religious-capitalist patriarchy has been limited to the identification of grave gender-related social problems, such as honor killing or female genital mutilation, and providing services for women victims of these heinous crimes.

In this war-torn society, U.S. control has helped the traditionalizing, retribalizing, and reprimordializing of society; the rather small community of feminist activists has abandoned the struggle against "patriarchy" and has fallen into the neoconservative gender plan of the

Bush administration. In an excellent study of the media coverage of the war in Afghanistan, Stabile and Kumar "unveil" the U.S. imperialist misogynist project in the region. They write that "[A]s long as women are not permitted to speak for themselves, they provide the perfect grounds for an elaborate ventriloquist act, in which they serve as the passive vehicle for the representation of U.S. interests."[39] In this project, the role of Islam in governing gender relations looms large. Kurdish women activists have also made a major strategic mistake. Their feminized nationalism has impeded their ability to build alliances with Arab women in Iraq. They have made Islam and Arabs their enemy, rather than patriarchy (with its religious-feudal-nationalist-imperialist characteristics) and capitalist forms of exploitation.

Patriarchy has survived two centuries of feminist theory and practice, and two centuries of women's and feminist struggle against it. Not only has it survived, it has launched a new round of offensives against women both in the developed capitalist world and in the developing world. Patriarchy has powerful allies in the developing world – these allies are imperialism, religion, nationalism, ethnic belonging, tribalism, and feudalism. In the West patriarchy also has powerful allies in capitalism, colonialism, religion, nationalism, and racism. Patriarchy, in the East and the West, reproduces itself through every means possible, but especially through mainstream media, popular culture, and the educational system. However, we should note that the liberal feminist project of achieving legal equality in the Western world has to a large extent been realized, but this historical project is at the end of its journey. The challenge is to achieve gender equality outside the sphere of charters, constitutions, and the law. I have argued that post-structuralist feminism fails to take us beyond liberal feminism. It is, in my view, no more than a form of sophisticated liberal feminism. We need materialist, socialist, Marxist, secular, and radical feminisms informed by complex dialectical-historical and materialist methodologies and modes of thinking in order to revive the international feminist movement.

NOTES

1. Bashara Dumani, "Academic Freedom Post-9/11," *ISIM Review*, 15, Spring 2005, pp. 22–23.

2. Letter from Karl Marx to Arnold Ruge, September 1843, in *Collected Works*, vol. 3, ed. Karl Marx and Frederick Engels (New York: International Publishers, 1975), pp. 141–145.

3. Middle Eastern cities such as Beirut, Cairo, Istanbul, and Tehran were lively centers of publishing, print media, and gramophone record production in the early twentieth century. The freedom of the press exceeded that of Western countries. For instance, Donald Fraser, a British observer, resented this freedom and found it harmful:

> Meanwhile there arose in Tehran a Press that for unbridled license in the discussion of things and people could not have been rivalled. Vituperation was its strong point, and the heights attained in the abuse of the Shah, Government, parliament, politicians, rival publications and finally private individuals, were calculated to shame the Yellow Press of the most civilized countries. Foreigners have from time to time said many hard things of Persians, but no outsider has ever said of them such unmerciful things as appeared daily in the Tehran press. . . . But the Tehran papers and their many imitators in the provincial towns penetrated far into the country districts and were widely read. (David Fraser, *Persia and Turkey in Revolt* [Edinburgh and London: W. Blackwood and Sons, 1910], pp. 32–33)

4. See, for example, Nancy Jay, "Dichotomies," *Feminist Studies*, 1(7), Spring 1981, pp. 38–56; Raia Prokhovnik, *Rational Woman: A Feminist Critique of Dichotomy*, 2nd edn. (Manchester: Manchester University Press, 2002); Maxine Sheets-Johnstone "Binary Opposition as an Ordering Principle of (Male?) Human Thought," in *Feminist Phenomenology*, ed. Linda Fisher and Lester Embree (Dordrecht: Kluwer, 2000), pp. 173–194; Joey Sprague and Mary Zimmerman, "Overcoming Dualisms: A Feminist Agenda for Sociological Methodology," in *Approaches to Qualitative Research: A Reader on Theory and Practice*, ed. Sharlene Nagy Hesse-Biber and Patricia Leavy (New York: Oxford University Press, 2004), pp. 39–61.

5. Lorraine Code, "Binaries/Bipolarity," in *Encyclopedia of Feminist Theories*, ed. Lorraine Code (London: Routledge, 2000), p. 44.

6. Lorraine Code, "Dichotomies," in *Encyclopedia of Feminist Theories*, ed. Lorraine Code (London: Routledge, 2000), p. 135.

7. Lorraine Code, "Patriarchy," in *Encyclopedia of Feminist Theories*, ed. Lorraine Code (London: Routledge, 2000), pp. 378–379.

8. Christel Stormhøj, "Feminist Politics after Poststructuralism," Research Paper no. 14/00, Research Papers from the Department of Social Sciences (Roskilde University, Denmark, 2000), p. 13.

9. Ibid., pp. 13–14; Gayatri Chakravorty Spivak, "In a Word" (interview with Ellen Rooney), in *The Second Wave: A Reader in Feminist Theory*, ed. Linda Nicholson (New York: Routledge, 1997), pp. 356–378.

10. Susan Ryan, "Errand into Africa: Colonization and Nation Building in Sarah J. Hale's *Liberia*," *New England Quarterly: A Historical Review of New England Life and Letters*, 68(4), 1995, p. 582.

11. Howard Williams, *Hegel, Heraclitus and Marx's Dialectics* (New York: Harvester Wheatsheaf, 1989), pp. 1–31.

12. Vladimir Ilich Lenin, "Conspectus of Hegel's Book *The Science of Logic*," *Collected Works*, vol. 38 (Moscow: Foreign Languages Publishing House, 1961), p. 223.

13. Vladimir Ilich Lenin, "On the Question of Dialectics," *Collected Works*, vol. 38 (Moscow: Foreign Languages Publishing House, 1961), pp. 359–360.

14. Women for Women International, "Windows of Opportunity: The Pursuit of Gender Equality in Post-war Iraq," Washington D.C., January 2005, p. 7. See http://www.womenforwomen.org/downloads/iraq_paper_0105.pdf

15. The anti-feminist credentials of the IWF can be gauged from its indictment of the United Nations Convention on the Elimination of All Forms of Discrimination Against Women. In "The Worst Treaty . . . With the Best Name," the IWF declares "10 reasons why the misnamed treaty should be rejected" (16 June 2002). See http://www.iwf.org/issues/issues_detail.asp?articleid=431 (retrieved 1 September 2005).

16. See, for instance, "IWF Awarded Grant to SUPPORT IRAQI WOMEN" (28 September 2004) at http://www.iwf.org/articles/article_detail.asp?articleid=677. See Melissa Dribben, "Two Visiting Iraqi Kurdish Women Thank the U.S. for Invading," *Philadelphia Inquirer*, 19 July 2004, pp. B1, B2, for other initiatives to teach democracy to Kurdish women.

17. The Iraqi Transition Government, http://www.iraqigovernment.org/index_en.htm (accessed 20 September 2005).

18. Afghanistan Government website, http://www.afghangovernment.com/ (accessed 20 September 2005).

19. Amnesty International, "Afghanistan: Women Under Attack: A Systemic Failure to Protect," AI Index: ASA 11/007/2005. See http://web.amnesty.org/library/index/engasa110072005?open&of=eng_afg (accessed 20 September 2005).

20. Bobby Sayyid, *A Fundamental Fear: Eurocentrism and the Emergence of Islamism* (London: Zed Books, 1997).

21. Marx noted in 1844 that "Man makes religion, religion does not make man," however, "religion is the self-consciousness and self-feeling of man who has either not yet found himself or has already lost himself again. But man is no abstract being squatting outside the world. Man is the world of man, the state, society. This state, this society, produces religion, a reversed world-consciousness, because they are a reversed world." Karl Marx, "Contribution to the Critique of Hegel's Philosophy of Law,"

Collected Works, vol. 3, ed. Karl Marx and Frederick Engels (New York: International Publishers, 1975), pp. 175–187.

22. See, for example, John Esposito, "Politics and Religion: Politics and Islam," *Encyclopedia of Religion*, 2nd edn. (New York: Macmillan, 2005), pp. 7284–7290. Esposito argues that the term obscures the diversity of governments or groups that have been called fundamentalist and prefers "political Islam."

23. All quotations are from the announcement of the prize cited from website of the Norwegian Nobel Committee: http://nobelprize.org/peace/laureates/2003/press.html (accessed 1 September 2005).

24. For a collection of media reports and other reactions to the event, see Hajir Palaschi, *'Hich ettefāq-e khāsi rokh nadāde ast! Jashn-nāme-ye nobel-e solh-eshirin-ebādi* (Back cover: *Nothing Remarkable Has Happened: Celebration of Shirin Ebadi's Nobel Peace Prize*) (Tehran: Enteshārāt-e Rowshangarān va Motāle'āt-e Zanān, 2003).

25. Yadollah Royai, "Zarbe-i kūr bar la'isite dar donyā," *Shahrvand*, 13(836), 7 November 2003, p. 44.

26. George Stauth, "Revolution in Spiritless Times. An Essay on Michel Foucault's Enquiries into the Iranian Revolution," *International Sociology*, 6(3), September 1991, pp. 259–280.

27. Janet Afary and Kevin Anderson, *Foucault and the Iranian Revolution: Gender and the Seductions of Islam* (Chicago, Ill. and London: University of Chicago Press, 2005), p. 162.

28. Karl Marx, "Contribution to the Critique of Hegel's Philosophy of Law," in *Collected Works*, vol. 3, ed. Karl Marx and Frederick Engels (New York: International Publishers, 1975), p. 182.

29. Ibid.

30. Mahmoud Sadri and Ahmad Sadri (ed. and trans.), *Reason, Freedom, and Democracy in Islam: Essential Writings of Abdolkarim Soroush* (New York and Oxford: Oxford University Press, 2000).

31. Abdolkarim Soroush, "Islam Doesn't Need the Clerical Guild," *Iran Star*, no. 527, 27 August 2004, p. 5 (in Farsi).

32. See Majid Anouar, *Unveiling Traditions: Postcolonial Islam in a Polycentric World* (Durham, NC: Duke University Press, 2000).

33. For a critique of these debates, see Shahrzad Mojab, "Islamic Feminism: Alternative or Contradiction?," *Fireweed*, 47, Winter 1995, pp. 18–25; Haideh Moghissi, *Feminism and Islamic Fundamentalism, The Limits of Postmodern Analysis* (London: Zed Press, 1999); and Hammed Shahidian, *Women of Iran* (Westport, CT: Greenwood Press, 2002).

34. Abdolkarim Soroush, "Text in Context," in *Liberal Islam: A Source Book*, ed. Charles Kurzman (New York: Oxford University Press, 1998), pp. 244–251.

35. Asthma Barlas, *"Believing Women" in Islam: Unreading Patriarchal Interpretations of the Qur'an* (Austin, Tex.: University of Texas Press, 2002), back cover and pp. 1–28.

36. Haida Mubarak, "Breaking the Interpretive Monarchy: A Re-examination of Verse 4:34," Ha*wwa: Journal of Women of the Middle East and the Islamic World*, 2(3), 2004, pp. 261–289.

37. Shaheen Sardar Ali, *Gender and Human Rights in Islam and International Law: Equal Before Allah, Unequal Before Man?* (The Hague: Kluwer Law International,1999).

38. Shahrzad Mojab, "Kurdish Women in the Zone of Genocide and Gendercide," *Al-Raida Magazine,* Institute for Women's Studies in the Arab World, Lebanese American University, VXXI(103), 2003, pp. 20–25.

39. Carol Stabile and Deepa Kumar, "Unveiling Imperialism: Media, Gender and the War on Afghanistan," *Media, Culture & Society,* 27(5), 2005, p. 778.

5

IMPERIAL NARCISSISM: MICHAEL IGNATIEFF'S APOLOGIES FOR EMPIRE

David McNally

The nemesis of empire was not just nationalism, but narcissism: the incorrigible self-satisfaction of imperial elites, their belief that all the variety of the world's people aspired to nothing else but to be a version of themselves.   (Michael Ignatieff, *Empire Lite*[1])

I Am Iraq.   (Michael Ignatieff, *New York Times Magazine*[2])

Michael Ignatieff presents himself as the thinking person's imperialist – thoughtful, anguished, decent. Bible-thumping imperial fundamentalism is not his thing. Instead, Ignatieff reads philosophy and literature, ponders the dilemmas of the human condition and throws in his reluctant lot with empire only after deep reflection. What I am doing is risky, he suggests, but I have thought long and hard about it all. I have spoken with experts, read deeply. To make sure we get the point, he drops names – of philosophers and literary greats – one after another. In the course of his meditations in defence of the new imperialism, for instance, he invokes Joseph Conrad's *Heart of Darkness*. "In 'Heart of Darkness,'" Ignatieff intones, "Joseph Conrad remarked that empire, when observed close-up, is not a pretty sight. What redeems it, he said, is only the idea."[3] It is not imperial practice, Ignatieff intimates, but this idea, approved by no less a critic than Conrad, that he too cherishes. And what is this idea? It is, he explains, a powerfully "spiritual" one: the notion of "assisting former enemies to reconcile."[4] In the face of this soaring rhetoric we might be advised, however, to pause for a moment to consult Ignatieff's source. Turning to *Heart of Darkness*, we quickly discover that Ignatieff has performed a sleight of hand: he has misappropriated the authority of Conrad's famous exposé of colonialism and disingenuously enrolled it in the imperial cause.[5] Attending to the details of this conjuring trick will instruct us greatly in Ignatieff's strategies in defence of empire.

In the passage in question, Conrad presents his protagonist, Marlow, as he recounts his gradual awakening to the madness of the colonialist imaginary. "The conquest of the earth," proclaims Marlow, "which mostly means the taking it away from those who have a different complexion or slightly flatter noses than ourselves, is not a pretty thing when you look at it too much. What redeems it is the idea only." But what is this ostensibly redeeming idea upon which Ignatieff so eagerly seizes? Marlow informs us – in a passage Ignatieff conveniently drops from the discussion – that it is "something you can set up, and bow down before, and offer a sacrifice to."[6] Now, anyone passingly familiar with the literature of African colonialism will recognize what Conrad is doing here. He is instructing us that the colonial idea is a *fetish*, something before which the worshipper bows down and delivers sacrifices. More than this, he is reversing the poles of the imperial imagination, making fetishism a practice of the colonizers, rather than the colonized. The fetishes attributed to Africans by Christian missionaries, European travel-writers, and colonial agents are thus repositioned as colonialist projections, parts of the imperial psyche projected onto its victims. But why engage in such projections? In order to resist the truth. As is well known, fetishism crucially involves structures of denial. In place of real objects and relations, the fetishist substitutes imaginary ones.[7] And where the psychology of fetishism is concerned, what is denied is projected on to "evil" Others. In the case of Western colonialists, practices of pillage and terror are denied, only to be replaced in the imagination by uplifting "ideas" – civilization, morality, progress – meant to redeem the imperial cause. Simultaneously, the violence and terror whose reality is denied are attributed to the "uncivilized" and "barbaric" colonized peoples themselves

By attributing fetishism to the colonizers Conrad is thus concerned, unlike Ignatieff, to *demystify* the imperial idea rather than to embrace it. As his novel advances, the colonialist imaginary is shattered by the overwhelming reality of imperialism's unrelenting hunger for wealth, property, and domination, a hunger that devours everything in its path. Forget the uplifting phrases and the storybook adventures of discovery, Conrad tells us, for colonialism is sheer, murderous barbarity. Behind its moral platitudes lurks appalling cruelty, summed up in the colonialist injunction to "Exterminate the brutes." This is why the moment of colonialist self-recognition, the moment when the colonizer actually sees himself for what he is, evokes the tortured cry, "The horror! The horror!"[8] And this returns us to Ignatieff. For he is a textbook case of an imperialist who compulsively resists the self-recognition towards which Conrad's characters drive, however reluctantly. Refusing self-recognition, Ignatieff fetishizes an idea, *his* idea, the better to substitute it for the reality of imperial practice. Empire is justified, he suggests, because I have an ennobling idea as to what it is, or could be. And, like a true fetishist, in defiance of overwhelming evidence to the contrary, he will insist on the reality of his idea as a substitute for the brutal and murderous realities of imperial practice. In short, Ignatieff proceeds narcissistically, seeing in empire only his own imagined self-image. This is why he leaves off from Conrad so quickly, having misleadingly pilfered his text. For read closely, *Heart of Darkness* is a warning to the Western apologist for empire that he is an accomplice of madness and horror. And Ignatieff is prepared to perform the most amazing somersaults to avoid this truth.

DISPENSABLE REASONS: THE SHODDY LOGIC OF THE IMPERIAL APOLOGIST

The logical contortions Ignatieff performs are on ample display in the most recent and decisive case, his brief for war against Iraq. Beating the drums in support of a U.S. invasion, Ignatieff informed us that Saddam Hussein "really is awful" and declared that the Iraqi dictator was "in possession of weapons of mass destruction."[9] Once his brief had been clearly demolished by the evidence that Saddam did not have weapons of mass destruction, the honourable thing would have been for Ignatieff to reverse his position, to take moral responsibility for a grievous error. Instead, his rationale falsified, he quickly shuffled it off stage. His strategy here was twofold. First, he joined the Bushites in claiming that the real issue was not whether Saddam had weapons of mass destruction, but whether he *wanted* to have them – not at all what he or they argued at the time and a somewhat less compelling case for war, to say the least.[10] Then, in an amazing act of bad faith, he condemned Bush and Blair for using the argument that Saddam possessed weapons of mass destruction, denouncing them for having done so in order to "manipulate democratic consent for war."[11] Not that any of this – deception, doctored intelligence, manipulation – gave him serious second thoughts. For Ignatieff also declared that his was in any event "an opportunistic case for war" based on the belief that invasion, apparently justified by any old rationale, was acceptable to get rid of "an especially odious regime."[12] Before this position might be fairly debated, however, our thoughtful warmonger proclaimed that all debate over the rationale for invasion is simply passé. In the face of a violent anti-occupation insurgency, "the old questions about the war in Iraq – Was it legal? Was it necessary? Was it done as a last resort? – now seem beside the point."[13] And if you don't quite grasp the logic of this, if your mind resists its evasions, that's because "thinking about this is hard."[14]

But let's persist anyway. Let's see if we can't wrestle with this hard stuff. First, Ignatieff campaigns for war on the basis of Saddam's alleged weapons of mass destruction. Then he acknowledges that no such weapons existed and condemns Bush and Blair for deceiving the public in this regard. But before the force of that acknowledgement is allowed to sink in, he instructs us that his support for war was in any case "opportunistic." Then he exclaims that none of this matters anyway. Now, that wasn't so hard. Simply summarized, it reveals the sequence of our apologist's positions as follows: (a) he uttered falsehoods in support of war, statements at odds both with the evidence and with his stated preference for deliberation and thoughtful reflection; (b) when the overwhelming preponderance of evidence demolished his rationale for war, rather than take moral responsibility for his egregious errors of judgement, he attacked others for making public declarations virtually identical to his own; (c) he then announced that his case for war was an "opportunistic" one, apparently prepared to countenance pretty much any argument for military action; (d) finally, he undertook to cut off the entire debate, declaring redundant the former terms in which he (and Bush and Blair) had couched it. Then, as if these schoolboy debating tactics were not bad enough, he shifted ground again, to what is thus far his most offensive argument of all.

This latest shift occurred in the face of mounting evidence of U.S. lies and atrocities – doctored intelligence, murder of civilians, human rights violations, abuse of Iraqi prisoners – that shook the confidence of some in the pro-war camp. In response to the evidence from Abu Ghraib that American soldiers have systematically tortured Iraqi prisoners, at least 90 percent of whom are guilty of nothing more than having been in the wrong place at the wrong time, Ignatieff changed tack once again. Yes, he laments, it is true that "Americans haven't been angels in the war on terror." However, we need not be excessively troubled by this. Why? Because "the willingness of American democracy to commit atrocity in its defense is limited by moral repugnance, rooted in two centuries of free institutions."[15] It doesn't take too much work to unpack this assertion. It is, after all, a pure and simple claim for moral superiority. Whatever our crimes, they need not delay us, since we are good people. This smugness is designed, of course, to quickly win the assent of readers steeped in the doctrine of the transcendent greatness of the West. And Ignatieff preaches this ethnocultural-centrism with fervour. The humanitarian empire he supports is, he intones, "the new face of an old figure: the democratic free world, the Christian West."[16] Because we are free, moral, Christian people it ostensibly follows that *our* atrocities can never be as bad as *theirs*. They, after all, are unfree, immoral and un-Christian. They are "evil" and they are "barbarians." And, yes, these are Ignatieff's actual terms, ones he uses repeatedly and ad nauseam.[17]

FLAGS OF CONVENIENCE: RIGHTS, ETHICS, AND THE NEEDS OF STRANGERS

Let us now examine the concept of ethics and the notion of human rights that inform these positions. It is difficult to pin Ignatieff down on such matters, in part because his outlook has consistently shifted to the right over a period of twenty-five years or more. While his first book adopted a mildly socialist approach to industrial capitalism in England, he soon vacated this position, touching down on moderate social democracy before settling, at least for the moment, into a free market liberal individualism.[18]

Of course, Ignatieff often pretends that his approach is an ethical, not a political one. He tries to position his doctrine of human rights as beyond politics.[19] But this is more than a trifle unconvincing, not only because of the actual political stances he adopts in the areas of foreign policy and war, but also in light of the wildly partisan speech he recently delivered to delegates to the convention of the Liberal Party of Canada.[20] Nevertheless, let us try to take his views on ethics and human rights on their own terms for the moment.

The point of human rights, Ignatieff opines, is to provide tools with which "to stop unmerited suffering and gross physical cruelty." To this end, human rights activism endeavours "to stop torture, beatings, killings, rape and assault and to improve, as best we can, the security of ordinary people."[21] It should be noted that this represents a controversial approach to human rights. Ignatieff's is a "minimalist" position, to use his own term, that is located within the tradition of doctrines of negative liberty. The purpose of freedom in this account is to defend individuals from society and government. This is consonant with a *market liberalism* in which the protection of the individual's right to maximize private wants becomes the benchmark of freedom. Committed to this framework, Ignatieff declares his hostility to "collective rights," by which he presumably means entitlements to the likes of education, healthcare, clean and affordable water, housing, and so on.[22] Here, Ignatieff cozies up to the *neoliberal* notion, popular these days with ideologues of the World Bank and the International Monetary Fund, that rights ought to revolve around free markets and the rule of law, not social entitlements or provisions. As Wendy Brown aptly notes, Ignatieff's discourse of rights thus "converges neatly with the requisites of liberal imperialism and global free trade, and legitimates both as well."[23]

Yet, even on Ignatieff's narrow definition, in which human rights are about stopping unmerited cruelty and suffering, the crucial question is *how* we are to do so. What if some means to this ostensible end – say, a military invasion – can reasonably be expected to produce tens of thousands of civilian casualties and an almost certain breakdown in social order? Ignatieff's doctrine of human rights provides absolutely no ethico-philosophical criteria in that regard. Instead, he offers a pragmatic judgement – and a highly dubious one – that only U.S. military power can be expected to advance human rights in the zones where "barbarians" rule. But note: this is an utterly ad hoc addition to his theory. In no respect can it be said to flow from any of his reflections on human rights per se. Moreover, others proceeding from the same principle of limiting cruelty and suffering have arrived at entirely opposite conclusions with respect to imperial war. Ignatieff's myriad proclamations for human rights thus lack any demonstrable tie to his support of empire and imperial war.

This is convenient, of course, since the chasm between moralizing rhetoric and imperial advocacy allows Ignatieff to pump out empty platitudes as if these contained real ethical guidance. Concrete moral choices, involving historical study and calibrations of real human risk, never enter the equation. So, Ignatieff can drone on about the world being a better place without Saddam, never so much as acknowledging the cost of this result: some 25,000 Iraqis killed as a result of armed conflict since the start of the U.S. invasion, and probably more than 100,000 dead as a result of all the consequences of the U.S. war.[24] Nowhere does he offer any kind of calculus for determining if these tens of thousands of deaths are ethically justified. Instead, banalities about being rid of Saddam are offered up without even countenancing the scale of human suffering that Ignatieff's preferred course of action – war and occupation – has entailed.

But then, Ignatieff shows little regard for ordinary people in the zones of military conflict. His concern is for the security of the West and of the U.S.A. in particular. Ruminating about America's new "vulnerability" in the world, for instance, he writes,

> When American naval planners looked south from the Suez Canal, they had only bad options. All the potential refuelling stops – Sudan, Somalia, Djibouti, Eritrea and Yemen – are dangerous places for American warships. As the attack on the U.S.S. *Cole* made clear, none of the governments in these strategically vital refuelling stops can actually guarantee the safety of their imperial visitors.[25]

The imperio-centrism here is mind-boggling. What matters about the Horn of Africa and adjacent regions is that they are unsafe from the standpoint of the imperium. The gaze to which Ignatieff subjects Africa and the Middle East is that of "American naval planners." It is their preoccupations, their priorities, their perceptions that count. And this is no anomaly. Ignatieff regularly reduces global problems to issues of "our safety." Writing in the *New York Times* about the decisions of the years ahead, he declares: "The choices are about what risks are worth running when *our* safety depends on the answer."[26] The safety of others is, of course, referenced from time to time as a concern. But this too is opportunistic. Other peoples, say those in the Horn of Africa, are regularly invisibilized in Ignatieff's account just as they are in the passage cited above. When they reappear, if they do at all, it is either as terrorists and "barbarians" or as mute victims for whom Ignatieff will have to speak.

Ignatieff could in fact serve as a sort of poster boy for the preoccupations of postcolonial theory, his constructions of the imperialized Other crudely obeying all the us/them, self/other binaries skewered by postcolonialists.[27] Even his one attempt to take up the problem of human solidarity, *The Needs of Strangers* (1984), regularly silences and marginalizes the Others at issue, appropriating their voices to his ends. *Needs of Strangers* sets out from the concern that rights discourses (of the sort Ignatieff now embraces) are "impoverished as a means of expressing individuals' needs *for* the collectivity."[28] Because its premise is atomized individuals, liberal rights doctrine lacks a language with which to express human sociality, interdependence, and solidarity. There is certainly considerable merit to this diagnosis. But when it comes to discussing these Others, even this work, his only effort devoted to "strangers," is utterly monological. Ignatieff, it appears, is incapable of a dialogue with the oppressed of the global South, even of hearing their voices. Instead, he converses with himself. He informs us that outside "the developed world" there are "strangers at our gates." Step beyond our "zone of safety – the developed world – and there they are, hands outstretched, gaunt, speechless or clamouring in the zone of danger."[29] This extraordinary passage overflows with colonialist imagery. These dangerous Others, reduced to mute body parts (threatening hands reaching out to grab us), utter frightful sounds (they clamour) or, what is effectively the same thing, they are "speechless." Given that speech and language are widely considered distinguishing features of humankind, this diagnosis implies that these strangers outside the developed world are not fully human – an inkling that is confirmed when Ignatieff announces that all we have in common with them is what "we share with animals."[30]

Yet, Michael Ignatieff is a decent man. So, if these people are incapable of speaking for themselves, then he will shoulder the burden of speaking for them. After all, he is not speechless. And it is words, he explains, "which give me the right to speak in the name of the strangers."[31] Unable to discover articulate humanity among these Others in the zone of danger, any more than he can locate it in the Horn of Africa, Ignatieff will be their voice. This typical exercise in imperial narcissism, this colonialist presumption that he knows what the Other needs and wants, has become something of his signature. Describing a trip to Afghanistan, Ignatieff takes us through a passing encounter with a Kabul brick-maker. "It would be too much to say that the brick-maker wants us infidels here," he writes, "but I would venture that he knows he needs us."[32] No evidence is offered for this claim, of course. But, then, having rendered these Others speechless, the problem of evidence is reduced to what Ignatieff chooses to claim on their behalf.

Twenty years earlier, Ignatieff proclaimed in *Needs of Strangers* that "there are few presumptions in human relations more dangerous than the idea that one knows what another human being needs better than they do themselves. In politics this presumption is a warrant to ignore democratic preferences and to trample on freedom."[33] Today it is precisely this dangerous politics that Michael Ignatieff practices – and the dangers to which he alludes have mounted precipitously, given that his arrogant presumption is used to justify imperialism and war.

This brings us to Ignatieff's notion of ethics. For our esteemed author repeatedly claims that his judgements pivot on ethical considerations. "Ethics matter," he has written, "to define the identity we are defending and to name the evil we are facing. The point of ethics is to enable us to encounter the reality of evil without succumbing to its logic, to combat it with constitutionally regulated lesser evils, without falling prey to greater ones."[34] One could certainly take issue with this definition – what has happened to the question of the good life, for instance? – but let us take it at face value for the moment. What Ignatieff claims is that his ethics, the ethics which lead him to embrace U.S. military imperialism, enable us to fight evil with "constitutionally regulated lesser evils." This is, of course, a return of the claim for moral limits imposed by free institutions on U.S. atrocities. American atrocities are lesser evils because, as free peoples, we constrain them through constitutional checks and balances. So, let us test Ignatieff's ostensible ethics on these grounds.

THEIR ATROCITIES AND OURS: IGNATIEFF'S DIALECTIC OF GOOD AND EVIL

I shall begin with the horrifying record of Vietnam and Indochina, especially as Ignatieff frequently mobilizes his opposition to America's war in Vietnam as evidence of his progressive credentials. Yet, curiously, Ignatieff's account of the Vietnam era skirts elementary facts such as mass murder. After all, scholarly estimates as to the numbers killed by the U.S. war machine during the years 1960–75 range from two to four million.[35] This was mass slaughter carried out against largely peasant societies by the world's most powerful techno-military imperium. Remarkably, Ignatieff manages to forget all of this, describing the Vietnam debacle as a failed attempt "to sustain a democratic republic in South Vietnam," an appalling piece of historical revisionism that does not even deign to mention napalm, Agent Orange, or massacres of civilians.[36] In fact, moral repugnance over the immense suffering of the Vietnamese people seems not to figure in Ignatieff's account of why he opposed the Vietnam war; nor does any expressed concern for the democratic rights of the peoples of Southeast Asia.[37] Instead, what troubled Ignatieff, he reports, what led him to join the anti-war protesters, was his conviction that "nothing could save the weak and corrupt South Vietnamese government."[38] The U.S. war on Vietnam was, apparently, a noble cause corrupted, a morally defensible objective (the creation of a democratic republic in the South) ineptly executed. The disappearance here of the colonized – their sufferings, their aspirations, their resistances – could scarcely be more complete. And this, cancelling out the reality of colonized Others, is something of a leitmotif in Ignatieff's defences of empire, as we have seen.

Still, it might be argued that Vietnam was an exception, an aberration. So, let us take an example with more obvious and direct connections to the U.S. occupation of Iraq: El Salvador. The connection here concerns both personnel and policy. After all, a number of high-ranking U.S. military advisors to the Iraqi government's war against insurgents honed their skills in the Salvadoran counter-insurgency of 1980–91, in which the U.S.A. backed a brutal right-wing government in its civil war against leftist rebels. The central individual at issue is James Steele, the U.S. Military Group commander during the counter-insurgency in El Salvador, now involved in assisting the battle against insurgents in Iraq.[39] Operating from a mission in El Salvador, Steele directed U.S. Special Forces which trained and advised pro-government troops and para-military death squads. And, as in so many cases throughout Latin America, torture, grotesque human rights violations, and massacres of civilians were run-of-the-mill tactics for these U.S.-backed forces. As Amnesty International reports,

Between 1980 and 1991 El Salvador experienced an armed conflict which led to gross and extensive human rights violations, including extrajudicial executions, other unlawful killings, "disappearances" and torture. Among the victims were human rights defenders, trade unionists, lawyers, journalists, opponents of the government (whether real or presumed) and, for the most part, innocent civilians who had no direct involvement in the conflict. Whole villages were targeted by the armed forces and their inhabitants massacred. Children were direct victims of extrajudicial executions (E.J.E.'s) or "disappearance".[40]

Overall, Amnesty estimates that 75,000 civilians were tortured and executed in the conflict. The United Nations Truth Commission Report (1983) found that the very soldiers trained by the United States were responsible for the vast majority of these massacres and civilian deaths, including the murders of Archbishop Romero, four U.S. churchwomen and six Jesuit priests. The U.N. also determined that more than two-thirds of the sixty military officers guilty of the worst atrocities were trained at the School of the Americas (S.O.A.), located at Fort Benning, Georgia. Ten graduates of the S.O.A. participated in the appalling massacre of about 1,000 civilians in the Salvadorean village of El Mozote.[41] Yet none of this prevented the U.S. government from coughing up $6 billion in aid to Salvadorean governments and their troops during the civil war. Indeed, Washington appears if anything to have been encouraged by these brutal tactics, many of which were learned at the S.O.A., from C.I.A. manuals and from U.S. military advisors on the ground. U.S. advisors even worked directly with Dr. Hector Antonio Regalado, the infamous San Salvador dentist dubbed "Dr. Death" for his use of pliers to extract teeth from those he tortured, before they were customarily executed.[42]

And El Salvador was no isolated case. As two intrepid reporters for the *Baltimore Sun* reported in 1995, the U.S. government was intimately involved with torturers and state-sanctioned murderers in Honduras, particularly Battalion 316, a secret military unit that housed death squads. Here there is another link to Iraq and the "war on terror," since the U.S. ambassador to Honduras at the time, John Negroponte, has played a central role recently in Iraq and was appointed in 2005 as Bush's director of national intelligence. This despite the fact that, as the

Baltimore Sun journalists pointed out, Negroponte tried to conceal U.S. involvement in "stalking, kidnapping, torturing, and killing suspected subversives" in Honduras. Describing Honduran–U.S. practices, they further report:

> The intelligence unit, known as Battalion 316, used shock and suffocation devices in interrogations. Prisoners were often kept naked and, when no longer useful, killed and buried in unmarked graves. Newly declassified documents and other sources show that the C.I.A. and the U.S. Embassy knew of numerous crimes, including murder and torture, yet continued to support Battalion 316 and collaborate with its leaders.[43]

It might be objected that Ignatieff does not study the Americas – which in itself would be a shocking revelation about someone who proselytizes on behalf of American empire. Yet, as I have noted, this is not simply a story about the Americas, since the very people who aided and abetted Salvadorean and Honduran forces guilty of torture and mass murder are now operating on behalf of the U.S.A. in Iraq. Furthermore, other key figures first committed documented crimes in Afghanistan – a country about which Ignatieff does write – before moving on to Iraq. And there too they excelled in torture. Consider the following report from the *New York Times* on one murder by U.S. guards there in 2002:

> Even as the young Afghan man was dying before them, his American jailers continued to torment him.
>
> The prisoner, a slight 22-year-old taxi driver known only as Dilawar, was hauled from his cell at the detention center in Bagram, Afghanistan, at around 2 a.m. to answer questions about a rocket attack on an American base. When he arrived in the interrogation room, an interpreter who was present said, his legs were bouncing uncontrollably in the plastic chair and his hands were numb. He had been chained by the wrists to the top of his cell for much of the four previous days.
>
> Mr. Dilawar asked for a drink of water, and one of the two interrogators, Specialist Joshua R. Claus, 21, picked up a large plastic bottle. But first he punched a hole in the bottom, the interpreter said, so as the prisoner fumbled weakly with the cap, the water poured out over his orange scrubs. The soldier then grabbed the

bottle back and began squirting the water forcefully into Mr. Dilawar's face.

"Come on drink!" the interpreter said Specialist Claus had shouted, as the prisoner gagged on the spray. "Drink!"

At the interrogators' behest, a guard tried to force the young man to his knees. But his legs, which had been pummeled by guards for several days, could no longer bend. An interrogator told Mr. Dilawar that he could see a doctor after they finished with him. When he was finally sent back to his cell, though, the guards were instructed only to chain the prisoner back to the ceiling.

"Leave him up," one of the guards quoted Specialist Claus as saying.

Several hours passed before an emergency room doctor finally saw Mr. Dilawar. By then he was dead, his body beginning to stiffen.[44]

Again, this was only one of many such killings of Afghans by American soldiers, one that U.S. officials went to great pains to cover up.[45] And, again, their behaviour was utterly predictable. It is worth remembering, after all, that six widely distributed C.I.A. manuals – also used at the S.O.A. – explicitly advocate executions of guerillas, false imprisonment, coercion, and extortion.[46] Yet, Ignatieff throws in his lot with these types without so much as a nod to their historical record – which is widely available in the public domain. He rushes to quote an Afghan or Iraqi who supports U.S. occupation, but never deigns to discuss the thousands jailed, tortured, or killed.[47] But then Ignatieff has his fetish, his idea of empire, and it shall not be disturbed by the realities of U.S. funded and trained death squads or prison guards and *their* evil doings.

What then of the revelations from Abu Ghraib prison? What, given his preoccupations with human rights, has Ignatieff had to say about them? To begin with the evidence, the International Committee of the Red Cross reports that prisoners at Abu Ghraib have been subjected to hooding, extended handcuffing, beatings with hard objects, slapping, punching, kicking, sleep deprivation, sexual humiliation, including forced masturbation in front of female guards, and forced participation in human pyramids composed of naked men, and a variety of forms of persistent psychological abuse.[48] The 171-page report issued by an army panel chaired by U.S. Major General George Fay further detailed brutal incidents in which prisoners were sodomized, subjected to extreme temperatures, led around on a leash while naked, and had electric shocks administered to their genitals. Reading through these hundreds of pages of documentation of beatings and humiliation, it is impossible for the fair-minded reader not to conclude that a *system* of brutality and a *logic* of torture are at work, in which prisoners are subjected to powerful sensations of isolation and helplessness (a key function of blindfolds and hoods). In an effort to break prisoners, military interrogators and guards assert their utter control over all the rudimentary aspects of life: food, clothing, sleep, urination, defecation, light, temperature, human contact, dignity.

Rather than extreme cases or the actions of "bad apples," these tactics are part of systematic policy laid out in the C.I.A.'s manual, *KUBARK Counterintelligence Interrogation*, first produced in 1963. And that text, which has been the handbook for U.S. military interrogators for over forty years, provides the template for the human rights violations committed at Abu Ghraib.[49] It comes as little surprise, then, when the American Civil Liberties Union reveals that illegal interrogation methods were approved by the top U.S. military official in Iraq.[50] The logic of torture practised by the U.S. military has been captured with remarkable insight by Elaine Scarry in her monumental work, *The Body in Pain*. Torture, notes Scarry, does not only inflict pain, though it certainly does that. It also establishes a relationship of domination in which the victim is rendered speechless, reduced to a suffering body pure and simple, while the torturer appropriates all speech to himself, emerging as a singular voice of power and authority. "Ultimate domination," Scarry claims, "requires that the prisoner's ground become increasingly physical and the torturer's increasingly verbal, that the prisoner become a colossal body with no voice and the torturer a colossal voice . . . with no body."[51] This is precisely the logic of torture in which U.S. forces engages – coupled with sexual humiliation and murder. It is also the reality of Ignatieff's "lesser evil," though one he refuses even to acknowledge, never mind defend.

Of course, Ignatieff does not condone torture. But he treats it as something of an aberration when, as we have seen, it was an utterly consistent and predictable aspect of established U.S. policy. What kind of ethics is it that cannot anticipate the highly probable *unethical* results of policies one advocates? What can it mean for Ignatieff to pronounce, long after his disquisitions on ethics, "Now I realize intentions do shape consequences"?[52] Now? How can it possibly be a revelation to anyone who has read and thought about ethics that intentions matter? Yet, even if confused about intentions, a glance at the historical record ought to have deterred Ignatieff from lining up with U.S. imperial militarism and its practices of torture. And assuming he is *now* shocked and distressed by recent revelations, we might also expect a more real and honest accounting. Instead, Ignatieff's responses to the evidence of abuse and torture have been evasive at best. At first, he tried to suggest that tactics involving "nothing worse than sleep deprivation, permanent light or permanent darkness, disorienting noise, and isolation" would merely constitute "coercion, rather than torture, and there might be a lesser evil justification for it."[53] Interestingly, this is precisely the sort of distinction U.S. Defense Secretary Donald Rumsfeld deployed in his claims that what occurred at Abu Ghraib constituted "abuse," not "torture."[54] The key issue here appeared to be whether physical pain was inflicted.[55] The fact that this distinction is not accepted in international conventions on torture seemed not to trouble Ignatieff (or Rumsfeld). For instance, the U.N. Convention Against Torture and Other Cruel, Inhuman or Degrading Treatment or Punishment (1984), an agreement to which the U.S.A. is a signatory, defines torture as "any act by which severe pain or suffering, *whether physical or mental,* is intentionally inflicted on a person for such purpose as obtaining from him or a third person information or a confession" (my emphasis). Perhaps this too is now irrelevant.

Once the evidence of physical and psychological torture at Abu Ghraib had become overwhelming and incontrovertible, Ignatieff tried out new strategies. The first involved ritual hand-wringing combined with Reagan-like American triumphalism. His most anguished article on the revelations from Abu Ghraib, for example, manages nevertheless to end on a note of imperial hubris. Commenting on public adulation of Ronald Reagan, following the former president's death, he opines, "It is good that America has wanted to be better than it is. It is good that the death of a president gave it a week to revive belief in itself."[56] Poor America, shaken by the revelations from Abu Ghraib, has now recovered the fortitude to do good thanks to its collective mourning of a dead president. Nowhere is Reagan's record in El Salvador or Honduras, to take but two examples, so much as hinted at. Death squads, illegal arms sales, White House cover-ups: none of these realities of Reagan's presidency exist in Ignatieff's universe. Instead, he promotes a fantasy world of jelly beans, Hollywood smiles, and hot dogs grilling on the Fourth of July. What matters are not the tens of thousands killed and "disappeared" thanks to Reaganite policies; what matters is that the president who "made Americans feel good about themselves again" might, with his death, inspire a new round of American self-congratulation. And so, America redeemed, Ignatieff turns to a second strategy, effectively carrying on as if Abu Ghraib were a mere footnote to the real story. In an article lashing out at "terrorism as pornography," devoted to the horrors of videotaping and transmitting terrorist executions in Iraq, he briefly countenanced the question of the "torturer as pornographer." Since U.S. troops did, after all, take photos and video of abused and humiliated Iraqi prisoners, Ignatieff dedicates one short paragraph (out of the twenty-one that comprise his article) to the pornography of torture. True, he registers his dislike of U.S. military practices at the Iraqi prison. But the effect of the article is again to bury the American abuses, belittling U.S. torture with the tacit suggestion that *their* atrocities are worse than ours.

Perhaps most galling, Ignatieff's evasion of the moral weight of the torture practised by U.S. forces sits uncomfortably with what he has written elsewhere on the topic. Formulating his case against torture in *The Lesser Evil*, he cites the example of Jean Amery, a Belgian anti-Nazi activist who was captured, then tortured, first by Hitler's S.S. in a Belgian jail and later by guards at Auschwitz. As Ignatieff poignantly notes, in reflecting on these horrific experiences, which cruelly marked the rest of his life, Amery "insisted that torture should be viewed not in individual terms as the psychosexual aberration of particular torturers but as a key to the identity of the society responsible for it."[57] Clearly the same moral observation ought to apply to the United States and its practices of torture on behalf of empire. Unless we are prepared to endorse a pure and simple double standard, we cannot avoid the conclusion that torture must also be seen as "a key to the identity" of U.S. society and American imperialism. But, where we would expect diagnosis and analysis, our imperial fetishist, so loquacious when he sets the agenda, again serves up . . . silence.

For moral responsibility in this area, compare the late Susan Sontag's analysis of the photos from Abu Ghraib and the reality they disclosed.

"The photographs are us," Sontag wrote. "That is, they are representative of the fundamental corruptions of any foreign occupation together with the Bush administration's distinctive policies." Then, probing the presence of smiling U.S. soldiers next to abused and humiliated Iraqi men, she continued: "If there is something comparable to what these pictures show it would be some of the photographs of black victims of lynching taken between the 1880s and the 1930s, which show Americans grinning beneath the naked mutilated body of a black man or woman hanging behind them from a tree."[58] With insight and precision, Sontag located the gleeful torture of Iraqi prisoners by Americans in a tradition of racism – at home and abroad. But just as Ignatieff's defence of empire ignores the history of U.S. torture, so it ignores the tradition of American (and Western) racism. At no point does he so much as gesture toward the racist practices at the heart of America's imperial history, even when the photos from Abu Ghraib rub our faces in it.[59]

Finally, because Ignatieff invokes human rights with such regularity, let us also note Amnesty International's well-documented claim that America's detention centre at Guantanamo Bay constitutes "the gulag of our times." Citing arbitrary and indefinite detention, abuse of prisoners, kangaroo courts, and torture as features of the U.S. "war on terror," Amnesty declares that as many as 125 U.S. officials, including the president and the secretary of defense, could be prosecuted under international law.[60]

But none of this matters. Perhaps all this too is now passé. In any event it is clear that little will divert Ignatieff from his drum-beating on behalf of U.S. imperialism – not lies, deception, racism, torture, or systematic violation of human rights. So intent is he on defending U.S. military might that he has even chastised delegates to the Liberal Party of Canada's convention for their refusal, thus far, to endorse George W. Bush's Ballistic Missile Defense plan (popularly known as "Son of Star Wars"). "We do not want our decisions to fracture the command system of North American defense," he exhorted.[61] And so, in the name of lesser evilism, he prods us to strengthen the military command structure of the world's greatest military power – one that keeps 2,000 warheads on high alert, each twenty times more powerful than the atom bomb that destroyed Hiroshima – and to take the further steps toward escalating the arms race and weaponizing space.[62]

IMPERIAL NARCISSISM, IMPERIAL HORROR

This, then, is the end point of our thinking person's imperialism. Starting from flowery platitudes about ethics and human rights, it leaves us with banal defences of an empire that practises torture, uses lies and deception to justify war, tramples on human rights, and launches a new arms race. In the process, our imperial apologist fractures logic, evades evidence, claims moral superiority for his kind, and demonizes imperialized Others.

And so we return to Joseph Conrad. For all the shortcomings of *Heart of Darkness*, Conrad intuited the metamorphosis of imperial identity that characterizes the likes of Michael Ignatieff. Key to Conrad's depiction is that the imperialist begins by lying to himself – he spurns reality in favour of his fetish. However much Ignatieff believes his own mutterings about ethics and human rights, his pronouncements must be measured against the murders and the torture carried out by those he nominates as humanity's benefactors – and whose crimes he both evades and back-handedly defends. Ignatieff's talk of morality is an exercise in imperial fantasy of a sort with which Conrad was familiar. Describing the con-versation among colonial agents in Africa, for instance, Conrad's protagonist, Marlow, proclaims: "It was as unreal as everything else – as the philanthropic pretence of the whole concern, as their talk, as their government." In fact, explains Marlow, notwithstanding their soaring proclamations, "there was no more moral purpose at the back of it than there is in burglars breaking into a safe."[63] The same, of course, is true of U.S. imperialism today. Its agents too have the morality of burglars breaking into a safe. But their crimes, just like those of an earlier era of colonialists, are of an exponentially higher order. Of course, they produce reports, make speeches, and utter declarations about civiliza-tion, freedom, and democracy. Where they differ from Conrad's obsessive colonialist, Kurtz, is that they *never* arrive at the truth. For Kurtz, after devoting seventeen pages to a report on behalf of the International Society for the Suppression of Savage Customs, finally records a truthful horror. It occurs at the end of his report, his "moving appeal to every altruistic sentiment," as Marlow describes it. Suddenly, the final words appeared and their message "blazed at you, luminous and terrifying, like a flash of lightning in a serene sky: 'Exterminate all the brutes!'"[64]

At the moment when he wrote those words, shortly before his death,

Kurtz finally "looked within himself," to discover that "his soul was mad."[65] And this Conradian truth might well be applied to Ignatieff. Defence of empire – of murder, pillage, torture, and deception – transforms the defenders themselves. Whatever values they might have once professed, the reality of what they defend takes possession of them, turns them into something other than what they intended. This is a central theme of *Heart of Darkness*, which, as I have noted, is a warning to the Western apologist for empire that he is an accomplice of madness and horror.

Michael Ignatieff too is an accomplice of madness and horror. But he seems not to know it. His imperial narcissism remains intact. While the body count rises, as civilians are killed and tortured, he continues to proclaim that he works "to stop torture, beatings, killings, rape and assault and to improve, as best we can, the security of ordinary people." He manages even to convince himself that he is the victim, the courageous moral crusader who has lost friends over his support of empire.[66] So enamoured is he of his fantastic self-reflection that he continues to take it for reality, blindly bowing down before his fetish, his idea of empire, his imagined self-image. The effect of this narcissistic operation is to obliterate others, particularly those whose acknowledgement would disrupt imperial self-absorption.[67] But, like all fetishes, Ignatieff's narcissistic self-image conceals something much uglier – the reality of an imperial war machine that trains death squads, tortures prisoners, murders civilians. Michael Ignatieff may never manage to see that truth. But we must. We must continue "to hear the whispered cry, 'The horror! The horror!'"[68] And we must also repeat it, loudly and urgently. In the process, we will need to continue the work of exposing the deceptions, the evasions, and the tortured logic of those who issue apologies for empire.

NOTES

1. Michael Ignatieff, *Empire Lite: Nation-building in Bosnia, Kosovo and Afghanistan* (Toronto: Penguin Books, 2003), p. 121.

2. Michael Ignatieff, "I am Iraq," *New York Times Magazine*, 23 March 2003.

3. Ignatieff, *Empire Lite*, p. 31.

4. Ibid., p. 32.

5. I recognize that there are distinct limits to Conrad's critique of colonialism. Among other things, his is still a Eurocentric vision in which Africans do not emerge as

subjects of their own resistance and emancipation, and his deployment of metaphors of darkness reinscribes fears of blackness. Despite these major flaws, *Heart of Darkness* does advance elements of a devastating critique of the psychology and practice of empire. For an intriguing assessment of this text see Edward Said, "Two Visions in *Heart of Darkness*," in Said, *Culture and Imperialism* (London: Chatto & Windus, 1993), pp. 20–35.

6. Joseph Conrad, *Heart of Darkness* (Harmondsworth: Penguin Books, 1995), p. 20.

7. The two most famous cases are the Freudian and Marxian accounts of fetishism. For Freud, the male fetishist denies the reality of sexual difference, while for Marx commodity fetishism involves a denial (or forgetting) of the origin of commodities in human labouring activity. On these points see my *Bodies of Meaning: Studies on Language, Labor and Liberation* (Albany, NY: State University of New York Press, 2001), pp. 66–71.

8. Ibid., pp. 84, 112, 118.

9. Michael Ignatieff, "Time to Walk the Walk," *National Post* (Toronto), 14 February 2003. The same basic position is expressed in Ignatieff, "The American Empire: The Burden," *New York Times Magazine*, 5 January 2003.

10. Michael Ignatieff, "Second, Sober Thoughts," *Toronto Star*, 26 March 2004.

11. Michael Ignatieff, *The Lesser Evil: Political Ethics in an Age of Terror* (Princeton, NJ: Princeton University Press, 2004), p. 163.

12. Ignatieff, "Sober, Second Thoughts."

13. Michael Ignatieff, "The Terrorist as Auteur," *New York Times Magazine*, 14 November 2004, p. 52.

14. Ibid.

15. Ibid., p. 58.

16. Ignatieff, *Empire Lite*, p. 17.

17. By my count, Ignatieff uses the term "barbarian" or "barbarians" eight times in the first twenty-one pages of *Empire Lite*.

18. Ignatieff's mild socialism is evident in his *A Just Measure of Pain: The Penitentiary in the Industrial Revolution, 1750–1850* (Harmondsworth: Penguin Books, 1978). Moderate social democracy/social reform liberalism would best describe *The Needs of Strangers: An Essay on Privacy, Solidarity and the Politics of Being Human* (Harmondsworth: Penguin Books, 1984). Rightward-moving liberal individualism is the motif of *Human Rights as Political Idolatry* (2001), *Empire Lite* (2003), and *The Lesser Evil* (2004). Ignatieff's positioning on the right of the federal Liberal Party of Canada is on display in his "Liberal Values in the 21st Century," Address to the Biennial Policy Conference, Liberal Party of Canada, 3 March 2005.

19. Michael Ignatieff, *Human Rights as Political Idolatry* (Princeton, NJ: Princeton University Press, 2001), p. 9.

20. See "Liberal Values in the 21st Century." For commentary on this speech see Jeffrey

Simpson, "The Sound of a Liberal Past, and a Martin Future," *Globe and Mail* (Toronto), 5 March 2005.

21. Ignatieff, *Human Rights*, p. 173.

22. Ibid., p. 90.

23. Wendy Brown, "'The Most We Can Hope For . . .': Human Rights and the Politics of Fatalism," *South Atlantic Quarterly*, 103, 2004, p. 461.

24. The figure of around 25,000 deaths due to armed conflict is based on calculations by Iraq Body Count, as of July 2005. See www.iraqbodycount.org, where detailed sourcing is provided. The figure of 100,000 is based on a wide-ranging survey of mortality rates conducted by the Center for International Emergency Disaster and Refugee Studies at the Johns Hopkins Bloomberg School of Public Health, Baltimore. See "Mortality Before and After the 20003 Invasion of Iraq: Cluster Sample Survey," published online 29 October 2004 at: http://image.thelancet.com/extras/04art10342web.pdf.

25. Ignatieff, *Empire Lite*, p. 12.

26. Ignatieff, "I Am Iraq" (my emphasis).

27. While I am quite critical of most postcolonial theory, it largely succeeds at demonstrating the discursive processes by which the oppressed of the world are marginalized and demonized. Its failures have largely to do with an overarching textualization that dehistoricizes and dematerializes key problems – such as imperialism and social class – that constitute the postcolonial condition. See, for example, E. San Juan, Jr., *Beyond Postcolonial Theory* (New York: St. Martin's Press, 1999).

28. Michael Ignatieff, *Needs of Strangers*, p. 13.

29. Ibid., p. 29.

30. Ibid.

31. Ibid., p. 142.

32. Ignatieff, *Empire Lite*, p. 108.

33. Ignatieff, *Needs of Strangers*, p. 11.

34. Ignatieff, *Lesser Evil*, p. 167.

35. By 1970, at least 1.4 million Vietnamese had been killed, alongside 600,000 Cambodians. In the next five years of war over half a million more Vietnamese people died. The actual figures may be considerably higher. See Frances Fitzgerald, *Fire in the Lake: The Vietnamese and the Americans in Vietnam* (New York: Vintage Books, 1989), p. 537. For the estimate of 600,000 killed in Cambodia see John Pilger, "A War in the American Tradition," *The Independent* (London), 15 October 2001.

36. Ignatieff, *Empire Lite*, p. 116.

37. These, of course, were the driving motives of the actual anti-war movement in the United States. In this regard, it is of course true that moral repugnance and political opposition contributed to forcing a U.S. withdrawal from Vietnam. But this had nothing to do with the moral underpinnings of American institutions. In fact, mounting opposition to war in Indochina was built, sustained, and organized by the

very *anti-imperialist* left toward whom Ignatieff displays such hostility. See, for example, Fred Halstead, *Out Now! A Participant's Account of the American Movement Against the Vietnam War* (New York: Monad Press, 1978).

38. Ignatieff, "I Am Iraq."

39. See Peter Maass, "The Way of the Commandos," *New York Times Magazine*, 1 May 2005.

40. Amnesty International, *El Salvador: Peace Can Only Be Achieved With Justice* (2001). While Amnesty does claim that leftist rebels committed human rights violations, it assigns overwhelming responsibility for civilian murders to the Salvadoran army and its associated death squads, the very groups supported by the U.S. state.

41. See Jack Nelson-Pallmeyer, *School of Assassins: Guns, Greed and Globalization* (New York: Orbis Books, 2001), pp. 27, 11; and Leslie Gill, *The School of the Americas: Military Training and Political Violence in the Americas* (Durham: Duke University Press, 2004), p. 137. In the face of mounting opposition, the SOA has recently changed its name to the Western Hemispheric Institute for Security Cooperation.

42. Nelson-Pallmeyer, *School of Assassins*, pp. 9–10.

43. Gary Cohn and Ginger Thompson, "Unearthed: Fatal Secrets," *Baltimore Sun*, 11 June 1995, available online at www.geocities.com/ravencrazy/baltimoresun.html.

44. Tim Golden, "In U.S. Report, Brutal Details of 2 Afghan Inmates' Deaths," *New York Times*, 20 May 2005.

45. Tim Golden, "Abuse Inquiry Bogged Down in Afghanistan," *New York Times*, 22 May 2005.

46. See James Hodge and Linda Cooper, "Roots of Abu Ghraib in C.I.A. techniques," *National Catholic Reporter*, 5 November 2004, p. 12.

47. For revelations of U.S. executions of Iraqi civilians see Doug Struck, "Former Marine Testifies to Atrocities in Iraq," *Washington Post*, 8 December 2004.

48. Mark Danner, "The Logic of Torture," in *Abu Ghraib: The Politics of Torture* (Berkeley: North Atlantic Books, 2004), p. 27.

49. As noted by Danner as well as Hodge and Cooper. A newer U.S. inquiry has also documented widespread abuse at the American prison camp at Guantanamo Bay. See Neil A. Lewis and Eric Schmitt, "Inquiry Finds Abuses at Guantanamo Bay," *New York Times*, 1 May 2005.

50. "Top Soldier in Iraq Okayed Illegal Methods, A.C.L.U. says," *Globe and Mail* (Toronto), 30 March 2005.

51. Elaine Scarry, *The Body in Pain: The Making and Unmaking of the World* (New York: Oxford University Press, 1985), p. 57.

52. Ignatieff, "Second, Sober Thoughts."

53. Ignatieff, *Lesser Evil*, p. 138.

54. See Adam Hochschild, "What's in a Word? Torture," *New York Times*, 23 May 2004.

55. Ignatieff does take his distance from "psychological abuse," but this seems inconsistent as his criterion for torture appears to be "physical duress or cruelty." See ibid.

56. Michael Ignatieff, "Mirage in the Desert," *New York Times*, 27 June 2004.

57. Ignatieff, *Lesser Evil*, p. 42.

58. Susan Sontag, "Regarding the Torture of Others: Notes on What Has Been Done – And Why – to Prisoners by Americans," *New York Times Magazine*, 23 May 2004. I recommend that the reader compare Sontag's piece to any of Ignatieff's defences of war against and occupation of Iraq in the same magazine. The trivial, banal, and disingenuous character of his analyses are thrown into sharp relief by comparison with the intelligence and moral wisdom of Sontag's piece.

59. On racism and empire see my *Another World is Possible: Globalization and Anti-Capitalism* (Winnipeg: Arbeiter Ring Publishing, 2002), ch. 4.

60. Amnesty International, *Annual Report 2005*, online at www.amnestyusa.org.

61. Ignatieff, "Liberal Values."

62. Of course, Ignatieff claims to oppose weaponizing space. But, then, so does George W. Bush, despite powerful analyses demonstrating how Ballistic Missile Defense (BMD) does just that. In fact, many supporters of BMD argue, not entirely without reason, that space is already weaponized and that they simply want to be the dominant power in that regard. See, for instance, the statements by editors for the *National Review* and others at www.missilethreat.com.

63. Conrad, *Heart of Darkness*, pp. 46, 55.

64. Ibid., pp. 83–84.

65. Ibid., p. 107.

66. Note the utterly pathetic endorsement of Ignatieff's self-pity from historian Margaret MacMillan: "It Takes Some Courage: He Lost Friends over his Support of the War on the Taliban." See her review of *Lesser Evil*: "Terrorism: The Democratic Dilemma," *Globe and Mail* (Toronto), 8 May 2004.

67. Freud makes an important distinction between primary narcissism, which literally cannot fully integrate the presence of others into its worldview, and secondary narcissism which respects the needs of others while maintaining a healthy sense of self. In charging Ignatieff with narcissism, it is primary narcissism that I have in mind. See Sigmund Freud, "On Narcissism: An Introduction," in Freud, *On Metapsychology*, vol. 11 of the Penguin Freud Library (Harmondsworth: Penguin Books, 1991), pp. 59–97.

68. Conrad, *Heart of Darkness*, p. 118.

6

NOSTALGIA FOR EMPIRE: REVISING IMPERIAL HISTORY FOR AMERICAN POWER

Colin Mooers

To allow frustration or nostalgia to incline us to the old-style imperial system is to disregard its racism, brutality and rapacity, as well as the self-delusion of its rulers.

(Karl E. Mayer, *Dust of Empire*)

I am fundamentally in favor of empire. Indeed, I believe that empire is more necessary in the twenty-first century than ever before.

(Niall Ferguson, *Colossus: The Price of America's Empire*)

BRINGING THE IMPERIAL STATE BACK IN

The apologists for the new imperialism, whatever we might say about the ideological nature of their project,[1] are also engaged in a debate amongst themselves concerning the proper balance between the military and economic aspects of empire. At stake from their perspective is the best strategy for securing nationally and regionally based capitalist interests in a world system composed of territorially limited states and the potentially limitless spread of capital. One solution to this dilemma has been the call for a return to formal empire. Formal empires of the kind which all of the great European powers constructed in the second half of the nineteenth century, and which were only finally dismantled after World

War Two, had the distinct advantage that the frontiers of capital were more or less coextensive with the geographical boundaries of the empire.[2] Put another way, what the advocates of the new imperialism have discovered is that the separation of economic and political power poses some concrete challenges for global capitalism which are not easily resolved.

The separation of politics and economics is both a blessing and a curse for capitalism. A blessing, because it enables class inequality to coexist with formal civic equality. The Victorians need not have feared the overthrow of property when suffrage was extended to include Burke's "swinish multitude." Civic and political rights could be extended widely across society without threatening the private powers of capitalists; formal democracy and citizenship rights could not affect class inequality and exploitation.[3] But the separation of economics and politics is also a potential curse because it establishes the conditions for the separation of territorial state power from the extra-territorial logic of capital accumulation. If the logic of territorial power stresses the state-political, diplomatic, and military aspects of capitalism, the latter highlights the diffuse and fluid flow of capital across national borders.[4]

The demise of the formal territorial empires in the second half of the twentieth century and the consequent decoupling of political power from the extensive reach of capital accumulation has posed special advantages and problems of its own. For the American empire, from Woodrow Wilson onward, it was taken for granted that economic prosperity could be secured without territorial aggrandizement.[5] The lack of a formal empire has allowed the American state to present itself to the world as a non- or even anti-imperialist power. It has been able to "conceal its imperial ambition in an abstract universalism . . . to deny the significance of territory and geography altogether in the articulation of imperial power."[6] But policing U.S. interests has had its own costs and perils. The dogma of economic "openness"[7] was dependent on either the cooperation of compliant local regimes or, failing that, an increasing number of "small wars" which, as one recent champion of such conflicts admits, "might as well be called imperial wars."[8] In the twentieth century alone, it is estimated that the United States sent troops or sponsored local forces to fight in sixty such "small wars."

The hazard of "small wars" of empire is that they can turn into major ones, resulting in the perennial danger of "imperial overreach" as happened most spectacularly for the U.S. in Vietnam. American defeat at the hands of the Vietnamese famously established the conditions for the "Vietnam syndrome" – the belief that the U.S.A. could not and should not fight wars it could not guarantee it would win. And winning in military terms meant the deployment of overwhelming force, preferably against much weaker enemies as in the Grenada or Panama invasions. The same guiding principle was in force in the 1991 Gulf War. It may have been premature for George Bush Sr. to declare an end to the Vietnam syndrome after that conflict since the very small number of allied deaths had not yet sufficiently tested the American public's willingness to accept a larger number of casualties. The Vietnam syndrome proved alive and well in the aftermath of the Somalian debacle of 1993 where 1,200 U.S. troops were routed by local warlords and forced to withdraw. The "Clinton Doctrine," which dominated military policy for the rest of the 1990s, sought to avoid U.S. casualties at all costs. Economic "openness," now enshrined under the equally euphemistic ideology of "globalization," would be secured by means of "a modern equivalent of old-fashioned 'gunboats' in cruise missiles and aircraft armed with precision-guided munitions."[9]

Clinton-era "globalization," backed by the occasional salvo of cruise missiles or a N.A.T.O.-sponsored bombing campaign, appeared to be all that was required to maintain U.S. hegemony. Indeed, state-military power seemed to recede into the background. Under the Clinton administration, the National Economic Council was more powerful than the National Security Council, and the Treasury and International Monetary Fund became the principal instruments of U.S. foreign policy.[10] The hidden hand of the market combined with "soft" and largely invisible policy intervention seemed to herald a new era of what the president of Microsoft liked to call "frictionless capitalism."[11] Those most mesmerized by globalization tended to mistake neoliberal down-sizing of the welfare state for its wholesale decline. Fluid flows of finance capital aided by new communications technologies had made the old state order itself redundant and the world safe for a kinder and gentler form of capitalism. Or so it seemed.

By the late 1990s, however, the state was undergoing a gradual rehabilitation. In their own version of "bringing the state back in," neoconservative intellectuals have become increasingly preoccupied with the role of state power both in the war on terror and more broadly in the protection of U.S. imperial interests. Francis Fukuyama saw in the 1990s by trumpeting the "end of history" doctrine, which held that liberal capitalism had vanquished all other contending ideologies; all that the "hidden hand" of the market required to work its benign magic was the minimalist "night watchman" state beloved of classical liberal theory. Lately, he has begun to question the wisdom of unbridled neoliberalism, arguing for a reassertion of the "*techne* of state-building."[12] "For the post-September 11 period," Fukuyama writes, "the chief issue for global politics will not be how to cut back on stateness but how to build it up . . . the withering away of the state is not a prelude to utopia but to disaster."[13] In a similar vein, Philip Bobbit links the emergence of what he calls, in a strikingly apt term, "the market-state" to U.S. victory in the epochal wars of the twentieth century.[14] The system of nation-states, and the right to self-determination upon which the concept of national sovereignty rested, has come to an end. In future, state legitimacy will rest less on welfare or democratic principles than on a state's ability to secure purely market-based rewards for its citizens. But the market itself is incapable of coordinating the defensive tactics required to guarantee these outcomes. The role of the "market-state" is precisely to deploy sufficient military might such that challenges to market-based societies are forestalled. Robert Kagan echoes these sentiments, arguing against what he takes to be the European delusion that the world has entered a "post-historical paradise of peace and relative prosperity, the realization of Immanuel Kant's 'perpetual peace'." Rather, "the United States remains mired in history, exercising power in an anarchic Hobbesian world where international rules and laws are unreliable, and where true security and the defense and promotion of the liberal order still depends on the possession of military might."[15] It is easy to see the fit between such cavalier dismissals of the supposed encumbrances of "old-fashioned" notions of state sovereignty and the right to self-determination – if these can ever be said to have been an obstacle for imperial states – and the Bush doctrine of "preemptive war."

An odd outcome, it might be thought, since what was supposed to distinguish neoconservatives from old-style foreign policy "realists" was their commitment to installing democracy throughout the world as an antidote to terrorism and other threats to U.S. hegemony. Yet the contradiction is only apparent: the ease with which neoconservative writers dispense with longstanding democratic ideals such as the right to self-determination should tell us something about the poverty of their conception of democracy. For them, "state-building" is not about bringing democracy to the disenfranchised. Rather, as Fareed Zakaria argues, "there can be such a thing as too much democracy – too much of a good thing."[16] On this view, freedom has been overtaken by "illiberal democracy" which threatens to undermine property rights and individual freedoms. Moving too quickly toward democracy, as the "failed states" of the postcolonial era ostensibly demonstrate, results in autocracy. Constitutionally limited democracy, "is about the limitation of power; democracy is about its accumulation and use. For this reason, eighteenth and nineteenth century liberals saw democracy as a force that could undermine liberty."[17] In other words, capitalism and the rule of law must be secured before any dangerous experiments in mass democracy are allowed. And, when they are permitted, democratic powers must be carefully contained so as not to threaten the rule of capital. Zakaria contends that the United States should therefore accept that its mission in the Middle East is not to install democracy but constitutional liberalism.[18] These sentiments have been echoed by a host of neoconservative intellectuals[19] and neatly dovetail with the Bush administration's National Security Strategy which holds that there is only "a single sustainable model for national success: freedom, democracy and free enterprise" firmly based in the rule of law, limited state power, political rights, and respect for private property.[20]

NIALL FERGUSON'S RESURRECTION OF EMPIRE

It is against this background, rather than any burning desire to bring democracy to the world's oppressed, that the term "imperialism" has come back into vogue. As Vivek Chibber has observed, "Commentators and ideologues no longer shy away from the E word and, indeed, openly embrace it – as well as the phenomenon it describes."[21] The rehabilitation of the discourse of empire and imperialism among mainstream intellectuals has produced a flurry of publications extolling the virtues of America's informal empire and the benefits to humanity wrought by the formal empires of the nineteenth century:

> A century of disastrous utopian hopes has brought us back to imperialism, that most ordinary and dependable form of protection for ethnic minorities and others under violent assault. . . .

Despite our anti-imperial traditions, and despite the fact that imperialism is delegitimized in public discourse, an imperial reality already dominates our foreign policy. . . . The very weakness and flexibility of such a non-traditional American-led empire will constitute its strength.[22]

The virtues of formal empire have been expounded by others,[23] but the British historian Niall Ferguson is unquestionably its most ardent contemporary advocate. For Ferguson, the resurrection of formal empire remains the only viable strategy in a world of fragmented and limited states: "In the absence of formal empire," Ferguson asserts, "it must be open to question how far the dissemination of Western 'civilization' – meaning the Protestant-Deist-Catholic-Jewish mix that emanates from modern America – can safely be entrusted to Messrs Disney and McDonald."[24] The solution to the problem of the territorially limited nature of the state in an age of global capital is to make the boundaries of the state once again coterminous with those of capital.

As bizarre as such a project might seem in the wake of half a century of anti-colonial struggles, Ferguson's work has been greeted with reverential gravitas by media commentators from across the political spectrum. Leading neoconservative Max Boot credits Ferguson with making

> a convincing case for the positive role played by the British Empire in world history. It exported liberal capitalism, parliamentary democracy, the rule of law, and the English language all over the world. . . . The British Empire made possible the first great wave of globalization and free trade. Britain benefited but so did less developed countries".[25]

The Economist congratulates Ferguson for "asserting . . . the virtues which acquit the British of really criminal imperialism. The empire emerges credibly, as the worst the world has ever known, except for all the others."[26] One would expect as much from political conservatives. However, what is truly astonishing is the welcome Ferguson's work has received in the mainstream liberal press as well. A reviewer in the *Atlantic Monthly* describes Ferguson as "the most gifted and prolific (too prolific) British historian of his generation."[27] Even mildly sceptical reviewers have seen his widely popular *Empire* as "timely as Americans try to work out their role in the post-cold war world."[28] Another review in the *New York Times Book Review*, by the historian John Lewis Gaddis, judges the most important lesson to be drawn from Ferguson's work to be "that the dismantling of formal empires and the near universal practice of self-determination have so far failed to produce the orderly, prosperous and equitable world for which liberals since Woodrow Wilson have hoped." Some form of imperial governance, he concludes, is therefore necessary and "only the United States is in a position to supply and secure international support for such tutelage."[29] The discourse of empire, it seems, has gone mainstream.

In several books and articles, Ferguson has sought to make the case that the United States needs to abandon its historic commitment to informal empire (what Ferguson calls "the imperialism of anti-imperialism"[30]) in favour of a twenty-first-century version of formal empire. America, "is an empire that dare not speak its name. It is an empire in denial."[31] The great success of Britain's empire was that it was prepared to send generations of colonial officials and missionaries to its colonies – the liberal imperialist version of non-governmental organizations (N.G.O.'s)[32] – who were ready to spend their entire careers ministering to the needs of empire. Unlike the British, the Americans are good at *conquering* but not at *ruling*:

> This is primarily because the American electorate is averse to the kind of long-term commitment that history strongly suggests is necessary to achieve a successful transition to a market economy and representative government . . . Americans lack the imperial cast of mind. They would rather consume than conquer.[33]

American efforts at informal rule have been largely inept: initial military success based on a strategy of limited war, usually followed by an escalation of military force due to a flawed reading of indigenous support, has inevitably led to domestic disillusionment and ultimate withdrawal.[34] Far more successful have been direct annexations or periods of prolonged occupation as occurred in Germany and Japan in the aftermath of World War Two.[35] The United States has failed in its imperial ambitions when it has attempted to fight limited wars of occupation and when public support – as in Vietnam – begins to wane and a sufficiently strong-willed leadership is lacking.[36] The loss of Iran in 1979 to theocratic fundamentalism was "a calamity whose ramifications were and remain incalculable."[37] The Khomeini regime legitimated terrorism for the next generation of "Islamo-bolshevism"[38] – the term Ferguson prefers to describe bin Laden and al-Qaeda. Bin Laden "is the offspring of the Middle East's distinctive civilization of clashes, a retarded political culture in which terrorism has long been a substitute for both peaceful politics and conventional warfare."[39] The Bush administration was therefore correct in claiming there was a connection between the sponsorship of terrorism and the policies of countries such as Afghanistan, North Korea, Sudan, Syria, and Iraq. They were right to claim that weapons of mass destruction were being produced by Saddam Hussein; right to claim that further U.N. inspections would be ineffective in finding them and, therefore, right in invading Iraq: "the only mystery is why Iraq was not invaded before 2003."[40]

The lack of any empirical evidence for such claims (or their subsequent official repudiation) does not seem to trouble Ferguson. His main worry is that the Bush administration will cut and run before the vital work of "nation-building" and the installation of a market economy is complete. To prevent this from happening, he has set himself the task of schooling the congenitally unhistorically minded leaders of Pax Americana in the lessons to be learned from Britain's empire. But in order for his pupils to appreciate the legacy of imperial history, Ferguson must first rewrite it.

REVISING BRITISH IMPERIAL HISTORY

Ferguson presents us not with a history of the British Empire but a history of empire for the British – and, of course, the Americans. His nostalgia for empire is not of the sentimental kind; he does not gaze back wistfully to the days before the lights went out on the British Empire. He is a neoliberal and "an unashamed modernist."[41] But despite these contemporary concerns, his is a curiously old-fashioned sort of story-telling redolent of a bygone age of imperial historiography; the makers of history are "great men" like Livingstone, Macaulay, and, inevitably, Churchill. His is a history of empire written by and for the "victors"; any interest in the lives of the conquered is incidental and its ill effects are systematically downplayed. Ferguson does acknowledge some unpleasantness– slavery, for example (though it is hard to imagine anyone who thinks that slavery wasn't so bad after all being taken seriously) – but as is typical of his method, he credits its demise to the decisions of wise imperialists and not to the struggles of the enslaved themselves.[42] Anticolonialism plays a negligible role in the end of empire; beyond a few minor mentions, the colonized are largely mute. The case for the British Empire is simply that it was better than the rest. A less brutal empire is apparently preferable to none at all.

The benefits of the British Empire, especially those bestowed in its liberal phase from the 1850s until the 1930s, have to do with the spread of capitalist social-property relations, the rule of law, "good governance," parliamentary democracy, and, to a lesser degree, Protestant Christianity and the English language.[43] According to Ferguson:

> Americans have more to learn than they are prepared to admit from their more self-confident British predecessors, who, after the mid-nineteenth century calamities of the Irish Famine and the Indian Mutiny, recast their empire as an economically liberal project, concerned as much with the integration of global markets as with the security of the British Isles, predicated on the idea that British rule was conferring genuine benefits in the form of free trade, the rule of law, the safeguarding of private property rights and noncorrupt administration, as well as government-guaranteed investments in infrastructure, public health and (some) education.[44]

Not only does a liberal empire make sense today "in terms of both American self-interest and altruism,"[45] it should also be seen, as with the post-1850 British Empire, just as much as a benefit to those *over whom* it rules; imperial rule should be seen as an unalloyed good for its *subjects*.[46] In many parts of the former colonial world, especially in Africa, people are worse off than they were under colonialism.[47] Since much of Ferguson's historical case rests on the account he provides of British rule in India, and to a lesser extent, the Middle East and Africa, it is worthwhile recalling some of the highlights of imperial rule in these regions, especially as they relate to the supposed benefits of capitalism, the rule of law, and "good governance."

INDIA

Modernization and Capitalism

India under the Raj was hardly the model study in the successful transition to industrial capitalism Ferguson seems to have in mind. Indeed the entire period of the British presence represented a kind of seesaw of advance and retreat from capitalist imperatives, owing mainly to the "military-despotic"[48] nature of the imperial state. During the rule of the East India Company, wealth was mainly based on commercial trade and the perquisites of office. The application of military force was central to sustaining and expanding these forms of wealth. Despite attempts to encourage forms of private property and agrarian capitalism, the Company constantly found itself squeezed by its debt requirements and the huge costs of administering the vast territories under its control. After the transfer of power from the Company to the British government, the colonial state continued to guarantee that productivity benefits would not return to the direct producers: financed by taxes on farm land, the state budget returned less than 2 percent to agriculture and education and 4 percent to public works, while one-third went to the army and police.[49] Even if English principles of property ownership had been successfully imported, the extractive toll of the state meant that the transformation of Indian ryots and zamindars into small capitalist farmers on the English model was a non-starter: "The colonial state was fully aware that this kind of relationship was inimical to development, [but] did little to bring capital into productive relationship with landed property. The colonial state [thus] came to resemble a classic agrarian bureaucracy rather than a capitalist state."[50] The thirst for higher profits was also the main motivator of further territorial expansion in the first half of the nineteenth century. As new territories were annexed, the Company increasingly relied on traditional landed elites to extract economic surpluses from the subject peasantry. Neither of these strategies, however, were successful in offsetting the growing fiscal crisis that was engulfing the British administration before the 1857 uprising finally put an end to East India Company rule once and for all. As Bayly observes:

> Insecurity on its extended frontiers and the desire to seize new revenues encouraged expansion. Expansion in turn generated new financial commitments which could only be met by trying to

ratchet up land revenue. But squeezing the Indian states for tribute and the dependent territories for land revenue merely gave a spurt to internal revolt and impaired the ability of India's peasant economy to generate new resources for itself. Between 1820 and 1857 therefore, Company government lurched from expansion to retrenchment and back and efforts at reform were implemented painfully slowly.[51]

Indeed this same, essentially non-capitalist, pattern of development would be repeated even after the British government took over the job of direct rule from the Company. Despite attempts to separate economic from political and military forms of wealth production and to promote private property, the threat of rebellion and territorial expansion constantly undermined efforts to create a capitalist economy in India. Ironically, the strength of Britain's own economy tended to exert cost/price pressures on Indian goods, forcing prices downward and inhibiting economic growth. This in turn encouraged a retreat to the earlier imperial practices based on revenues extracted through extra-economic means:

> But capitalist imperialism required property forms different from those of a revenue-extracting non-capitalist empire and conditions that would allow market imperatives to regulate the economy. This, on balance, may have been the direction in which the imperial state was trying to move, but conditions in India and the logic of the empire itself – not least, the danger of rebellion, culminating in the Mutiny of 1857 – constantly reasserted the primacy of the military state. The evolution of the British Empire would continue to display these contradictory tendencies, oscillating between "modernization" and "traditionalization", as the imperatives of capitalism were constantly offset by the logic of an imperial military state, which imposed its own imperatives.[52]

But this is not the story Ferguson chooses to tell. Rather, while other colonies were in decline India "was booming. Immense sums of British capital were being invested in a range of new industries: cotton and jute spinning, coal mining and steel production."[53] This is, at best, only a partial truth; very few economic historians would agree with this rosy picture of Indian development. After 1860 British-manufactured textile exports picked up sharply. Nearly one-third of demand for cloth in Bengal and Bihar was met by British imports.[54] The era of free trade was one in which Britain's powerful export economy dominated not only the world economy but those of its colonies as well:

> Between 1885 and 1913 India took two-fifths of Britain's total exports of cotton goods, based on low customs duties which worked to Britain's advantage. India's share of Britain's imports fell to about 10 percent by 1900 and its share of India's total exports fell from one-third in 1890 to one-quarter twenty years later, less than either Europe or Asia.[55]

As Davis summarizes: "The looms of India and China were defeated not so much by market competition as they were forcibly dismantled by war, invasion, opium and a Lancashire-imposed system of one-way tariffs . . . the use of force to configure a 'liberal' world economy is what Pax Britannica was really about."[56]

Famine and Free Trade

But it was not for lack of ideological commitment that India failed to overcome its essentially pre-capitalist dynamic in the second half of the nineteenth century. Colonial officials both at home and in the colonies saw their "civilizing mission" as imparting the benefits of economic "improvement" and Christian piety. The "gentlemanly capitalism"[57] that dominated in the colonial administration sought to link the social-property relations which lay at the heart of England's seventeenth- and eighteenth-century agrarian capitalist revolution with the newer forms of financial and service capital that came to prominence in the later nineteenth century. These officials had read their Locke on property, enclosure, and "improvement." They were also avid proponents of the latest principles of political economy espoused by Malthus, Bentham, and Mill. It was the *liberal* empire – so vaunted by Ferguson – which encouraged not just chronic economic underdevelopment, but which bears responsibility for the deaths of millions due to starvation during the two great waves of famine which swept India in 1876–79 and 1896–1900.

Between 5.5 and 12 million died in the famine of 1876–79 and mortality rates were highest in areas best served by railways. As Mike

Davis has shown in painful detail, it was the fanatical commitment to free-market and Malthusian dogmas which made famine a death sentence for millions while British officials railed against "enthusiastic prodigality" as they shipped huge grain exports out of the country. Malthus's injunctions against feeding the poor and hungry because "mother nature had not set enough places at her table" were taken up by British viceroys from Lytton to Curzon with methodical and murderous abandon. Just as in England, poor relief in times of poor harvest was considered a slippery slope leading to more permanent forms of relief. In India, Lytton reasoned, "The doctrine that in time of famine the poor are entitled to demand relief . . . would probably lead to the doctrine that they are entitled to demand relief at all times, and thus the foundation would be laid for a system of general poor relief, which we cannot contemplate without serious apprehension."[58]

When Lytton dispatched Sir Richard Temple to deal with the famine in Madras, the latter was under considerable pressure to prove that he had overcome his previously "profligate" ways in dealing with the famine in Benghal and Bihar (where he had imported half a million tons of grain from Burma, thus avoiding a mass catastrophe). As a result, official figures had shown only twenty-three deaths. Temple's job was to clamp down on such expenditures in order to finance the war in Afghanistan. He quickly set about reducing the rice ration to one pound per day, far below what medical authorities thought necessary for survival, especially under conditions where famine victims were incarcerated in camps and forced to do hard physical labour. What became known as the "Temple Wage" resulted in a monthly death rate of 94 percent: "Temple's perverse task was to make relief as repugnant and ineffective as possible. In zealously following his instructions to the letter, he became in Indian history . . . the personification of free market economics as a mask for colonial genocide."[59]

In the Madras districts, at least 1.5 million perished; in the Deccan one-quarter of the population died; and in Madras city 100,000 starved around the precincts of the grain stockpiles being guarded by troops. In the northwestern provinces and the Punjab, famine could have been avoided in 1878–79 if the government had foregone the collection of the land tax. But in the name of principles of "good governance" and sound fiscal management, it refused to do so. Such policies were directly impli-cated in the deaths of 1.25 million poor peasants and labourers. Lytton's officials promptly ordered officers to "discourage relief works in every possible way. . . . Mere distress is not a sufficient reason for opening relief work."[60]

Nor was the situation any different nearly twenty years later during the famine of 1896–97. Under Lord Elgin the same policies were pursued with a vengeance. Not only had the famine fund been looted to pay for the Afghan war but the administration was prepared to divert huge sums toward celebration of Queen Victoria's sixtieth year of rule. Rioting and the assassination of a British official did not trouble them so much as the threat that famine and plague posed to Britain's balance of payments. This, and the prospect of a French embargo, prompted the Secretary of State in London to tell the Viceroy that "he was more concerned about the plague and famine" because "a market once lost, or even partially deserted, is not easily regained."[61] Lord Curzon, appointed in 1898, likened "prodigal philanthropy" in the form of relief works to a "public crime."[62]

Ferguson devotes a scant few lines to the disastrous policies pursued by British officials during the famine years, admitting that free-market policies may have made things worse than they might have been, but dismissing criticism that the British did nothing to avert starvation. He rejects the view that their actions can be likened to other modern genocides on the grounds that Lytton never planned to kill millions of Indians whereas the Nazi genocide was intentional.[63] However, it is difficult to imagine a more *intentional* outcome than that pursued by Lytton and Temple: they *knew* that other measures were available and that mass starvation could be averted (as Temple had done previously in Bengal and Bihar) and yet they proceeded to do the opposite. Indeed, even by Malthusian standards, it was hardly a situation of letting "nature" run its course. The reduction of rations, insistence on hard labour, and collection of the land tax could have no other outcome than drastically increasing mortality rates. Instead of viewing such actions for what they were – intentional acts of imperial genocide – the most that Ferguson can muster is the rhetorical query: "But would Indians have been better off under the Mughals? Or for that matter, under the Dutch – or the Russians?"[64] In fact, there is considerable evidence to suggest that the Moguls and Marathas did attempt to tailor their rule to fluctuating ecological and climactic conditions, especially in drought-prone regions. Moreover, as Davis asserts,

There is persuasive evidence that peasants and farm laborers became dramatically more pregnable to natural disaster after 1850 as their local economies were violently incorporated into the world market. What colonial administrators and missionaries perceived as the persistence of ancient cycles of backwardness were typically modern structures of formal and informal imperialism.[65]

Indirect Rule and Traditionalization

The policies pursued by imperial officials during the famine years greatly strengthened the powers of "traditional" chiefs and other intermediaries who were able to enrich themselves at the expense of their poorer neighbours. Ferguson likes to contrast the so-called liberal phase of indirect rule advocated by the Whig historian and Indian administrator Thomas Babington Macaulay from the "Tory-entalist"[66] and despotic policies of Curzon. Macaulay promoted the idea of creating "a class of persons, Indian in blood and colour, but English in taste, in opinions, in morals, and in intellect."[67] The key to the latter strategy was to create an educated middle-class elite which identified its fortunes with those of its imperial masters. Indeed, Macaulay's strategy met with some initial success, by the 1870s enrolling some 60,000 Indian students in higher education and 200,000 more in anglophone secondary schools.[68]

But there were two obvious shortcomings to this strategy. As time went on, the continued allegiance of intellectuals and middle-class professionals, despite their privileged status, was strained by the growing popularity of anti-British sentiment. Even the mildest concessions to self-rule at the local level "were an encouragement to nationalism."[69] Secondly, the idea that such a social pact could be sustained in the face of the essentially pre-capitalist cast of the Indian state and economy was unrealistic. Indeed, Indian society was becoming more traditional, caste-ridden, and economically backward and the number of Indians drawn toward Christianity was extremely small. But the revival of fundamentalist forms of Hinduism and Islam grew disproportionately, making India more "religious" than it had been prior to British rule. Moreover, colonial institutions like the law courts reinforced the caste system through reference to "ancient" prerogatives based on the self-sufficient village community.[70] Far from being the progressive modernizing period of imperial rule that Ferguson believes it to have been, Indian society during its most liberal phase was rather, a society founded on the perpetuation of "Oriental" difference, as Edward Said has put it. India became a subordinate agricultural colony under the dominance of metropolitan, industrial Britain; its basic cultural institutions were disempowered and "fixed" in unchanging traditional forms; its "civil society" was subjected to the suzerainty of a military despotic state. British rule before the Mutiny may be credited with having fundamentally changed Indian society. But the change moved against the anticipations of "modernization" and left it with a vast legacy of "backwardness" subsequently to undo.[71]

That is why the shift toward a more apartheid-like form of indirect rule was made in the aftermath of the 1857 uprising. In India and elsewhere there was a hardening of racial attitudes toward all sectors of the local population but especially "a revulsion occurred against educated and Westernized members of indigenous societies who threatened to over-turn the 'difference' sustaining British superiority."[72] Thereafter, physical distancing and the invention of imperial traditions like the Indian durbar which drew in equal measure from imagined English and Indian feudal ceremonies and customs, became the order of the day. As Lytton cynically observed in 1877, "the further east you go, the greater becomes the importance of a bit of bunting."[73]

In sum, British rule in India sustained a pre-capitalist economy by means of a "military-despotic" state based on an alliance with the most backward religious and caste-ridden elements of Indian society. Its fanatical attachment to Malthusian political economy during the two great waves of famine that swept India in the late nineteenth century guaranteed the deaths of millions. And yet Ferguson concludes from this history "that there can . . . be little doubt that British rule reduced inequality in India. And even if the British did not greatly increase Indian incomes, things might conceivably have been worse under a restored Mughal regime had the Mutiny succeeded. China did not prosper under Chinese rulers."[74] This is a familiar tactic designed to exonerate British rule because other scenarios might have been worse. It is also a grotesque distortion of the facts:

> If the history of British rule in India were condensed into a single fact, it would be this: there was no increase in India's per capita income from 1757 to 1947. . . . Moreover, in the age of Kipling,

that "glorious imperial half century" from 1872 to 1921, the life expectancy of ordinary Indians fell a staggering 20 percent, a deterioration in human health probably without precedent in the subcontinent's long history of war and invasion.[75]

AHISTORICAL HISTORY: LEGACIES OF EMPIRE

At its zenith the British Empire encompassed nearly a quarter of the globe, or nearly 13 million square miles of the world's total land mass. Its overriding imperial ethos was that of a "civilizing mission" on the basis of which it would school the "uncivilized" non-Christian peoples of the planet in the virtues of Christianity, private property, parliamentary democracy, and free trade. "The imperial impulse," Ferguson contends, "arose from a complex of emotions: racial superiority, yes, but also evangelical zeal; profit, perhaps, but also a sincere belief that spreading 'commerce, Christianity and civilization' was as much in the interests of Britain's colonial subjects as in the interests of the imperial metropole itself."[76] Such passages belie Ferguson's tendency to take "sincere belief" at face value, whatever its consequences. Not only is this a calculatingly naïve view of imperial ideology – the "civilizing mission" was simply a rationalization for imperial plunder – it also downplays the brutality of imperial rule. Ferguson has merely dressed up old imperial "morality tales"[77] in new clothing for contemporary consumption. But the tale he tells, riddled as it is with distortions and half-truths, is also at its core profoundly ahistorical; there is no place in his narrative for the resistance of the colonized in their ultimately successful struggle to end to British rule.[78]

Indeed, Ferguson makes a point of diminishing the significance of anti-colonial struggles. The costs of imperial rivalry were of much greater importance.[79] This is a telling omission which has the effect of reversing the legacies of colonialism and anti-colonialism. It allows him to repeat the old lie that Britain bestowed the benefits of colonial administration, parliamentary democracy, and citizenship on a supine Indian nation. The real legacy of empire is in fact quite the opposite. As Aijaz Ahmed argues at length:

The fact . . . is that, to the extent that India is a nation at all, it became so not through British administration but in the course of the anticolonial movement, which was internally far more democratic than the colonial state and which mobilized some 20 million peasant households in the struggle against colonialism; the main British contribution to this process was that, at the beginning of the second world war, and in response to the Quit India Movement, Britain made an irrevocable commitment to Jinnah and thereby contributed to the Partition of the country. . . . Similarly, Indian democracy has nothing to do with the "heritage of imperialism". As late as 1946, one year before Independence, franchise had been extended to only a small minority of the population. By contrast, the most important – virtually the only worthwhile – political achievement of the modern Indian state is that it became a secular, democratic republic immediately after Independence.

The same applies to citizenship, which exists only to the extent that the people in their collectivity are able to give laws to themselves. No one can be a citizen of a colonial state, and citizenship itself cannot be a so-called "heritage of imperialism". The precise aim of the anticolonial movement in India was to institute citizenship and to put in place a constitutionality that was derived not from colonial authority but from a constituent assembly. None of it amounts to a "heritage of imperialism".[80]

Moreover, the centrepiece of colonial administration – indirect rule – contributed to precisely the postcolonial pathologies that Ferguson uses to justify the call for a return to formal empire today. Pioneered in India but practised almost universally throughout the British Empire, indirect rule institutionalized what Mamdani labels in the African case a "decentralized despotism" – a form of rule with closer affinities to apartheid than is usually acknowledged.[81] As in India, the policy was based on the co-optation or, if necessary, wholesale creation, of pliant local elites willing to carry out and enforce the dictates of the colonial administration. In Africa, colonial officials manipulated indigenous traditions of decentralized power while discarding customary forms of constraint on despotic rule. Indirect rule was justified as an enlightened form of customary rule sensitive to African culture. However, the reality was quite different. The "customs" so admired by the British were based on the encouragement of religious and ethnic divisions as part of a classic strategy of "divide and rule."[82] Moreover, as Mamdani points out, there was "nothing voluntary about custom during the colonial period. More than being reproduced through social sanction, colonial custom was enforced with a whip, by a constellation of customary authorities – and, if necessary, with the barrel of a gun, by the forces of the central state."[83] The ethnic and tribal conflicts that have so plagued postcolonial Africa – opposed but never fully overcome by postcolonial governments – are the direct legacy of colonial rule. In short, far from forging a lasting legacy of democratic citizenship based on accountable administrative and political institutions, Britain's most lasting contribution "may lie in the inherited impediments to democratization."[84]

Similar policies were implemented with the same predictable outcomes in the Middle East. After World War One, the victorious imperialist powers set about carving up the remnants of the Ottoman Empire. Britain was to get Palestine – where it favoured setting up a Zionist state – Arabia and Mesopotamia; Syria and Lebanon were to go to France. Egypt was to serve as "a laboratory of indirect rule."[85] The British had effectively ruled Egypt since the opening of the Suez Canal in 1869 and remained there until 1952. Indirect rule was now redefined as a "mandate" to satisfy U.S. opposition to formal empire and the terms of the League of Nations.[86] But its substance remained the same. The British established regimes with compliant rulers: in Arabia, Ibn Saud and Hussein served the purpose; in Mesopotamia (modern Iraq) they imported Faisal from Mecca and established the Hashemite monarchy. In order to impose the Hashemite regime the British resorted to gassing and bombing resistance by the local population, inflicting 98,000 casualties.[87] They then set about shoring up decaying tribal structures through the creation of large landed estates ruled by a class of "government sheikhs." Their aim, as Peter Gowan observes, was to,

> *revive* dying traditional authority relations, resulting in economically and socially regressive consequences, undertaken for thoroughly modern imperialist political purposes – namely, to create a ruling class dependent upon British military power and therefore committed to imperial interests in the region.[88]

Ferguson casts all of this in a positive light. He likens the challenge facing the Americans in Iraq today to that faced by Britain in its seventy-four-year-long, but officially unacknowledged, military occupation of Egypt. The main lesson to be drawn from Britain's "veiled protectorate" in Egypt "is that it is possible to occupy a country for decades, while consistently denying that you have any intention of doing so. This is known as hypocrisy, and it is something to which liberal empires must sometimes resort."[89] But Ferguson's cynical view, however repugnant, also blinds him to an irresistible fact. Throughout the history of its so-called liberal empire, from the earliest stirrings of Indian nationalism to the Arab revolts after World War One, down to its brutal suppression of the Mau Mau uprising in Kenya in the final days of formal rule,[90] British colonialism faced growing resistance from the populations over which it ruled.[91] In the postcolonial world resistance to imperialism has found different expressions – nationalism, communism, and, more recently, in the form of religious fundamentalism. Whatever its sources, anti-imperialism is deeply sedimented in the collective memory of the formerly colonized and cannot be erased simply because Ferguson wishes it so. As Gilbert Achcar observes:

> When the population of an occupied country today is hostile to an occupying force and sees it as such, it is incomparably more dangerous for the occupiers than in the nineteenth or even the first half of the twentieth century. A century ago the bulk of colonized peoples was often resigned to their subjugation. Since then people have taken note of the national liberation struggles that character-ized the era of decolonization. In addition, levels of education and therefore national consciousness are now at a qualitatively higher level.[92]

This may represent the ultimate *reductio ad absurdum* of Ferguson's entire case for formal empire. He may believe that he has resolved the most pressing problem of contemporary global imperialism, namely how to make the world safe for capitalism in a world of fractured territorial states. But even here, he fails to appreciate the benefits such a system represents for capitalism. The fact that capital has spread far beyond the borders of any individual state makes a system of many nation-states inevitable and necessary.[93] The dream of a return to formal empire is as unrealistic in this context as the dream of establishing some form of "global governance." Ferguson's purported solution, therefore, is a chimera, conjured by an ahistorical imagination (an odd outcome for an historian), determined to ignore and forget the real testament of the past, especially of those whose struggles helped bring an end to empire.

Orwell famously wrote in *Nineteen Eighty-Four*: "Who controls the past controls the future. Who controls the present controls the past." Although we have not yet descended to the dystopian depths depicted by Orwell, "newspeak" has become ubiquitous and mendacity commonplace. Lies and half-truths of breathtaking scope are paraded about in the media and polite academic circles with little apparent embarrassment. Perhaps more alarming is that many seem to recognize that they are being lied to by their leaders, but choose to ignore it in favour of more comforting "morality tales" of the kind told by Ferguson.[94] It is hard to disagree with the judgement that Ferguson's historical revisionism is all about imperial self-image.[95] The debate, in other words, is not about history per se but about the role that Ferguson's sanitized version of events plays for those embarking on the latest round of imperial conquest; it is a hymn to the past glories of empire designed to heighten the moral tone of today's tawdry imperial enterprise. In the end, therefore, it is a debate not about the facts of imperial history – for these have been plain for decades – but about a version of the past that speaks to the self-deluding fantasies of those who control the present, but whose imperial hubris by no means guarantees their control of the future.

NOTES

1. See the introduction to this volume.
2. Although Britain also had extensive imperial interests throughout Latin America this region never became a major part of its colonial empire in the nineteenth century.
3. See Ellen Meiksins Wood's contribution to this volume.
4. David Harvey, *The New Imperialism* (New York: Oxford University Press, 2003).
5. Peter Gowan, *Global Gamble: Washington's Faustian Bid for World Dominance* (London: Verso, 1999), p. 159.
6. Harvey, *New Imperialism*, p. 50.
7. Andrew J. Bacevich, *American Empire* (Cambridge, Mass.: Harvard University Press, 2003), p. 26.
8. Max Boot, *The Savage Wars of Peace* (New York: Basic Books, 2002), p. xvi.
9. Bacevich, *American Empire*, p. 148.
10. James Mann, *Rise of the Vulcans: The History of Bush's War Cabinet* (New York: Penguin Books, 2004), p. xvi.
11. Bill Gates, *The Road Ahead* (New York: Viking Press, 1995).
12. Francis Fukuyama, *State-building: Governance and World Order in the 21st Century* (New York: Cornell University Press, 2004), p. 99.
13. Ibid., p. 120.

14. Philip Bobbit, *The Shield of Achilles: War, Peace, and the Course of History* (New York: Alfred A. Knopf, 2003), p. xxi.

15. Robert Kagan, *Paradise and Power: America and Europe in the New World Order* (London: Atlantic Books, 2003), p. 3.

16. Fareed Zakaria, *The Future of Freedom: Illiberal Democracy at Home and Abroad* (New York and London: W. W. Norton and Company, 2003), p. 27.

17. Ibid., p. 102.

18. Ibid., p. 152.

19. Kagan, *Paradise and Power*, p. 154; Bobbit, *Shield of Achilles*, p. 639; Robert D. Kaplan, *Warrior Politics: Why Leadership Demands a Pagan Ethos* (New York: Random House, 2002), p. 83. Niall Ferguson praises Zakaria's "brave and ambitious book" for pointing out "that the power of the masses has grown at the expense of the elites who once ruled the United States." Ferguson, "Overdoing Democracy," *New York Times Book Review*, 13 April 2003, p. 9. He reprises essentially the same argument in his latest book, *Colossus: The Price of America's Empire* (New York: The Penguin Press, 2004), pp. 179–180.

20. Quoted in Mann, *Rise of the Vulcans*, p. 329.

21. Vivek Chibber, "The Good Empire," *Boston Review*, http://bostonreview.net/br30.1/chibber.html, p. 1.

22. Kaplan, *Warrior Politics*, p. 149. Kaplan enlists the "warrior virtues" of Hobbes, Machiavelli, and Malthus against the "utopian" cosmopolitanism of the Kantian tradition. For the policy-makers of the American empire "projecting power comes first; values come second" (p. 61).

23. Fukuyama writes that the most notably successful historical examples of state-building come from the history of European colonialism: "The British above all succeeded in creating durable institutions in a number of their colonies, such as the Indian civil service and legal systems in Singapore and Hong Kong that are widely credited as laying the basis for post-independence democracy in the first case and economic growth in the latter two." This is a familiar refrain among the defenders of the historical legacy of empire. As will be argued at length below, it never seems to occur to them that the postcolonial democratic institutions (however limited) forged by postcolonial states such as India were achieved not because of but in spite of the legacy of imperial rule.

24. Niall Ferguson, *Empire: The Rise and Demise of the British World Order and the Lessons for Global Power* (New York: Basic Books, 2002), p. 310.

25. Max Boot, "Imperial Ambitions: How Britain Won and Lost the World," *Weekly Standard*, 24 February 2003.

26. *The Economist*, 22 March 2003.

27. *Atlantic Monthly*, April, 2003.

28. Margaret MacMillan, "Queen Victoria's Secret," *New York Times Book Review*, 20 April 2003, p. 12.

29. John Lewis Gaddis, "The Last Empire, for Now," *New York Times Book Review*, 25 July 2004, p. 11.

30. Ferguson, *Colossus*, p. 78.

31. Ferguson, *Empire*, p. 317.

32. Ibid., p. 98.

33. Ibid., pp. 28–29.

34. Ibid., p. 48.

35. Ferguson provides an astonishing defence of General MacArthur's desire to end the Korean War by dropping up to fifty atomic bombs on Chinese cities. "Politically he had miscalculated. But had he been wrong on the strategic question of how to win in Korea? It is at least arguable that he had a case. . . . MacArthur was at least partly vindicated. Limited war had not succeeded in securing an end to the war; only the threat of an atomic escalation had" (*Colossus*, pp. 91–92).

36. Ibid., p. 99.

37. Ibid., p. 117.

38. Ibid., p. 121.

39. Ibid., p. 120.

40. Ibid., p. 154.

41. Jon Wilson, "Niall Ferguson's Imperial Passion," *History Workshop Journal*, 56(1), 2003, p. 180.

42. See the exchange between Ferguson and Bernard Porter in the *London Review of Books*, 19 May 2005 and 2 June 2005.

43. Ferguson, *Empire*, pp. 303–4.

44. Ferguson *Colossus*, p. 25.

45. Ibid., p. 27.

46. Chibber, "Good Empire," p. 2.

47. Ferguson, *Colussus*, p. 173.

48. C. A. Bayly, *Indian Society and the Making of the British Empire* (Cambridge: Cambridge University Press, 1988).

49. Burton Stein, *A History of India* (Oxford: Blackwell Publishers, 1998), p. 263.

50. Kaiwar quoted in Mike Davis, *Late-Victorian Holocausts: El Nino Famines and the Making of the Third World* (London: Verso, 2001), p. 324.

51. Bayly, *Indian Society*, p. 120.

52. Ellen Meiksins Wood, *Empire of Capital* (London: Verso, 2003), p. 115.

53. Ferguson, *Empire*, p. 164.

54. Bayly, *Indian Society*, p. 200.

55. Robin J. Moore, "Imperial India 1858–1914," in *The Oxford History of the British Empire: The Nineteenth Century*, ed. Andrew Porter (Oxford: Oxford University Press, 1999), p. 441.

56. Davis, *Late-Victorian Holocausts*, p. 295.

57. P. J. Cain and A. G. Hopkins, *British Imperialism: Innovation and Expansion 1688-1914* (New York: Longman Publishing, 1993).

58. Davis, *Late-Victorian Holocausts*, p. 33.

59. Ibid., p. 37.

60. Ibid., p. 52.

61. Ibid., p. 152.

62. Ibid., p. 162.

63. Ferguson, *Empire*, pp. 157, 181.

64. Ibid., p. 182.

65. Davis, *Late-Victorian Holocausts*, p. 288.

66. Ferguson, *Empire*, p. 173.

67. Macaulay quoted in ibid., p. 158.

68. Ibid., p. 158.

69. Moore, "Imperial India," p. 433.

70. D. A. Washbrook, "India, 1818–1860: The Two Faces of Colonialism," in *The Oxford History of the British Empire: The Nineteenth Century*, ed. Andrew Porter (Oxford: Oxford University Press, 1999), pp. 397–398.

71. Ibid., p. 399.

72. Peter Burroughs, "Imperial Institutions and the Government of Empire," in *The Oxford History of the British Empire: The Nineteenth Century*, ed. Andrew Porter (Oxford: Oxford University Press, 1999), p. 182.

73. Lytton, quoted in ibid., p. 183.

74. Ferguson, *Empire*, p. 182; *Colossus*, p. 196.

75. Davis, *Late-Victorian Holocausts*, p. 312.

76. Ferguson, *Colossus*, p. 208.

77. Wilson, "Imperial Passion," p. 176.

78. In his review of Ferguson's six-hour television documentary on which *Empire* is based, Wilson notes that "only six non-Europeans are mentioned by name: Ghulam Hussein Khan, Jagat Bose, Paul Bogle, George William Gordon, Motilal Nehru and Mohandas K. Gandhi" (ibid., p. 177).

79. Ferguson, *Empire*, p. 246. In his book on World War One, *The Pity of War* (New York: Basic Books, 1999), the "pity" lies not so much in the human carnage as in the fact that the financial burden of the war made Britain's empire unsustainable (p. 435). The slow decline of British power after World War One could have been avoided if only British and European politicians had grasped that Britain and Germany had more in common than divided them. An Anglo-German alliance "was not only desirable but possible" (p. 45). Britain should have "stood aside" and possibly saved its empire from terminal financial collapse (p. 460).

80. Aijaz Ahmad, "The Politics of Literary Postcoloniality," *Race and Class*, 36(3), 1995, p. 4.

81. Mahmood Mamdani, *Citizen and Subject: Contemporary Africa and the Legacy of Late Colonialism* (Princeton, NJ: Princeton University Press, 1996), p. 48.

82. Burroughs, "Imperial Institutions," p. 179.

83. Mamdani, *Citizen and Subject*, p. 51.

84. Ibid., p. 25.

85. Karl E. Mayer, *The Dust of Empire: The Race for Mastery of the Asian Heartland* (New York: Century Foundation Public Affairs, 2003), p. 19.

86. David Fromkin, *A Peace to End All Peace: The Fall of the Ottoman Empire and the Creation of the Modern Middle East* (New York: Avon Books, 1989), p. 283.

87. Gowan, *Global Gamble*, p. 164.

88. Ibid., p. 167.

89. Ferguson, *Colossus*, p. 222.

90. It estimated that the entire Kikuyu population of 1.5 million was detained in order to thwart the Mau Mau uprising in Kenya. In a recent study, the historian Caroline Elkins disputes the official figure of 11,000 deaths, reckoning it much higher. In the course of putting down the rebellion the British pioneered such imperialist tactics as "forced villagization" (later taken up by the Americans in Vietnam in the form of "protected hamlets") in which they incarcerated the Kikuyu in 804 villages. Colonial officers also compiled personal photo albums of the camps including images of starvation and torture reminiscent of those captured by the torturers of Abu Ghraib. See, Caroline Elkins, *Imperial Reckoning: The Untold Story of Britain's Gulag in Kenya* (New York: Henry Holt and Company, 2005), pp. xv, 259–260, 287.

   In the introduction to *Empire*, Ferguson waxes lyrical about his boyhood in 1960s Kenya: "thanks to the British Empire my earliest childhood memories are of colonial Africa . . . it was a magical time, which indelibly impressed on my consciousness the sight of hunting cheetah, the sound of Kikuyu women singing, the smell of the first rains and the taste of ripe mango" (p. xv). He doesn't say what the Kikuyu women were singing about.

91. It may well be that the inability of liberal imperialists like Ferguson fully to appreciate the power of such movements speaks to a more general failure on the part of liberals to appreciate the affective attachments associated with territory and place. This is the argument put forward by Uday Singh, *Liberalism and Empire* (Chicago: University of Chicago Press, 1999). It is certainly the case that formal empire in the liberal imagination has always been more deeply allied to a different notion of territoriality, namely, that associated with "enclosure," and private property.

92. Gilbert Achcar, *Eastern Cauldron: Islam, Afghanistan, Palestine and Iraq in a Marxist Mirror*, trans. Peter Drucker (New York: Monthly Review Press, 2004), pp. 41–42.

93. See Wood, *Empire of Capital*, p. 141.

94. See on this point, "An Interview with Slavoj Zizek," *Left Business Observer*, August 2003.

95. Chibber, "Good Empire," p. 16.

7

WHEN MIGHT IS RIGHT: ANCIENT LAMENTATIONS, STRAUSSIAN MINISTRATIONS, AND AMERICAN DISPENSATIONS

Thom Workman

INTRODUCTION

Straussian scholars and thinkers have received growing popular attention in recent years. Earl Shorris's essay entitled "Ignoble Liars" in *Harper's* in the summer of 2004 attests to this growing fascination with the writings of Leo Strauss and the circle of academics inspired by his thought. Shorris claimed that Straussianism is the "the worst in American Politics" and, in an effort to make sense of the spurious claims about weapons of mass destruction in Iraq, he focused upon the cultivated commitment to dishonesty and deception that supposedly lies at the heart of the intellectual tradition.[1] Straussians, if we can use this moniker, do regularly surface in the news – Paul Wolfowitz, Richard Perle, Leon Kass, Francis Fukuyama, Alan Keyes, Irving Kristol, William Kristol to name a few – and these public intellectuals are open and frank about their intellectual heritage.[2] They are also perceived to be the architects of the domestic and foreign policy agenda of the Bush administration, including the controversial doctrine of pre-emption. From one perspective, however, those concerned with the Straussian influence in U.S. foreign policy might be faulted for having an inadequate grasp of history. What we have learned throughout the twentieth century is that U.S. conduct has not been contingent upon the political predilections of its ruling administration.

Republican and Democratic presidents come and go, and this seems to have remarkably little to do with the conduct of America, as a Nicaraguan, whose country has been meddled in or invaded by the U.S. upwards of a dozen times in the last century, might incline to remind us. In the last half of the twentieth century Democratic regimes were as keen to ramp up wars – witness Vietnam before 1968 – as their Republican counterparts. Even the Carter presidency coincided with extensive political interference and military manipulation by the U.S.A. in many of the world's hotspots, especially southern Africa and in the southeast Asian region. While the rationalizing principles come and go – the "containment doctrine" at the height of the Cold War, the Reagan doctrine of "roll-back" in the 1980s, or Bush's "doctrine of pre-emption" in the aftermath of 9/11 – the intrusions of empire have varied little across most of the world. Nevertheless, we recently witnessed a revival of the sentiment that administrations do matter, as the American "left" rallied behind Democratic hopefuls in the summer of 2004 with a view to reversing American fortunes in Iraq.

There is good reason to be wary of both the rallying Democratic forces in the 2004 presidential election, and of the popular concern with the Straussian presence in the senior echelons of the Bush administration, for they are similarly framed by a rather benign, voluntary view of U.S. imperial practices. The cultivation of a firm, critical standpoint with respect to the politics of American empire must aim for more than gentrified imperialism – a kinder, gentler brand of empire vaguely premised upon the notion of "good" and "bad" wars, "real" and "fabricated" enemies, or "vulgar" and "refined" court philosophers. With this in mind, it is here stressed that Straussian thought is worthy of critical scrutiny because it contributes to the ideological subtext of empire, helps to establish the shared visions of interlocutors who embrace overtly different policies, and assists in the formation of a disarming consensus that lies at the heart of much Western intellectual life.[3] To begin to unpack Straussian claims about war and empire it is helpful to note the basic conclusion reached by Kenneth Waltz in his provocative *Theory of International Relations*, that is, his claim that a bipolar system is the most stable system of international alliances.[4] The book formed an important part of the Realist revival in international relations thought in the 1980s, and critiques of the work also helped spawn the so-called "third debate" which broadened the intellectual foundations of the field.[5] Waltz's conclusion about bipolarity could mercifully be ignored except for the fact that a critique by Robert Cox, in a manner reminiscent of Marx's claim in *The German Ideology* that the social needs of the ruling class will encourage the ascendancy of validating ideas expressed as "eternal laws,"[6] drew attention to the ideological nature of his conclusions: "There is an unmistakably Panglossian quality," Cox wrote, "to a theory published in the late 1970s which concludes that a bipolar system is the best of all possible worlds. The historical moment has left its indelible mark upon this purportedly universalist science."[7] This one brief remark wisely drew the academy's wandering attention about war back to the profound relationship between intellectual life and the evolving social relations of power within and across societies.

A similar sensitivity with respect to the relationship between knowledge claims and the social relations of power inform this assessment of Straussian ideas about empire. Writers in the Straussian tradition share the same phenomenological horizons as all late moderns, horizons that include imperialism centred in the north, especially Washington and London, and dispiriting wars which exact a heavy toll across the majority of the world. At its core, however, Straussian thought urges us to relax our judgement of this very same world – indeed, to accept this world with all of its blemishes and failings. Straussian writings advise us that the rise of empires is a natural function of our all-too-human weakness for power. Empire is an outgrowth of humanity qua humanity; to condemn either war or empire without discretion is to condemn a natural part of our selves. In this age of empire, then, Straussian intellectuals have risen to supply the apologetic "eternal laws" of international life, but their place at the feet of the emperor is less important than the fact that they roam the corridors of the academy. As we shall see, their provision of an ideological subtext to American empire amounts to little more than a restatement of the realist theory of international politics, an outlook that dominated the field of international relations for decades, as writers in the Straussian tradition now acknowledge.

The more involved contribution of Straussian thought regarding war and empire, however, is their rigorous reshaping of the ancients as would-be apologists for the course of modern history. Thucydides in particular has been made to appear as a prototypical thinker in the Straussian vision of international life. The great historian of antiquity, they argue, recognized the limitations of humanity as he surveyed the

Hellenes at war, just as Straussian intellectuals in the twentieth century acknowledge the true character of humanity as they behold the disquiet of contemporary history. It will be argued here that Thucydides cannot be used to supply the foundational thought that naturalizes war and empire. The Straussian reading of Thucydides is untenable, and prompts one to reflect on the ideational requisites of modern empires. The ancients were certainly concerned about war and empire, and cynicism about the character of international life emerged from time to time. As the Cretan traveller from the opening of Book One of Plato's *Laws* declared: "Peace is just a name. The truth is that every city-state is, by natural law, engaged in a perpetual undeclared war with every other city-state." But Greek intellectuals, especially Thucydides, did not ratify such cynicism. Indeed, the opening Book of Plato's *Laws* just cited proceeds to attack and dismantle this cynical view. The ancient intellectual standpoint did not regard war and empire as necessary or ineluctable features of international life. The fact that Straussians find traction for their views among Thucydides specifically and classical thinkers more generally is most unfortunate, especially since the ancient critique, forged despite the ubiquity of both war and empire, could offer us so much inspiration in our troubled age.

THE STRAUSSIAN NATURALIZATION OF EMPIRE

Leo Strauss was a historian of political thought and a critic of modernity. He believed that the rationalistic arrogations of modernity severely limit our appreciation of ancient commentary, undermine convention and therewith the wisdom it typically bears, and render our society rudderless precisely when our technical capacities vastly outstrip all previous epochs of human history. Leo Strauss is also known well for his claim that all great thinkers write both exoterically and esoterically, that is, in a manner for public consumption that sustains many of the myths and illusions integral to any society, and in a philosophically more truthful way that can only be discerned by initiated readers, respectively. Intellectuals writing in the Straussian tradition broadly embrace most of the insights of Strauss himself, and have contributed to contemporary American conservative thought by writing widely on subjects ranging from sexuality to modern warfare.[8] The focus here is on the intellectual character of one particular aspect of Straussian thought, namely, its standpoint regarding war and empire. We can begin to unpack this region of Straussian thought by addressing its conception of political history, a conception inspired by the writing of the ancient Greek historian Thucydides.[9] Strauss claimed that political history sets out to unearth the eternal truths about human history through a careful excavation of its foundations. Attentive empirical observation and astute reflection are the tools of the political historian, and decisive in the generation of knowledge and wisdom. Modes of thought not observationally immersed in history as it actually unfolds, particularly philosophy, are not regarded by the political historian as being all that helpful when it comes to the generation of insight into the course of human history.[10] In a complementary language, the ground of history for the political historian is immanence, and its methodology is largely empirical.

At this point, the intellectual temper of political history shares the same assumption as modern sociological analysis, namely the notion that the truths of humanity are to be revealed through the direct study of humanity itself. But we also learn that the political historian turns further inward, and comes to account for the course of human history with reference to our "human nature," regarded as invariable or fixed. That is, the political historian traces world history back to the properties of a relatively permanent human nature. This enduring or unchanging human nature issues in a range of involuntary or compulsive behavioural norms, and thus establishes the parameters of actual history; the story of humanity, especially war and empire, then, is that acting out of our human natures.[11] The truth of empire and war is laid bare by exposing the *natural history*, if you will, of *human history*. Strauss wrote that Thucydides regards "human nature as the stable ground of all its effects."[12] Seeing this relationship is not easy, for the political historian realizes that history is alloyed, shrouded in hyperbole and cloaked in protestations, and thus one must discover the foundational nature of humanity amidst the welter of historical affection. In the last instance, nevertheless, the political historian regards the world as a manifestation of human nature that is ultimately incapable of being significantly modified or tamed. The wisdom of the political historian ultimately comes to tell us that the course of history is rooted in our immuring natures.

What particular lessons of history did the quintessential political historian Thucydides draw from analysis of the Peloponnesian war according to Straussian thought? We learn that at its deepest level the *History* is framed metaphorically in terms of the interplay of "motion" and "rest," a "fundamental opposition" between those forces that move the world along and those forces of relative stability, orderliness, and calm.[13] These forces play themselves out in two complementary directions, a more expansive ontological one in which the basic tension seems to permeate the entire natural world, and a more limited, historical one concerned with human nature and the *poleis*.[14] Of course, Thucydides focuses upon the latter, and particularly upon the play of motion and rest in human history. The metaphorical understanding of human history as the countervailing tension of motion and rest, moreover, maps respectively onto a number of derivative themes of the *History* including barbarism and Greekness, civic concord and discord, naval power and land power, the few and the many, and, importantly, Athenian daring and Spartan moderation as the subtext of the greatest counterpositional tension of all: war and peace. The Peloponnesian war was a great motion, indeed, the greatest motion to shake the ancient world.

In the Straussian interpretation, the metaphors of motion and rest capture the historical tensions rooted in an all-too-human struggle between our desire for justice (*dikē*) and our acquiescence to compulsion (*ananke*).[15] Regarding *dikē*, Thucydides' study recognizes the importance humanity places upon "right" or respect for international law, although it also affirms that its influence in the affairs of states is weakly enforced. Regarding *ananke*, Thucydides' study acknowledges that political leaders never miss an opportunity to add to the power of their respective states for reasons relating to fear especially, but also for reasons of greed and honour, and that the reality of these ineluctable drives "compels" or disciplines all states in their relations with one another. International life, then, exhibits this tension between *dikē* – which lends itself to rest – and *ananke* – which lends itself to motion – both of which are but expressions of our immuring human natures. This interplay of motion and rest, of justice and power, structures the *History* from its opening pages onwards. The *History* is basically an account of human nature manifest through Hellenic time.

It is in this sense that the growth of Athenian power compelled the Spartans to embark on a path of war. But we also learn that the Athenians were compelled to compel Sparta and its allies. In other words, the Athenians, bound by the same need to expand their power vis-à-vis other *poleis* across the Hellenic world and beyond, were destined to alarm the Peloponnesian League. Fear compelled the Spartans to respond to the growing power of Athens, a fear rooted in the natural calculations that emerge out of the basic character of power relations in international affairs. The chilling view of international relations expressed by the Athenian envoys at Melos just before they massacred the adult males of the island and enslaved the Melian women and children, namely that the strong rule the weak whenever they can – the "Athenian thesis" as it has come to be called – is affirmed by Thucydides. It expresses a most fundamental truth about the character of international life. But this is a doctrine of all international relations, not merely a doctrine justifying Athenian expansionism. As Leo Strauss wrote: "The Athenians' assertion of what one may call the natural rights of the strong as a right which the stronger exercises by natural necessity is not a doctrine of Athenian imperialism; it is a universal doctrine; it applies to Sparta for instance as well as to Athens."[16] At this point the Straussian reading of Thucydides resembles in all respects the standard reading of Thucydides made by the field of international relations, a connection now fully acknowledged by later Straussian writers including Thomas Pangle and Peter Ahrensdorf. One of the earliest expressions of this understanding of the relations among nations – commonly called Realism in the field of international relations – came from Hans Morgenthau, a colleague of Leo Strauss at the University of Chicago, in a celebrated work entitled *Politics Among Nations*.[17] In this book Thucydides was identified as a thinker who saw the basic Realist character of international life clearly, and most international relations thinking since then assumes that Thucydides prefigured Realist thought of the twentieth century.[18]

This basic tension between "right" and "power" frames all discussion about Thucydides among those who accept Leo Strauss's basic teachings. Thucydides expresses the truth of power politics in international life, and he recognizes the dilemmas that bear down upon statespersons in international relations who "naturally" factor in our more ethical or humanist dimensions. We are powerless to resist the lure of interest and power, just as we are powerless to resist thinking about right and justice. Our basic natures tug at us in two different directions, yet all state leaders come to realize that considerations of justice are relatively weak in the affairs of nations. As Pangle elegantly expressed it: "Through his account of the great and terrible war between Athens and Sparta, Thucydides nourishes in his readers a *resigned realism*, one that perceives the necessary weakness of justice among nations but does so without exulting in that insight."[19] Straussian thought never abandons the idea that Thucydides grasped the enduring truth of the Athenian thesis. Ann Norton's recent claim that later Straussian writing reverses an earlier, more tempered interpretation of Thucydides as a critic of empire in favour of one that sees him as embracing imperial Athens is utterly unfaithful to the scholarly texts themselves.[20] Whatever the Straussian thinkers may have been saying in their lectures at the University of Chicago, Straussian texts evince impressive continuity when it comes both to Thucydides and to the naturalization of empire. If anything, later thought emphasizes the so-called "ethical" side of life even more than the writing of Leo Strauss himself. The well-known work of Clifford Orwin, whose study of the ancient historian is entitled *The Humanity of Thucydides*, underscores the tension between considerations of power and justice, and equates "humanity" with the struggle to insert the latter into international relations practice. The titular intimation of the work is noteworthy given the fact that, time and again, the book returns faithfully to the central truth of the Athenian thesis that purportedly lies at the centre of the *History*. On Straussian terms, however, one should not be led astray by the deliberately deceptive nature of Orwin's title, for it should be regarded as a response to an anticipated line of criticism emerging from uninitiated readers, a response framed in a way that does not compromise the basic Straussian tenets regarding human history, war and empire, power politics, and the Athenian thesis.

Straussian thought on empire is virtually indistinguishable from its reading of Thucydides. The work of the ancient historian contains one of the great lessons of history. Empire and war are inescapable facts of international life. Thucydides accepted that the world cannot be changed; it can be more or less vulgar, but it cannot be changed. The sophistication of Pericles is to be preferred to the ignoble Cleon, but in the end Thucydides' "austere humanity" and his "somber but human realism" counsel us to resign ourselves to the basic Realist character of international life. All Straussian thought forges the idea that the corollary of the wisdom of the political historian is the relaxation of our judgement of war and empire. Severe judgement is tantamount to a self-loathing or the futile condemnation of our very own natures. The political historian in any epoch steadfastly refuses to hold humanity in such indirect contempt. Leo Strauss admonished his readers not to form unfair judgements about the verities of international life disclosed by the great historian: "One may say that the theme of political history is human power," he wrote, "but power viewed sympathetically."[21] Indeed, there are elements of Straussianism that shade into unabashed admiration of the supposed grandeur of war and empire, of their enduring achievements and of their legacies: "Political history presupposes that freedom and empire are, not unreasonably, mankind's great objective – that freedom and empire are legitimate objects of admiration."[22]

GETTING TO EMPIRE THROUGH THUCYDIDES

Can Thucydides be read as an accidental apologist of American empire? Over the last century there has been a rich debate about the interpretation of Thucydides' history of the Peloponnesian war. The interpretive poles of this debate congealed with the publication of Cornford's *Thucydides Mythistoricus* in 1907 and Cochrane's *Thucydides and the Science of History* in 1929.[23] On the Cornford side of the debate there is the claim that the *Peloponnesian War* of Thucydides assumes the shape of a tragedy in the Aeschylean tradition, while the opposing reading of Thucydides contends that he was a scientific observer in the manner of the early Hippocratics and Democritus.[24] In the former view Thucydides uses dramatic techniques to select and reshape the events of the war in a way that would be rejected by contemporary historians, while the latter tradition regards Thucydides as a dispassionate observer of human nature and history in the spirit of modern science. And the former view regards Thucydides as infusing his account of the Peloponnesian war with judgement and censure, while the latter is more inclined to regard the great historian as conveying the truths about human nature and history irrespective of his beliefs and preferences.

Straussian thought explicitly gravitates towards the "scientific" reading of the *History*. Leo Strauss dismissed the Cornford reading of Thucydides, especially the connection it establishes between the Melian massacre and the Athenian defeat in Sicily, as "stories delightful to the ear," that is, he dismissed Cornford's thesis in the language that Thucydides employed to attack Herodotus.[25] Strauss stressed that Thucydides "is silent about the gods or the strictly superhuman," but that he shows time and again that our inclination to believe in the gods can have a profound effect on the course of events.[26] Accordingly, Thucydides' strong support for the virtue of moderation – a Delphic maxim at the core of ancient culture – is read as a form of prudential understanding grounded in his astute reading of history. Not only is Thucydides' support for the virtue of moderation purely pragmatic in character, but Strauss stressed that Thucydides also balances his fondness for Sparta with support for Athenian daring and determination. States face natural limits in international relations imposed by the "logic" of international life, and this encourages moderation; but states are also given to expand and test their limits in the manner of Athens. Thucydides admires both Athens and Sparta. But while Thucydides' admiration for the moderation of Sparta leaps off the pages of the text, his support for Athens, we learn, is conveyed "only between the lines of his work."[27] For our purposes these observations are less important for the fact that they infuse the schematic Straussian hermeneutic regarding exo/esotericism with dogmatism, and rather more important for the fact that they permit us to underscore the Straussian claim that Thucydidean virtues, namely his open embrace of Spartan moderation and his altogether unwritten praise of Athenian daring, are grounded exclusively in immanence.

Straussian thought repudiates the idea that there are transcendent aspects to Thucydides' manner of thinking. The standards of political history can only be political and historical; the Straussian contention is that the very core of political history rests on the conviction that international life is impervious to transcendent measure, and that no such moments ever appear in the *History*. Indeed, the wisdom of the philosopher easily runs the risk of being inferior to the wisdom of the political historian in so far as the former is naïve to one's own historical irrelevance. Strauss held that "philosophy," for Thucydides, "has no point of entrance into political life. . . . The Peloponnesian War . . . is wholly independent of philosophy."[28] To underscore this aspect of political history, Strauss contends that Plato believed that philosophy could shape political life directly, and accordingly we are told that his judgement of political life is more severe. But, in stark contrast, Thucydides harboured no such beliefs, and his judgement of politics is correspondingly muted or tempered. There were things about the Peloponnesian war that Thucydides may have disliked, like the Athenian demagogue Cleon, and things he admired, like Spartan moderation, but he did not shrink from presenting the truths about the character of human history irrespective of how unpleasant they might sound to more refined ears.

Although there have been calls to avoid reading Thucydides exclusively in terms of either interpretive pole over the years,[29] the premise of this essay is that the interpretive polarity itself is framed by an understanding of science, knowledge, and truth peculiar to we late moderns. It is in this post-Nietzschian atmosphere that such a sharp wedge is driven between judgement and science, between notions of the good and claims about pristine sociological truths, between the upward-lifting transcendent moments of thought and the more grounded, immanent aspects of understanding. Nietzsche's anti-metaphysical diatribes reinvigorated modernity's repudiation of philosophy that began in earnest with Hobbes's materialism and his attack on the "*schooles.*" In particular, Nietzsche's denial of a transcendent ground of knowing (scepticism or Nietzschian perspectivism) and his denial of a transcendent ethical ground (nihilism) establish a sharp polarity in the relationship between philosophy and history, and it would be hard to overestimate its impact in the last century. In the language of Eric Voegelin, modernity itself might be essentialized in terms of its "radical immanence"; we proceed as though the separation between both aspects of being and thought can be hard and fast, and often proceed to develop one-sided perspectives (like the Hobbesian or Nietzschian ones) on a variety of philosophical and historical subjects.[30]

The frequent claim that Thucydides likely gravitated to one or another of these poles reveals more about our tendency to insist on the radical disconnection between the immanent and transcendent moments of thought than it does about the ancient historian himself.[31] We must relax this severe separation and not insist that it guided the analytical character of intellectual traditions in distant times. Accordingly, we can begin to provide a brief counter to the Straussian reading of Thucydides by bearing in mind observations of Alfred North Whitehead: "This notion of historians, of history devoid of aesthetic prejudice, of history devoid of any reliance on metaphysical principles and cosmological generalizations, is a figment of the imagination."[32] This essay submits that Thucydides neither bracketed notions of the good nor suspended ideas about "lives lived properly" as he recounted the history of the struggle between the Spartan and Athenian empires. Thucydides' history rather clearly establishes the basic outlines of ideal conduct rarely being met in a world convulsed by war. Thucydides was guided by a sense of measure oriented cosmologically; the *History* is infused with the sense of a world turned bad. He is never merely sizing things up as an empiricist bent on revealing the sociological or all-too-human truths *in* the world; the *History* is never exclusively grounded in immanence. The analytical character of the *Peloponnesian War* is not premised upon the radical suspension of the more transcendent aspects of thought in a manner typical of we late moderns, and to read the *History* so is to interpret it in a way that says more about the intellectual pretensions of ourselves – pretensions that have caught the critical eye of Whitehead and others – than it does about Thucydides' work.

This essay contends that the deepest ideological moment of the Straussians' reading of Thucydides is, ironically, their very modern rejection of the transcendent element in the *History*, an interpretive fallacy that presupposes a sharp disjunction between metaphysical speculation and empirical sociology, and a rejection that ultimately comes to rest on the claim that the historian *merely* disclosed the truths about human nature and its propensity for war and empire. Their reading of Thucydides is striking because Straussian thought is fond of harvesting ancient thought to expose the ills of modernity, and thus the irony of their Procrustean reading of Thucydides from a distinctively modern perch. It is also ironic because Straussian thought has occasionally seen the folly of pretentiously repudiating the idea of judgement in modern social science.[33] The interpretive fallacy of modernity prevents Straussian thinkers from seeing the richness of Thucydides' work, and more particularly leads to their repudiation of the claim that there are cosmological or transcendent aspects in the *History*. As we release ourselves from such interpretive shackles, as we disentangle the entwined aspects of the ancient historian's thought, we can begin to see that the transcendent aspects of the *History* furnish the critique of war and empire, and establish continuity between the historian and the poetic reflex of the time. Although the foremost concern of the intellectuals of Thucydides' day was the health and stability of the *polis*, especially the scourge of *stasis* (factionalism possibly leading to civil strife), the matter of war and empire figured prominently in their thinking. Certainly, the tendency to celebrate and even glorify war hung in the air as is evident in the following passage from the *Iliad*:

The men whom Zeus decrees, from youth to old age,
must wind down our brutal wars to the bitter end
until we drop and die, down to the last man.[34]

This cultural current, however, did not translate into a resignation about war and empire among most Greek intellectuals. The general thrust of their observations strongly suggests that they often regarded war as a sickness. This strain of ancient criticism is evident in Euripides' *The Women of Troy*. As the drama opens the god Poseidon mourns the sacking of Troy, thereby recasting the greatest event of the past as the greatest occasion of sorrow and misery,:

How are ye blind,
Ye treaders down of cities, ye that cast
Temples to desolation, and lay waste
Tombs, the untrodden sanctuaries where lie
The ancient dead; yourselves so soon to die![35]

Writing in the same period, the comic poet Aristophanes claimed that a permanent peace from generation to generation is both natural and possible. In the *Acharnians*, the first of his famous peace plays that include *The Peace* and *Lysistrata*, the protagonist Dicaeopolis (broadly meaning *just city*) has just been presented with three options for a private peace with Sparta – imagine a play about a farmer from Nebraska negotiating a private peace with Saddam Hussein! Each peace offering appears metaphorically in the form of a wine:

Dicaeopolis: You've got the peaces?
Amphitheus: Yes, here they are – three of them – taste them. This one is for five years. Have a sip.
Dicaeopolis: Ugh! [*He spits out the wine and thrusts the skin from him*]
Amphitheus: What's wrong?
Dicaeopolis: It's nauseating! It simply reeks of turpentine and shipyards.
Amphitheus: [*offering him the second, larger skin*] Well, try the ten-year one.
Dicaeopolis: [*after tasting it*] No, this one is too acid. More diplomatic missions, I bet, and trying to get the allies to send troops for when the fighting starts again.

Amphitheus: [*offering the third skin*] Ah, but now this one – this is the real thing. Thirty years, by land and sea.

Dicaeopolis: [*drinking deep, and gradually breaking into an enormous smile*] Why, by all the feasts of Dionysus! It has the taste of nectar and ambrosia.[36]

The first wine reminds Dicaeopolis of Athenian imperial activities such as shipbuilding, and he associates the second with the strategies of alliance building during the *interbellum*, and so he rejects them both. It is only the third one, the wine suitable for a divine repast, and one which has matured over the span of a generation, that is acceptable to our Athenian farmer. The underlying point stresses the possibility of a permanent peace, but one that can be engendered only when older generations are given an opportunity to forget about the present war and younger generations can mature in peace.

These poetic examples express sentiments that were hardly exceptional in ancient commentary. It can be claimed that the poets Aeschylus, Sophocles, Euripides, and Aristophanes, the historian Herodotus, and the philosophers Plato and Aristotle shared grave concerns about war and empire, particularly the Persian and Athenian empires. The sobering condemnation of war in Aeschylus' *Orestian* trilogy, Aristophanes' unrelenting reproof of the Athenian demagogues during the Archidamian phases of the Peloponnesian War, and his rehearsal of these same themes much later in *Lysistrata*, Herodotus' tragic depiction of Persian imperialist designs or Plato's speculative critique of empire attest to this general disquiet among Hellenic thinkers. When considered together they effectively mounted a sustained critique of war and empire from their unique intellectual standpoints.

Thucydides' *History* is in step with this tradition. Most notably, his account of the war has the feel of a poetic tragedy, especially as it moves through the latter books. At its most fundamental level the tragic idiom is premised upon the notion of a cosmological order with inviolable boundaries. Within this cosmology humankind must take care not to transgress the natural order, a violation destined to invite correcting hands. As a literary form, tragedy presents us with a subject (individual or nation) succumbing to *hybris*, that is, to an overreaching or exaggerated optimism rooted in the inability to recognize one's place in the natural order of things. The deities typically function as superhuman custodians of the natural order of things, especially the goddess Nemesis. The tragic personage or nation, in the face of this transgression, then suffers a reversal of fortune understood as divine vengeance on over-weening mortals.

In the *History* the Athenian massacre at Melos is immediately followed by the account of the Sicilian expedition. The Athenian massacre at Melos had shaken Athens to its core, and any reader of the *History* would have known that the formidable Athenian forces were routed in Sicily. Thucydides immediately establishes that when the Athenians launched the Sicilian expedition they "were for the most part ignorant of the size of the island and of the number of its inhabitants, both Hellenic and native, and they did not realize that they were taking on a war of almost the same magnitude as their war against the Peloponnesians."[37] Despite Nicias' warnings about the folly of far-flung aggression, the Athenians, drunk with *hybris*, pressed on to Sicily. When "this most costly and finest-looking force of Hellenic troops up to that time" was poised to set sail, Thucydides tells us that crowds gathered on the shore "merely to see the show and to admire the incredible ambition of the thing." Wine was poured, prayers were made, and the spectacular armada of the "most far-reaching kind" set sail for disaster.[38] The overweening Athenians suffered ignominious defeat at Syracuse, and would eventually lose the Peloponnesian War to Sparta.

Thucydides' narration continues in the tradition of Herodotus' tragic *Histories*. In their circumference the *Histories* of Herodotus present the rise and fall of four successive Persian emperors beginning with Cyrus in 559 and ending with Xerxes' final defeat at Plataea in the summer of 479 at the hands of Spartan hoplites. Each king of the Achaemenid empire – Cyrus (559–529 B.C.E.), Cambyses (529–522), Darius (521–486), and his son Xerxes (486–465) – follows a distinct cycle of consolidation, terri-torial expansion, and military defeat at the edges of their realm. Each defeat is final and irreversible; each defeat comes on the heels of wise counsel strongly admonishing the emperor in question to reconsider his expansionist plans; and each emperor appears as a living violation of the Delphic maxims "know thyself" and "nothing in excess" as he succumbs to the belief that he is god-like, and that the expansion of his realm has no natural limits. At the moment of their most frivolous annexation their fortunes are dramatically reversed. Herodotus' story of the Persian invasions is cast as a story of over-reaching emperors who invite godly retribution.[39] Yet Thucydides also breaks free of Herodotus and the narrative reflex of the poets. The gods no long appear on the battlefield as they do in Homer's *Iliad*, nor do the wishes of the gods appear indirectly in oracles and dreams as they do in Herodotus. The gods have largely faded out of Thucydides' picture; the correcting hand of Nemesis seems more like a vague correcting force rooted in the order of being. The transcendent element in Thucydides, to put this in complementary terms, is not reduced to the presence or absence of the supernatural in a personified form.

The cosmological order in the *History* is not policed by a constabulary of gods. But the sense of a proper order of things is unmistakable, a cosmology with a clear hierarchy and a clear sense of inviolable boundaries. Leo Strauss sometimes made distinctions between "the gods," "the divine law," and "the divine" in his discussions of Thucydides, discussions that should have opened the door to a recognition of the transcendent aspects of Thucydides' thought as they pertained to *being* most broadly conceived, but they were never taken beyond this.[40] Thucydides' more cosmological sensibilities can be seen when we observe that the narrative of the *History* establishes the primacy of the rational element of being over the appetitive or merely animalistic element, and it accordingly extols the virtues of moderation and restraint that issue from such primacy. The narrative site of these cosmological sensibilities is the emergent notion of human being that permeates the *History*, a notion that expresses the tension between the appetitive dimensions of our existence and our capacity for reason; to be human is to be existentially *in between* the poles of mere appetites shared with other animals and the more divine quality of pure reason.[41] Our appetitive dimension cannot be altogether disregarded, but in a good person or a good leader, the appetites and passions must be subordinated to the deliberative side of our soul. This existential tension at the heart of human being tended to be understood culturally as the struggle between *logos* – rational, thoughtful speech – and *ergon* – action. In a good leader the balance between *logos* and *ergon* involves the manifest ascendancy of the former, and when in proper balance Delphic ideals – nothing in excess – would have the best chance of being preserved. A good leader must be thoughtful and reflective, and never rush headlong into unmediated action. The virtue of moderation (*sophrosyne*) is the natural outcome of the person so balanced. Importantly, this sense of goodness articulated with metaphysical intuitions, is a goodness expressing harmony between human being and the cosmological order of things. Plato would later recast these conventional ideas or *doxa* in a more rigorous, philosophical *epistēmē*. Plato formulated a tripartite division of the *psychē* or soul including the appetitive element, the spirited element, and the reason element, with each of these three having a corresponding excellence (*aretē*) – moderation, courage, and wisdom respectively. A virtuous person was characterized as having a properly ordered soul with the reasoning element governing the appetitive element, with the spirited element or *thumos* providing assistance. Most importantly, the Platonic formulation rigorously preserved the spirit of ancient culture, and thus a person succumbing to unrestrained appetitiveness could not be good or just, that is, in Platonic terms, would not achieve the overarching *aretē* of the properly ordered soul.

Thucydides' notion of the good person or the good leader, unlike Plato's, is not grounded in a transcendent philosophical *epistēmē*, but is rather premised upon metaphysical sensibilities about the proper order of things as they were expressed through conventional cultural beliefs or *doxa*. A good person balances *logos* and *ergon* properly with the former manifestly ascendant. The *History* reveals a number of good leaders over the course of the narrative, including the Spartan king Archidamus, and Themistocles, Pericles, Diodotus, and Nicias on the Athenian side. But these thoughtful and temperate leaders (*sōphrōn*) are slowly eclipsed in influence by leaders who are rash and impulsive, and who attack the very idea of reflection and debate.[42] Leadership qualities rooted in the lower-order elements of human being coalesce in the demagogue, one who is rash and impulsive, and who will pander to, manipulate, or exploit the *demos* without compunction and for personal gain. The quintessential Athenian demagogue, Cleon, appears in Thucydides' recounting of the war.[43] The famous Athenian who rose to power after the death of Pericles was attacked relentlessly by the comic poet Aristophanes, especially in the *Knights*. But for all of the truculence of Aristophanes' attacks, it is Thucydides who provides the most damning indictment of the famous leader. The intemperate qualities of Cleon appear most clearly in the Mytilenian debate, a debate about whether to rescind a law condemning all Mytilenian men to death in the face of an attempted uprising by some. Cleon spoke against any reversal of the earlier decision despite the fact that Athenians were uncomfortable with it, and his speech epitomizes the imbalance of *logos* and *ergon* characteristic of the demagogue. Thucydides introduces Cleon as a leader who "was remarkable among the Athenians for the violence of his character."[44] Cleon criticizes the Athenians for beings "regular speech-goers" and for failing to comport themselves in the manner of imperialists: "You are simply victims of your own pleasure in listening," he reproached, "and are more like an audience sitting at the feet of a professional lecturer than a parliament discussing matters of state."[45] Cleon claims that the best punishment is one where "reprisals follow immediately," but that the Athenians, unfortunately, "merely listen to accounts" of action. Cleon tellingly admonishes that *logos* mixes poorly with empire: "As for the speech-makers who give such pleasure by their arguments, they should hold their competitions on subjects which are less important, and not on a question where the state may have to pay a heavy penalty for its light pleasure."[46]

When Cleon's opponent Diodotus rose to speak in favour of rescinding the original decree he immediately set about to attack the most basic assumptions of his opponent:

> I do not blame those who have proposed a new debate on the subject of Mytilene, and I do not share the view which we have heard expressed, that it is a bad thing to have frequent discussions of matters of importance. Haste and anger are, to my mind, the two greatest obstacles to wise counsel – haste, that usually goes with folly, anger, that is the mark of primitive and narrow minds.[47]

In deciding the proper course of policy Diodotus emphasizes the importance of persuasion and fair argument, of avoiding cynicism, of speaking truthfully and ingenuously, of trust, and of empathy and compassion, especially in situations where one's circumstances drag them down. The speech of Diodotus essentially outlines the ideal balance of *logos* and *ergon*, and therewith of our deliberative capacities on the one hand and our appetites and passions on the other, and his remonstrations provide the model for the good leader.[48]

At this point is should be emphasized that the Straussian claim that a good leader essentially chooses between *interests* on the one hand and *right* on the other, and that the latter more or less constitutes our humanity, is severely flawed.[49] Thucydides never poses the problems of good leadership or wise statecraft in terms exterior to the *drama of the soul*. The good leader is not confronted with voluntary choices between *interest* on the one hand and *right* on the other, as though these options were somehow exterior to the existential tension at the centre of human beingness. Nothing in Thucydides' manner of thinking pushes the notion that the texture of experience resolves itself into choices about "interest" and "right." Rather, the struggle for wise leadership *is* a struggle *of* the soul – interior to human beingness understood transcendently – and the nature of that struggle is not contingent upon the immediate welter of options established by historical contingency. And most importantly, as a pole in this struggle reason is assigned primacy; a good leader must be reflective and thoughtful – period. Wise and moderate policy emerges out of careful consideration and deliberation.

In its general thrust the *Peloponnesian War* is a history of the decline of good leaders capable of pushing through moderate policies steeped in deliberation and forged with care. This degradation was exacerbated by the plague in Athens and by the outbreak of civil strife or *stasis* throughout the Greek world. As Thucydides wrote of the Corcyrean civil war:

> What used to be described as a thoughtless act of aggression was now regarded as the courage one would expect to find in a party member; to think of the future and wait was merely another way of saying one was a coward; any idea of moderation was just an attempt to disguise one's unmanly character; ability to understand a question from all sides meant that one was totally unfit for action.[50]

The signatures of this decay in Athenian political life included a decline in the restraining force of convention (*nomos*), excessive pride and self-satisfaction (*hybris*), self-seeking and overreaching ambition (*pleonexia*), hope unmediated with thoughtfulness (*elpis*), a general lack of foresight (*apate*), and infatuation (*ate*).[51] The convergence of these failings poignantly sets the narrative mood for the Melian dialogue and the Sicilian debate. The inhabitants of Melos were given the option of surrendering to the Athenians. Over the course of the dialogue the Athenians claim that the gods are just as likely to be on their side as that of the Melians,[52] chastise the islanders for merely *hoping* for the best,[53] reprove the Melians for *failing to see* that the Spartans would not come to their rescue,[54] and mock the Spartan lack of daring.[55] The Melians, of course, were destroyed by the Athenians, but any reader would have been aware of the irony of such reproof coming from a state that would soon be infatuated by the idea of adding to its empire, openly rely upon *hope*, fail to heed admonishments, and suffer from a grievous *lack of foresight* as they daringly opened up a second front of the war in Sicily.[56]

"Remember that success comes from *foresight*," Nicias pleaded as he tried to dissuade the Athenians from the Sicilian undertaking, "and not much is ever gained by *simply wishing* for it."[57] Indeed, it could be argued that Nicias' interventions during the debate over the Sicilian expedition constitute the climactic moment of the *History*. For the outcome of good leadership, of careful and thoughtful debate, of deliberate policies, is moderation of a state's conduct, and such a presence and process will not incline the state towards the unbridled aggrandizement of empire. The decline of good leadership, in complementary terms, coincides with excessive state conduct; the *History* forges an unmistakable connection between good leadership, thoughtful policies, and moderation. Thucydides' fondness for the moderation of the Spartans permeates the entire work. His praise for Pericles explicitly links his intelligence and thoughtfulness with moderation.[58] Diodotus' speech in the Mytilenian debate is also imbued with the spirit of moderation and restraint. And so it is telling that when Nicias rose to warn his fellow Athenians against reaching for too much, he resigned himself to the fact that he could not dissuade the Athenians with argument. One cannot help but compare this predicament of Nicias with Thucydides' explicit praise of Pericles: "Certainly when he [Pericles] saw that they [the *demos*] were going too far in a mood of over-confidence, he would bring back to them a sense of their dangers; and when they were discouraged for no good reason he would restore their confidence."[59] But Nicias lacked these persuasive powers at a moment when the *demos* was brimming with overconfidence, and he chose rather to focus on the logistical impossibility of the task: "I know that no speech of mine could be powerful enough to alter your characters," Thucydides has Nicias admit tellingly, "and it would be useless to advise you to safeguard what you have and not to risk what is yours already for doubtful prospect in the future. I shall therefore confine myself to showing you that this is the wrong time for such adventures and that the objects of your ambition are not to be gained easily."[60] When he rose to speak a second time Nicias desperately inflated the logistical requirements of the expedition, but the overweening Athenians "became more enthusiastic than ever" and the Sicilian expedition, so to speak, was on. Thucydides has already told us that Pericles would have prevented the "mistake" of the Sicilian expedition.[61]

In the intervening moments between Nicias' climactic speeches the larger-than-life figure of Alcibiades rose to argue in favour of the Sicilian expedition, and Thucydides paints him as a lavish, self-serving figure who pushes for the unrestrained expansion of the Athenian empire:

> And it is not possible for us to calculate, like housekeepers, exactly how much empire we want to have. The fact is that we have reached a stage where we are forced to plan new conquests and forced to hold on to what we have got, because there is a danger that we ourselves may fall under the power of others unless others are in our power.[62]

At the decisive moment of the *History* the "Athenian thesis" is put in the mouth of a living embodiment of extravagance, licentiousness, and excess. The sway of the *History* exhorts us to recognize the connection between the decline of wise leadership on the one hand and the continuation of the war, especially the Sicilian expedition, on the other. Plutarch's reflections on the struggles of Nicias are informed by his attentive reading of these connections in Thucydides:

> At this time, too, Alcibiades was beginning to become a power in Athens. He was not an out and out demagogue such as Cleon. But just as the soil of Egypt because of its very richness is *said to produce many a whole drug growing side by side with a poison*, so his was one of those exceptional natures which possessed immense potentialities both for good and for evil, and produced the most far-reaching changes in Athenian affairs. The result was that even when Nicias was rid of Cleon, he had no time to stabilize Athenian politics or to compose the differences within the city. No sooner had he set his country's affairs on the path of safety than the force of Alcibiades' ambition bore down upon him like a torrent, and all was swept back into the tumult of war.[63]

The decline of wise leadership and therewith the prolongation of the war and Athenian expansionism were outside the boundaries of proper living as established by the general order of things. These links give the *History* a transcendent cosmological ground – vague and imprecise to be sure, and lacking in the philosophical rigour of Plato, but unmistakable nevertheless. Thucydides' reflections on the Hellenic war come to have a contingent or qualified historical status. By grounding the discussion of the war transcendently he assigned an air of untruthfulness to his worldly observations about the misshapen, woe-begotten life unfolding before him – those hardships of war captured so poignantly in Aristophanes' *Acharnians*, especially the close of the play when a Megarian trader attempts to sell his daughters, disguised as piglets, only to use the proceeds, sadly, to buy cloves of garlic, a well-known Megaran export before the outbreak of war. Thucydides deliberately forges the impression that the world he held before him, one where the Hellenes were tearing each other apart, was not a world lived truthfully in the sense of being in step with the proper order of things. As we might say more colloquially, for Thucydides the Peloponnesian war was *very real* but *all wrong*. The measure of the war is never war itself; through its idiomatic tragic framing we learn that the whirling events that constituted the Peloponnesian war were outside the pale of a properly lived life, and that the war exacts an accounting precisely because it *was* but should not *have been*. What was *true* about the Peloponnesian war – those contemporary thoughts, behaviours, and events discussed by Thucydides with so much richness and perspicacity – was also *false* in so far as the tragic outline of the *History* advises the reader that those same behaviours etcetera fail to conform to the requirements of a world unfurling as it should. Therefore, to cash in Thucydides at the level of his rich, empirical observations, that is, to take him at his empirical face value and nothing more, leads to a limited appreciation of this magisterial work by necessarily missing the accidental or contingent status of the world he supposed before him.

Moreover, the foregoing discussion also advises us to be sensitive to the richness of Thucydides' empirical side or sociology.[64] Thucydides does speak of human nature in the manner of the Hippocratics, a nature that responds to certain stimuli in predictable ways.[65] However, the qualities of fixity in our natures are not played up, but it is clear that Thucydides' notion of human being establishes the importance of sitting on our "natures" through rational deliberation. The concept of a fixed human nature seems too limiting given the breadth and richness of Thucydides' thinking; the concept of a human nature must give way to a notion of human being as discussed above. Things like the plague and *stasis* can unleash our natural and somewhat unsavoury natures by destroying convention (*nomos*) and undermining the basis for deliberation and thoughtfulness.[66] And such developments can have a profound effect on the character of international life, suggesting that Thucydides accepted that there is a certain *seamlessness* of life within the *polis* and life between the *poleis*.[67] If there is a fluidity to our humanity there is bound to be a certain fluidity to the character of international life – and it is correspondingly impossible to assert on behalf of the historian that all relations between states have a Realist flavour. The *History* tells us that international life was bellicose in the fifth century precisely because the Hellenes could not reign in their natural selves in a manner true to human beingness. The *History* tells us that the Athenian thesis is a pathological expression of a troubled *polis*. Things could have been, and should have been, much more irenic; a better-ordered world is bound to be a more peaceful one.

CONCLUSION

Expressed baldly, writers in the Straussian tradition contend that empire is a natural outgrowth of the "logic" of international life as conditioned by our "natures." The ancient historian Thucydides, they claim, prefigures their own thinking about the inevitability of empire. It can be said that the Straussian reading of Thucydides' *History* is indistinguishable from their understanding of "small-h" history. All history can be traced back to an essential human nature. This human nature consists of ineluctable drives – fear, greed, and honour – that shape the character of international life and, indeed, of all history. Although we concern ourselves with justice in the affairs of nations, we ultimately recognize that considerations of power dominate international life. In the end, states seek power and power – the Athenian thesis as captured bluntly in the Melian dialogue – expresses a very simple truth about the causes of war and empire. Hence, like Thucydides, we should not judge war and empire too harshly, for this amounts to turning our backs on our basic natures, a denial of the all-too-human truths that condition the character of international life.

We have argued here that Thucydides cannot be appropriated on behalf of the Straussian intellectual project, for the Athenian historian generated a sobering indictment of the Peloponnesian war and its excesses. Nevertheless, the Straussian claims about empire elevate a cynicism about international life to the status of theory – not theory self-consciously grounded in a rich appreciation of its terminological character and its historical origins, but rather a "spin" on the world based upon a superficial phenomenological survey of history and a sensitivity to the pleasures of power. Why should we be concerned about a theory that naturalizes empire? Why be concerned about the Straussian reading of Thucydides? Because it lends a sense of historic continuity, perhaps even destiny, to U.S. imperialism; because it compromises judgement when it can least afford to be compromised; and ultimately, and most importantly, because the reading does its part to help the capitalist class pursue its renovated accumulation strategies globally and thereby "unmake" the working class of North America. I suspect that when the Athenian composed his history "for all time" he could not have imagined that court advisers down the road would be cozying up to their leaders with a copy of the *History* under their arms, but I do believe that he would have quickly recognized that their efforts would have much to do with the struggles of the *demos*.

NOTES

1. Earl Shorris, "Ignoble Liars," *Harper's Magazine*, June 2004, pp. 65–71.
2. A chatty but compelling account of the Straussian connections to the Bush administration from someone who has broken ranks with the tradition can be found in Anne Norton, *Leo Strauss and the Politics of American Empire* (New Haven, Conn.: Yale University Press, 2004).
3. Accordingly, our focus is on the scholars rather than the newsmakers, including Leo Strauss himself and his students who populate the modern academy, especially at the University of Chicago and the University of Toronto.
4. Kenneth N. Waltz, *Theory of International Relations* (Reading, Mass.: Addison-Wesley, 1979).
5. For a review of these developments see Y. H. Ferguson and R. W. Mansbach, *The Elusive Quest Continues: Theory and Global Politics* (Upper Saddle River, NJ: Prentice Hall, 2003).
6. Karl Marx, *The German Ideology* (Moscow: Progress Publishers, 1976), p. 67.
7. Robert W. Cox, "Social Forces, States and World Orders: Beyond International Relations Theory," in *NeoRealism and its Critics*, ed. R. O. Keohane (New York: Columbia University Press, 1986), p. 248.
8. For an excellent overview of this relationship see Shadia B. Drury, *Leo Strauss and the American Right*, (New York: St. Martin's Press, 1999), especially chs 4 and 5.

9. The principal text employed here is Leo Strauss, "Thucydides: The Meaning of Political History," in *The Rebirth of Classical Political Rationalism: An Introduction to the Thought of Leo Strauss*, ed. Thomas L. Pangle (Chicago: University of Chicago Press, 1989), pp. 72–102.

10. Straussian thinkers do speak of "universals," but they simply mean enduring features of human nature or enduring trends in human history. Orwin's language is revealing. As Clifford Orwin wrote: "Thucydides aims to articulate the parameters of political life, its permanent patterns and thus also its permanent dilemmas" (*The Humanity of Thucydides* [Princeton, NJ: Princeton University Press, 1994], p. 4).

11. See especially Strauss, "Thucydides: Meaning," p. 84.

12. Leo Strauss, *The City and Man* (Chicago, Ill.: Rand McNally, 1964), p. 159.

13. See discussion in ibid., especially pp. 154–163, quote from p. 156.

14. Ibid., p. 159.

15. See discussion in ibid., pp. 174–192.

16. Ibid., p. 191.

17. Hans J. Morgenthau, *Politics Among Nations: The Struggle for Power and Peace* (New York: Alfred A. Knopf, 1973).

18. Straussian thought on Thucydides is construed by drawing out his "revealing silences" and uncovering the "deepest stratum" of the ancient historian's thought (quotes from Strauss, *City and Man*, pp. 152 and 231) in a manner consistent with its esoteric reading of texts and the peculiar Straussian hermeneutic outlined in Leo Strauss, *Persecution and the Art of Writing* (Westport, Conn.: Greenwood Press, 1952).

19. Thomas L. Pangle and Peter J. Ahrensdorf, *Justice Among Nations: On the Moral Basis of Power and Peace* (Lawrence, Kan.: University Press of Kansas, 1999), p. 31.

20. See Norton, *Leo Strauss and the Politics of American Empire*, p. 200.

21. Strauss, "Thucydides: Meaning," p. 73.

22. Ibid.

23. F. M. Cornford, *Thucydides Mythistoricus* (London: Edward Arnold, 1907) and C. N. Cochrane, *Thucydides and the Science of History* (London: Oxford University Press, 1929).

24. It is thought that the library of over seventy works known as the Hippocratic corpus was written by several physicians who made careful physiological observations relating to ailment and disease. Democritus (*c.* 460–370 B.C.E.) was a most learned thinker who wrote on a wide variety of topics ranging from music to history, but only fragments of his works have survived.

25. Strauss, *City and Man*, spends considerable time attacking the connection, pp. 192–209.

26. Ibid., p. 161.

27. Strauss, "Thucydides: Meaning," p. 96. It is striking, as an aside, that the most casual readings in international relations have come to the same conclusion about Thucydides by focusing on a few key passages and ignoring the bulk of the text. For

example, see Michael W. Doyle, "Thucydides' Realism," *Review of International Studies*, 16 (1990), p. 223.

28. Strauss, "Thucydides: Meaning," p. 99.

29. For example, see W. P. Wallace, "Thucydides," *Phoenix*, 18(4), Winter 1964, pp. 256–257.

30. See Eric Voegelin's discussion of the "radical immanence" of modernity in *The New Science of Politics: An Introduction* (Chicago, Ill.: University of Chicago Press, 1952), especially ch. 6.

31. Even upon the publication of Cochrane's work the critique was made that the scientific method does not preclude metaphysical considerations and Aristotelean questions about "the good life," but the point of this paper is that such considerations are inescapable. See A. W. Gomme, "Thucydides and Science," *Classical Review*, 44(4), September 1930, p. 124. Even the best class analysis of Thucydides, namely, G. E. M. de Ste. Croix, *The Origins of the Peloponnesian War* (Ithaca, NY: Cornell University Press, 1972), disappointingly commits the same error and collapses into a purely immanentist reading of the *History*.

32. A. N. Whitehead, *Adventures in Ideas* (New York: Macmillan, 1961), p. 4.

33. For Leo Strauss's sensitivity to ideas about "the good" and the character of "historicism" see "What Is Political Philosophy?," in *What is Political Philosophy? And Other Studies* (Westport, Conn.: Greenwood Press, 1959), pp. 9–55. Moreover, these ironies point to a most fundamental contradiction in all Straussian thought that is merely teased to the surface through our examination of their appropriation of Thucydides in the name of empire, namely their fondness for the robustly metaphysical ancients and the stridently anti-metaphysical Nietzsche, shared affections that cannot be sustained by philosophical sensibilities. For a most insightful account of the Straussian fondness for Nietzsche – one that centres on the conservative politics of their work – see Shadia B. Drury, *The Political Ideas of Leo Strauss* (New York: St. Martin's Press, 1988), ch. 9.

34. Homer, *The Iliad*, trans. Robert Fagles (Harmondsworth: Penguin Books, 1990), 14.105–107.

35. Euripides, *The Trojan Women*, trans. Gilbert Murray (New York: Oxford University Press, 1915), p. 16. This particular play also spoke directly to popular feelings in Athens, especially their apprehensions regarding the recent attack on the island of Melos and ongoing debates about the Sicilian expedition. In fact, the subject matter of the play was so immediately relevant that almost nothing happens. As Philip Vellacott writes: "So topical a performance would certainly hold attention without the help of a plot; and the author evidently felt free to develop a reflective theme unencumbered by suspense or surprise" ("Introduction," *The Bacchae and other Plays* [Harmondsworth: Penguin Books, 1954]).

36. Aristophanes, *The Acharnians*, trans. Alan H. Sommerstein (Harmondsworth: Penguin, 1986), pp. 57–58.

37. Thucydides, *The Peloponnesian War*, trans. Rex Warner (Harmondsworth: Penguin Books, 1954), VI.1.

38. Ibid., VI.31.

39. Herodotus' lament of war is celebrated: "For no one is of himself, so foolish as to prefer war to peace; in the one, children bury their fathers; in the other, fathers their children" (*The Histories*, trans. David Greene [Chicago, Ill.: University of Chicago Press, 1987], 1.87.

40. See Leo Strauss, "Preliminary Observations on the Gods in Thucydides' Work," in *Studies in Platonic Political Philosophy*, ed. Thomas L. Pangle (Chicago, Ill.: University of Chicago Press, 1983), p. 96.

41. Although all accounts of Thucydides as a tragedy are indebted to Cornford's work, his themes were often presented erratically and incompletely. For a different presentation of many central themes – reason and passion, *logos* and *ergon*, *nomos* and *physis*, and *pleonexia* – see David Bedford and Thom Workman, "The Tragic Reading of the Thucydidean Tragedy," *Review of International Studies*, 27, 2001, pp. 51–67. This paper centres on Thucydides' notion of human being to draw out the cosmological grandeur of the *History*, and would hold that Cornford's work failed to do this adequately.

42. The fact, as Winspear tells us, that this view of a good leader reflects the predilections of the aristocracy does not lessen our observations about Thucydides' intentions. Indeed, the origins of his thinking are quite separate from his literary conveyances. See A. D. Winspear, *The Genesis of Plato's Thought* (New York: S. A. Russell, 1940), pp. 216–217. For a more thorough account of the class origins of ancient Greek philosophy see E. Wood and N. Wood, *Class Ideology and Ancient Political Theory: Socrates, Plato, and Aristotle in Social Context* (New York: Oxford University Press, 1978).

43. For an excellent survey of demagoguery in the political context of Athens see M. I. Finley, "Athenian Demagogues", *Past and Present*, 21, April 1962, pp. 3–24.

44. Thucydides, *Peloponnesian War*, III.36.

45. Ibid., III.38.

46. Ibid., III.40.

47. Ibid., III.42.

48. For a similar reading of the Mytilenian debate see A. Andrewes, "The Mytilene Debate: Thucydides 3.36–49," *Phoenix*, 16(2), Summer 1962, pp. 64–85.

49. I think this is what Orwin meant by humanity, although his lack of clarity in this respect has been duly noted. See Simon Hornblower, "Humane Thucydides," *Classical Review*, 47(1), 1997, pp. 31–32.

50. Thucydides, *Peloponnesian War*, III.82. On the plague in Athens see II.55–65.

51. These themes were surveyed by Cornford, *Thucydides Mythistoricus*, although without an explicit discussion of the emergent notion of human being.

52. Thucydides, *Peloponnesian War*, V.105.

53. Ibid., V.103.

54. Ibid., V.105.

55. Ibid., V.107.

56. For direct connections between Thucydides' treatment of the Melian debacle and the tragedian Euripides see Grace Harriet Macurdy, "The Fifth Book of Thucydides and Three Plays of Euripides," *Classical Review*, 24(7), November 1910, pp. 205–207.

57. Thucydides, *Peloponnesian War*, VI.13 (my emphasis).

58. Thucydides devotes an entire section to the policy of Pericles, and unlike Plato and Aristotle, who date the rise of demagoguery much earlier, the turning point for the historian is the post-Periclean world. See *Peloponnesian War*, III.65. Plato's dating of the decline is much earlier and extends to Miltiades, Themistocles, Cimon, and Pericles. See Plato, *Gorgias*, trans. W. C. Helmbold (Indianapolis, Ind.: Bobbs-Merrill, 1952), pp. 75–82, 502–507. It has also been argued that Thucydides' praise of Pericles was qualified. See F. Melian Stawell, "Pericles and Cleon in Thucydides," *Classical Quarterly*, 2(1), January 1908, pp. 41–46.

59. Thucydides, *Peloponnesian War*, II.65.

60. Ibid., VI.9.

61. Ibid., II.65.

62. Ibid., VI.18.

63. Plutarch, *The Rise and Fall of Athens: Nine Greek Lives* (Harmondsworth: Penguin Books, 1960), p. 217, emphasis in original.

64. The sociological influence of the ancients has been acknowledged for generations, but the specific debt to Thucydides tends to be understated. The emphasis has been on the rich influence of Aristotle upon writers like Marx and Weber, especially Marx's theory of political economy. For example, see the recent work by George E. McCarthy entitled *Classical Horizons: The Origins of Sociology in Ancient Greece* (Albany, NY: State University of New York Press, 2003), where Thucydides is rarely mentioned. It is the case, however, that Thucydides, especially in Book I, more or less invents socio-logical analysis, that is, he organizes his discussion around ideas that are vaguely Marxian – basic analysis of classes and class factions – and vaguely Malthusian – basic assumptions about the limits to population growth which affect migratory behaviour, and that these two dynamics combine to affect inter-poleis relations. It is true, however, that Thucydides' thought cannot be harvested in the way that the philosophy of Plato and Aristotle permit one to refine sociological categories and concepts central to grasping the ills and limits of modernity.

65. See, for example, D. L. Page, "Thucydides' Description of the Great Plague at Athens," *Classical Quarterly*, 47 (N.S. 3), 1953, pp. 97–119.

66. Thucydides says this repeatedly. See especially Thucydides, *Peloponnesian War*, II.53 and III.84.

67. Although it is beyond the scope of this essay, throughout *Peloponnesian War* Book I in particular Thucydides offers his account of the world that sunk Hellas into a

drawn-out and injurious war, and claims that the character of international life is fluid, and that wars come and go largely as a result of the configuration of class relations and the nature of the governing constitutions in any given region. In a familiar language once again, Thucydides' analysis does not reify international life, but is rather premised upon the seamlessness of life within the developing *poleis* on the one hand and the relations between the *poleis* on the other. When we finally learn that the growing scope of the Athenian empire caused alarm among the Spartans (I.23) the unmistakable sweep of the introduction instructs us to understand that it was the oligarchs in the Peloponnesian empire who were troubled, and who felt compelled to take action.

8

PRAISING EMPIRE: NEOLIBERALISM UNDER PAX AMERICANA*

Adam Hanieh

In the months following the U.S.-led invasion of Iraq, a series of little-noticed military orders were passed in Baghdad by then-administrator of the Coalition Provisional Authority, Paul Bremer. Order no. 39, signed on 19 September 2003, allowed for the privatization of around 200 state-owned enterprises with leases given for at least forty years. Overnight it became illegal to restrict foreign ownership in any part of the Iraqi economy except resource extraction. Order no. 37 set the tax rate for multinational companies at a flat 15 percent, with no distinction between corporations and individuals. A poor Iraqi farmer would pay the same tax as the U.S. multinational Bechtel, the company contracted to run Iraq's privatized water system. Foreign companies were given authorization by Order no. 39 to withdraw dividends, profits, and investments from the country without restriction. Earlier in 2003, Bremer had signed a trade liberalization law that abolished "all tariffs, customs duties, import taxes, licensing fees and similar surcharges for goods entering or leaving Iraq, and all other trade restrictions that may apply to such goods." Order no. 17 gave any foreign company immunity from Iraqi law in regards to "acts performed by them pursuant to the terms and conditions of a Contract."

* The author would like to thank Greg Albo, Sam Gindin, Colin Mooers, Ananya Mukherjee-Reed, and Rafeef Ziadah for many helpful comments and suggestions on various drafts of this chapter.

These military orders provide a remarkable insight into the contours of U.S. imperialism in the twenty-first century. Underpinning Iraqi "reconstruction" – as it has come to be known – is the economic program of neoliberalism. Drawing its ideological roots from classical liberal theory, and Austrian and monetarist economics, this logic has dominated international economic policy since the mid-1980s. Its prescriptions are now familiar across the globe: privatization, cutbacks to state and public spending, the reduction of barriers to capital flows worldwide, and the imposition of market imperatives throughout all spheres of human activity. Despite a number of prominent economists who have moved away from the orthodoxy in the face of the financial crises of the late 1990s and early 2000s, the neoliberal economic paradigm remains virtually unchallenged in policy-making circles and most of academia.

The current imperialist order is fundamentally driven by an economic logic – a fact explicitly recognized by the key ideological supporters of U.S. global supremacy. Iraq provides a perfect illustration of this intimate connection between neoliberalism and imperialism. The significance of the Iraqi case lies in the manner with which neoliberalism has been so thoroughly driven by U.S. military force.

This chapter examines the basic assumptions of neoliberalism and its connection with the global expansion of U.S. power. Of particular focus is the argument of a leading neoliberal economist, Deepak Lal, whose work has been widely promoted in U.S. government circles and neoconservative think-tanks. Lal's writing is an ideal case study for understanding the current economic program of imperialism. His output has been voluminous, with over twenty years of writing and teaching dedicated to the defense of capitalism. His 1983 work, *The Poverty of "Development Economics,"* was the initial, highly significant attack on the types of state-led development thinking that characterized dependency theories and some versions of Marxism. Published by the most influential neoliberal think-tank in Britain, the Institute of Economic Affairs, it was immediately championed by Britain's establishment press and the most prestigious economic journals. Lal is closely associated with key neoconservative think-tanks, in particular the American Enterprise Institute, the Adam Smith Institute, and the Liberty Institute. He has advised the finance ministries of South Korea, the United Kingdom, Australia, Zimbabwe, and Sri Lanka.

The central premise of this chapter is that neoliberalism must be understood as more than just a right-wing economic ideology based on faulty assumptions or a set of policy choices designed to enrich wealthy global elites. Rather, the neoliberal imperialist project expresses the systemic logic of the current material and social reality of the capitalist mode of production. We can learn much about this reality from the way in which the defense of the system is articulated. This reality, and the defense of imperialism offered by the proponents of neoliberalism, is examined below through the Marxist concept of the "circuit of capital."

LAL: THE "LIBERAL" INTERNATIONAL ECONOMIC ORDER

A few months prior to the invasion of Iraq, a leading neoconservative think-tank, the American Enterprise Institute (A.E.I.), held its Henry Wendt Honorary Lecture. This eponymous annual lecture is named after a trustee of the A.E.I. and former C.E.O. of the world's second-largest pharmaceutical company, Glaxo-SmithKline. Deepak Lal, Professor of International Development Studies at U.C.L.A. and former advisor to the World Bank and International Monetary Fund (I.M.F.) in the late 1980s, gave the keynote address.

Lal's lecture, entitled "In Defense of Empire," was to form the basis of a book, *In Praise of Empires: Globalization and Order.*[1] His argument is clear and unequivocal: as a matter of urgency the U.S.A. must embrace its global responsibility and establish a world empire. Lal put it in no uncertain terms: "The continued unwillingness of Americans to recognize that their role is now an imperium makes it difficult for them to sensibly discuss the imperial tasks they must undertake. Words do matter, and it is no aid to clear thinking to avoid calling a spade a spade."[2]

Lal's argument follows a straightforward neoclassical economic logic. People engage in exchange in order to satisfy their own subjectively defined needs. They wouldn't exchange if they didn't believe those needs would be fulfilled. When people can exchange freely, everyone benefits. Therefore the unimpeded action of the free market will promote a maximization of happiness and pleasure because it maximizes the number of exchange interactions that take place. Global prosperity and happiness are directly correlated with the unfettered spread of capitalist exchange relations. The larger the space in which these exchange relations can operate free from any interference, the greater the prosperity that will result.

For Lal, the history of the global economy is essentially the story of successive attempts at maximizing the area of the market through the creation of a "liberal international economic order" (L.I.E.O.). The first of these occurred under the British Empire, which "was hugely beneficial for the world, particularly its poorest. It saw the integration for the first time of many countries in the Third World into a global economy and the consequent first stirring of modern intensive growth."[3]

Following the decline of the British Empire the world failed to create a new L.I.E.O. Instead, Third World governments adopted what Lal described as the *dirigiste dogma*, and attempted to steer economic policy through state intervention and Keynesian economic policies. For Lal this was a terrible error. States were inevitably "predatory" and tried to capture wealth for their own purposes. Their policies created "rent-seeking" behavior, as economic agents tried to benefit through state monopolies and corruption.

In the place of *dirigisme*, Lal argues that the role of the state should be simply to ensure that the "rules of the game" are fair and that the free market is able to function. The state's actions should be restricted to the provision of law and order, national security, and property protection. The rest should be left to private individuals. Lal believes, "the primary role of government is not to maximize the social good, but rather to maintain a framework of rules within which individuals are left free to pursue their own ends."[4] And, "A good government is one which promotes opulence through a policy of promoting natural liberty by establishing laws of justice which guarantee free exchange and peaceful competition, the improvement of morality being left to non-govern-mental organizations."[5]

According to Lal, the *dirigiste* era fell apart during the 1980s with the onset of neoliberalism. The U.S.A. helped to support transnational insti-tutions such as the I.M.F. and World Bank with the aim of opening world markets. Following the 1980s debt crisis and the collapse of the U.S.S.R., the Third World embraced globalization, which Lal tellingly defines as the creation of a common economic space.[6]

Under the current U.S. hegemony, Lal sees a direct correlation between the presence of a supranational imperial structure and the maintenance of a new L.I.E.O. The role of the empire is to ensure the free flow of trade and commerce with minimum government intervention.

This structure of empire can link "previously autarkic states into a common economic space" and within this common economic space, everyone will benefit from "the mutual gains from trade adumbrated by Adam Smith. . . . [D]espite their current bad name, empires have promoted peace and prosperity."[7]

In order for this to happen, individual states must be brought completely under the control of the imperium. Lal makes this point forcefully, contrasting it with any softer notions of hegemony: "Empires need to be distinguished from mere hegemony. *Empires seek to control both the domestic and foreign policies of their allies*; hegemons, only their foreign policy."[8] In other words, individual states must be forced to adopt free-market policies regardless of their own preferences. If the globe will not conform to the neoliberal prescription by choice, then an empire is necessary to guarantee this outcome by force.

The doctrine propagated by the Bush administration serves to "maintain the Pax necessary for globalization."[9] For Lal, there should be no underestimating the danger from those opposed to the unfettered spread of exchange relations:

> The war on terror can be seen as merely an extension of [defending the capitalist market]. The terrorists, despite their utopian millennial objectives, are best seen as pirates of yore . . . their major targets are directed not so much at lives as at the complex market infrastructure of the modernizing world. They are as much warriors against globalization . . . as the activists marching at the anti-Davos summits of N.G.O.'s in Porto Allegre. Both need to be resisted.[10]

Nevertheless, Lal sees an "Achilles Heel of the American imperium." While the U.S.A. has "created the military structure to project its power . . . it has failed to build the complementary imperial administrative structure required to run an empire."[11] The lessons must be drawn from the Roman Empire: "with the growth of a cosmopolitan class of primarily American-trained technicians and executives (culturally and often personally linked) at work in many different countries . . . [there exists] the core of a global 'Roman' political and economic elite . . . which could run this new U.S. imperium."[12]

THE MATERIAL AND SOCIAL ROOTS OF NEOLIBERAL IDEOLOGY

To large sections of the anti-globalization and anti-war movements, visions such as Lal's are seen as indicative of the power of a small group of neoconservatives influencing White House policy. According to this framework, the present round of U.S. unilateralism and "permanent war" is girded by a messianic, right-wing zeal promoted through think-tanks such as the Project for the New American Century and the A.E.I., and by individuals such as Paul Wolfowitz and Richard Perle. The victory of this ideological current is seen as the explanation for the ascendancy of U.S. military might. The problem lies with Bush and his administration, as well as their business partners in the oil companies and neoconservative think-tanks.

This argument, however, casts an overly rosy glow on most of twentieth-century history. As the peoples of Africa, Latin America, Asia, and the Middle East understand all too well, imperialism is *not* the novel feature of the "new imperialism." Indeed, the classic anti-imperialist formulations made in the early part of the twentieth century appear more prescient in today's world than ever before. The writings of Rosa Luxemburg, Vladimir Lenin, Nikolai Bukharin, and Rudolf Hilferding each capture specific features of today's imperialism. Most of the world has now come under the sway of massive blocs of capital organized via the imperialist core. The centralization and concentration of capital means that virtually every industry is dominated by a handful of corporations. Mass impoverishment in the exploited South alongside prodigious concentrations of wealth in the North is the most striking and overwhelming feature of the global economy. The gap between the poorest and richest people on the planet is greater than at any other point in human history.

Furthermore, as John Bellamy Foster has recently pointed out, there has been "a remarkable consensus on underlying assumptions and goals"[13] concerning U.S. foreign policy from both the liberal and conservative wings of the U.S. elite. The current political program of George W. Bush enjoys broad bipartisan support and builds upon the imperial successes of the Clinton era.

Clearly though, something did change in the last quarter of the twentieth century. We live in a largely unipolar world order in which U.S. military power appears to hold relatively unchallenged supremacy. While tensions exist between North American, European, and Asian states and capital blocs, decisive U.S. military superiority appears to outweigh any emergence of an inter-imperialist "hot" war, at least in the short term. The last few decades have also witnessed a vast acceleration in what Christian Palloix identified as the internationalization of capital.[14] Processes of production and consumption now occur across the globe and involve a myriad of different national spaces and interdependent activities of internationally organized capital units. This internation-alized capital – dominated in particular by finance – seeks the highest rates of return on investment, moves rapidly between geographic spaces and abhors barriers to its free movement.

The internationalization of capital has been accompanied by the almost universal sway of neoliberal dogma. Governments across the world are adopting policies promoting "free" enterprise, liberalized capital markets, deregulation, privatization, and cut-backs in social spending. How should we understand this global embrace of the neo-liberal paradigm? One argument sees neoliberalism – the dominant form of mainstream economics – as a policy choice of international financial institutions such as the I.M.F. and the World Bank. With the sometimes-willing and often-forced acceptance of neoliberal economic prescriptions by most governments around the world (the so-called "Washington consensus"), capital has been able to break free from its territorialized moorings and is now imbued with a global reach.

Criticisms such as this accuse neoliberalism of faulty assumptions designed to enrich ruling elites through mechanisms such as the driving down of wages and the cutting back of the public sector. The ascendancy of neoliberalism – as many post- and left-Keynesians argue – is simply a consequence of its victory in the ideological debate with Keynesianism during the 1970 and 1980s. Palley, for example, sees the triumph of neoliberalism as made possible by the weakened internal coherence of Keynesianism due to the ideological schisms between its European and U.S. versions.[15] The challenge, according to theorists of this persuasion, is to demonstrate the false assumptions of neoliberalism. From there it is possible to reconstruct and advocate an alternative, socially grounded perspective to tackle the inevitable "market failures" of the neoliberal paradigm.

The U.S.-led neoliberal imperial project, however, needs to be seen as more than solely an ideological choice or strategy of the capitalist class (or a fraction thereof). In the same way that imperialism is not new, neoliberalism is based upon a set of neoclassical ideas that have long been present. Fundamentally, neoliberalism is based upon a neoclassical, liberal view of human nature, combined with a faith in the market drawn from the Austrian school of economics.

THE NEOLIBERAL BELIEF SYSTEM

An underlying axiom of neoclassical economics is the assumption that the basic analytical unit of larger aggregates such as society and nation is the self-contained individual – captured in the pithy phrase of mainstream economics, "the individual economic agent." All individuals are driven fundamentally by the desire to maximize their self-gain, and it is this drive that defines "rational behavior." Following Adam Smith, the urge to "truck and barter" is considered a transhistoric feature of human nature.[16] People fulfill needs through engaging in exchange – the buying and selling of goods. Because these needs are self-defined and no one would freely participate in exchange if they did not think they would benefit, everyone gains in the process. The unimpeded action of the free market will therefore promote a maximization of utility because it maximizes the number of exchange interactions that take place.

For the neoclassical economist the individual desire to consume is the driving force of human progress. This assertion is known in economic parlance by the phrase "consumer sovereignty." Everyday we participate in a democratic vote on society's production options as we enter the marketplace to purchase our goods and freely demonstrate our desires. This view of consumption is key to the neoclassical/neoliberal worldview. Our consumption drives production. The market meets our needs because we demonstrate what we want every time we go shopping and the spread of human progress can be equated with the size of the market.

In order for this conclusion to hold, a number of extremely restrictive assumptions must be made. The individual must be considered a completely isolated, self-contained unit – an assumption of neoclassical economics known as "no externalities." This is an absolutely necessary analytical standpoint: without it, individual preferences could not be considered the basic driving force from which all subsequent economic processes spring. If individual preferences were themselves related to or caused by a factor external to the individual, then the basic building block would no longer remain the self-contained individual. Another factor would exist at a more basic level than individual preferences and the individual and society would need to be seen as mutually constituted.

Likewise, it is necessary to assume that all market participants have perfect knowledge of market conditions (what is available, competing products, and how much they cost). If knowledge is incomplete there is no necessary connection between what an individual chooses and the benefits they obtain as an outcome of that choice. If this is the case, then individual choice may not lead to the best outcome.[17]

A third assumption is that of perfect competition in which all market participants are price-takers. If some market participants are price-makers and are able to influence the price of a good through their strength in the market (that is, a monopolistic position), then the market price does not reflect subjective individual preferences but the actions of producers.

Clearly these assumptions do not hold in reality. Real-life markets are imperfect and monopolized, and people are influenced by a range of factors. For some mainstream economists, this means that state intervention is permissible in order to increase social welfare, alter distribution outcomes, and address "market failure." This intervention may include taxation measures, public spending programs, central bank intervention in monetary policy, or social welfare spending.

Most neoliberals, however, strongly disagree with this attempt to "fix the market." Drawing from the Austrian school of economics, neoliberalism believes that the market will automatically tend to produce optimum outcomes. Consequently, this school generally opposes any attempt to make ethical judgments on social welfare outcomes: the only judge of an individual's welfare is the individual in question. There is no way for an outside observer to judge the utility or rationality of an individual's decision; the individual is the sole arbiter of whether they are better or worse off.[18] It is ethically wrong, therefore, to utilize the state to impose any "patterned end-state" on social outcomes.

Lal, for example, denies that it is possible to provide any value judgment on the fairness of social outcomes, distribution, or inequality. Only the process by which the outcome has been achieved can be judged ethically. He explicitly denies that egalitarianism or questions of distribution should be considered in judging the relative performance of countries. "[Welfare judgments based on the size and distribution of national income] must be based upon accepting egalitarianism as either a self-evident or universally accepted moral imperative. Neither position is tenable."[19] Or:

> We deny there is some universal egalitarian moral code to which we can appeal in defining social justice . . . it is insufficient merely to examine the existing distribution of income and assets and recommend its alteration purely on the basis of its divergence from some egalitarian norm. It is equally important to judge whether the resulting coercive redistribution of incomes or assets is in consonance with other moral ends, such as liberty and equity.[20]

In contrast to the "market failure" approach, Lal and other neoliberals offer a different solution to the clear divergence between conditions found in the real world and the assumptions of neoclassical economics. While affirming that these assumptions are ideal forms that do not exist in reality, they argue that we should aspire to get as close as possible to the perfect free market because doing nothing will probably be better than trying to fix these market "imperfections." Indeed, the chances are that any attempt to fix "market imperfections" will lead to a less-than-optimal outcome. Any form of state intervention, for example, breeds "rent seeking" behavior and thereby "politicizes income streams."[21] The solution is to let the free market work its magic through its inevitable evolution towards the ideal.

As an example, when considering the implementation of a floating exchange rate system, Lal argues that such a system enables optimizing behavior by rational individuals freely participating in exchange. These individuals:

> will be able to choose through their portfolio behavior many possible combinations of exchange rates, ratios of traded to nontraded goods prices, and present versus future consumption choices. Only some of these will correspond to the choices they would have to make if they were committed to a fixed exchange rate. The fixed-rate combinations are always open even under a flexible-rate system. If they are not chosen by optimizing agents, we can assume that the alternative choice is better. Put differently, a commitment to a fixed exchange rate (or to particular rules for managed floats) is a constraint, and it will necessarily reduce the range of present and future consumption choices.[22]

Lal's fundamental assertion is that the choices of "optimizing agents" will always lead to outcomes that are good for all. The proof he offers is simply that these were the choices that were made and therefore they must be the best decisions. It is, in other words, completely tautological. This position also contains an unspoken assumption on how the real world relates to the model. Due to the "imperfections" that exist, the free market, if left to its own devices, will automatically tend towards (evolve in) a direction to reduce those imperfections. Variants of this argument are repeatedly found throughout the neoclassical approach. Indeed, much of the current economic literature is devoted to explaining how the real world spontaneously develops institutions to reduce market "imperfections" automatically.

In the final analysis, therefore, neoliberalism is nothing more than an assertion of faith based on false assumptions. It can be essentially reduced to the (unproven) belief that the unfettered spread of exchange relations will automatically produce the best result through the unintended consequences of selfish acts. The only way to reach that conclusion is by making a series of assumptions that do not fit with the real world.

While the assumptions and conclusions of neoliberalism are plainly false, it remains to be asked where these ideas come from. They did not just emerge from the heads of economists such as Deepak Lal. What is it about the capitalist system that produces a particular ideology like neoliberalism, and how is this ideology related to the current form of imperialism?

THE CIRCUIT OF CAPITAL

The neoliberal view asserts that the purpose of production under capitalism is exchange, and that our individual consumption choices drive this production. The reality is exactly the opposite: the aim of capitalist production is the accumulation of profit and it is production that shapes our consumption choices.

One way of picturing this production process is suggested in Karl Marx's notion of the circuit of capital. Marx understood capitalism as a system driven by the pursuit of profit with an inherent tendency to expand its spatial borders while reducing the temporal distance between places.[23] Capitalist economic ideology can therefore be interpreted in light of the continual drive to expand the spatial reach of capital, epitomized in Marx's evocative phrase of the tendency to "annihilate space with time."[24] Capitalism can be understood as a process of continual movement in space and time, where an individual capitalist starts with a sum of money, M, which is exchanged for commodities, C, (including the commodities labour power, Lp, and means of production [raw materials, factories, and so on], Mp). These are combined in the process of production, P, to produce a commodity with an increased value C' which can then be exchanged for an increased M'.[25] The circuit also captures the basic capitalist *social relation* – workers are employed by capital in order to produce a commodity C' with a value greater than that of commodity C.

$$M \ldots C \ldots P(Lp + Mp) \ldots C' \ldots M'$$

If we take this representation of the processes driving the accumulation of profit in space and time, the essential features of the neoliberal economic ideology underpinning the current imperialism can be clearly understood. Increased profits depend on maximizing the number of commodities that undergo the transformation $M \rightarrow C \rightarrow P \rightarrow C' \rightarrow M'$ and on increasing the speed at which capital can move through this circuit. Moreover, it is necessary to ensure the circuit remains unbroken. The logic of the circuit can thus be summarized in four basic themes: (1) maximizing the sphere of human activities encompassed by capitalist social relations; (2) maintenance of a system of private property rights; (3) minimizing any restrictions or barriers to the flow of capital; and (4) the role of the capitalist state as a guarantor of capitalist social relations.[26]

THE EVER-EXPANDING MARKET PLACE

Capitalism is a system driven fundamentally by the accumulation of profit. The more human activities encompassed by the basic capitalist social relation, the greater the profit. In his powerful work on the spatial implications of capital accumulation, David Harvey points out that "the tendency to eliminate spatial barriers becomes the key to understanding the rapid dispersal of the circulation of capital across the face of the earth."[27] The expansion of capital to the Third World can be seen, as Harvey describes it, as a "spatio-temporal fix" to the inevitable and recurring crises of the hegemonic centre.[28] The "empire of free trade" advocated by Lal and others, reflects this basic tendency of capital to expand across the globe. In recent decades the most striking expansion at this level has been the spread of capitalist exchange relations into the former Soviet Union, eastern Europe, and more recently China.

Christian Palloix described this process as the internationalization of capital.[29] He stressed that internationalization of capital should not be understood as an increase in the multinational nature of a firm's capital or even the increasing international movement of capital. Rather, internationalization should be seen in light of the circuit of capital, specifically, the increasing spread of capitalist social relations. The reasons behind internationalization are "the need to produce, reproduce, and constantly expand the basic capitalist relation, the class relation."[30]

Occurring alongside the internationalization of capital is the tendency towards its concentration and centralization. Increasing amounts of capital become concentrated in fewer hands, generally located in the richest countries. This phenomenon was identified in the classical theories of Lenin, Bukharin, and Hilferding as central to the development of imperialism. As capital comes under the control of a handful of huge conglomerates it seeks to expand across the globe in search of higher profits.

The centralization and concentration of capital is clearly shown in the domination of all sectors of the world economy by a handful of corporations. Look at the food sector: five companies control 90 percent of the world's grain trade, six companies control nearly 80 percent of the world pesticide market, three companies control 85 percent of the world's tea market, two companies control 50 percent of the world trade in bananas, and three companies control almost 80 percent of the confectionary market. Four companies control 75 percent of all retail trade in the U.K. In media and entertainment, nine large conglomerates dominate the sector, with five companies controlling around 80 percent of the music industry worldwide.[31]

Capital becomes centralized and concentrated not just in specific corporations but also in particular geographic regions. This is the reason for the uneven spatial development that is germane to modern capitalism and is reflected within nations and regions as well as between nations.[32] Indeed, it is a striking and undeniable fact that global inequality has consistently widened over the last 150 years of capitalist history. This observation stands in stark contrast to the neoliberal predictions of convergence and equilibrium. Indeed, it is precisely the *convergence* of neoliberal policies across the globe that causes the *divergence* characteristic of the global economy today.[33]

The dispersal of capital, however, implies more than geographical extension. Perhaps more significant in the current period is the deepening penetration of capital into increasingly numerous and variegated spheres of human activity. This process is known as commodification (that is, turning more and more of the objects we make and consume into things produced and sold by capitalist businesses).

This has been a continual tendency of capitalism throughout its history. The 1950s, for example, witnessed the penetration of capital into the sphere of domestic production. White goods, pre-packaged food, and so on – representing activities that were previously performed in the family and outside of the basic capitalist social relation – became subject to the profit motive and controlled by capitalist industry.

Today this drive manifests itself in one of the central policies advocated by neoliberalism, privatization, which is an attempt to (re)commodify spheres of human activity that have been partially removed from – or not yet become subject to – the profit motive. One of the key elements of imperialist control today is a program of mass privatization of Third World assets and natural resources. In the advanced capitalist countries, privatization of state-run sectors is central to neoliberal austerity measures, often phased in through stages of corporatization or "public–private partnerships."[34]

The commodification of water provides one example of this process. The three biggest water companies in the world – Suez and Veolia Environment of France and R.W.E. A.G. of Germany – serve almost 300 million people in over 100 countries. These three companies are predicted to control over 70 percent of the water systems in Europe and North America within a decade.[35] All over the Third World, water supplies are becoming the exclusive property of large transnational corporations. In Bolivia, for example, the Aguas de Tunari consortium – majority controlled by two multinational companies: Bechtel (U.S.A.) and Edison (Italy) – was in 1999 awarded a forty-year water concession for the Cochabamba province. Following this privatization, the price of water was raised by 400 percent.[36]

Iraq also provides a striking illustration of neoliberal privatization.

Even before the invasion began, plans had been put in place to privatize large parts of the Iraqi economy. Fittingly, even the process of drawing up the plan to privatize was itself privatized with the U.S. company BearingPoint (a company that was initially a division of K.P.M.G. Accounting) awarded the contract to steer the restructuring of the Iraqi economy. This contract was estimated in December 2003 to be worth over $240 million. The phenomenon of utilizing private multinationals to steer the implementation of neoliberalism is itself a product of neoliberal "reforms." BearingPoint won its first contract in El Salvador in the early 1990s. It has worked in Serbia on a plan to redesign the banking system and implement neoliberal financial reforms, and in Montenegro and Kosovo to implement new regulations in taxation, banking, pensions, and the privatization of energy utilities and business regulation.[37]

BearingPoint's plan for Iraq involved putting up for privatization ports, roads, banks, water and electricity, schools, and even textbook production. As noted above, military orders passed by the U.S.-run Coalition Provisional Authority prevent any restrictions on foreign ownership and allow complete repatriation of profits by multinational companies in addition to one of the lowest corporate tax rates in the world. Foreign companies that engage in criminal or fraudulent activity while working on a contract are essentially immune from Iraqi law.

The results of this privatization to date have been disastrous. Bechtel, for example, was awarded one of the largest post-war contracts: a massive contract to rebuild everything from schools, roads, and water systems to hospitals. The contract was set up as "cost-plus" – meaning that profits are calculated as a percentage of expenses: the more costly the work the higher the profits. This arrangement has encouraged widespread graft as companies simply charge high costs that are then passed on to the U.S. government. Much of the work performed under the contract is substandard, with companies aiming to do the job as quickly as possible with little regard for quality. The *Los Angeles Times* reported on 10 April 2005 that at least forty water, sewage, and electrical plants refurbished by Bechtel are no longer working properly. Baghdad has witnessed large increases in child mortality rates and water-borne illnesses as water treatment and sewage plants are malfunctioning. "Schoolchildren have to step over rancid brown puddles on their way to classrooms. Families swim in, fish from and get their drinking water from the polluted Tigris and Euphrates rivers."[38]

One of the key institutions of imperial control, the U.S. military, is itself finding its operations outsourced to private companies. The number of private military contractors operating in Iraq is unprecedented in U.S. history, exceeding the number of British troops and making up the second biggest contributor to the U.S.-led forces in Iraq after the Pentagon. One-third of the monthly war budget is spent on private contractors. Companies such as Halliburton, DynCorp, Vinnell, and Blackwater dominate these contracts in areas such as police training, logistics, construction, and even prison interrogation.[39]

This process of privatizing military functions began in tandem with the onset of neoliberalism in the late-1980s. In 1992, then-U.S. Defense Secretary Dick Cheney pushed the U.S. military in the direction of outsourcing its logistical functions following recommendations from a $9 million classified study conducted by a Halliburton subsidiary, Kellog, Brown & Root (K.B.R.). Cheney was made C.E.O. of Halliburton in 1995, a position he held until he became U.S. vice-president in 2000. K.B.R. now has a logistics contract with the U.S. military worth $13 billion for feeding, housing, and transporting troops.[40] Ironically, Halliburton was established by an act of violation of capitalist property rights. Earle Halliburton stole patented information from his former employer, Almond Perkins, and founded the company in 1919.[41]

THE RIGHT TO PROPERTY

Commodification and privatization represent the domination of increasing spheres of human activity by the profit motive. It is necessary, therefore, *to establish a system of property rights* that (1) guarantees ownership rights of these commodities; and (2) prevents unrestricted use of objects that are outside of capitalist production by forcing their conversion into commodities. For this reason, a regime of enforceable property rights is the constant "legal" companion of the imperialist order.

A particularly influential argument in defense of capitalist property rights has been offered by Hernando De Soto, who argues that a system of formal property rights is a mechanism akin to a "hydroelectric plant" that enables the potential energy of capital to be utilized.[42] De Soto believes that people in the Third World are poor because the property they own (houses, small shops, equipment, and so on) does not possess a visible property title. Many people living in slums, for example, do not hold rental contracts or have any proof of ownership for their living space. This property, therefore, cannot be used as collateral when applying for loans or to create securities that can then be bought and sold on secondary markets.[43] Property, formally recognized by title, not only leverages debt but also provides a link in the owner's credit history, a place to collect debts and taxes, and acts as a distribution point for utilities.[44]

Consequently for De Soto, the poor are poor because they lack the means of leveraging their property into capital due to a lack of a formal property system. What distinguishes the affluence of the Nile Hilton Hotel from the poverty found in the rest of Cairo is simply the fact that the world outside the hotel is without "legally enforceable property rights."[45] While Haiti might be the poorest country in the western hemisphere, with a history dominated by a rapacious colonialism and slavery, the value of untitled rural and urban real estate in that country is $5.2 billion according to De Soto.[46] If the "extra-legal" apartments, businesses, and other property present throughout the slums of Haiti entered the market in a system that gave property titles to their owners, then Haiti would presumably require no foreign aid.

Reaffirming the pioneer myth, De Soto praises the determination of early North American settlers who marked out their new farmlands by simply squatting on them. He naturally avoids any mention of the devastation of the indigenous population of North America and the theft of most of the continent as the fruits of this genocide. Instead he chooses to marvel at the "superabundance of land in British North America [that] presented the first settlers with opportunities unimaginable in the Europe they had left."[47] To De Soto, the secret of U.S. global supremacy lies in a legal system that gradually incorporated, recognized, and integrated these "extra-legal" property rights, establishing a unified property system that recognized squatter rights and created "the expanded markets and capital needed to fuel explosive economic growth."[48]

Plainly speaking, the implication of establishing the system of property rights advocated by De Soto is to make accessible to global capital the large swathes of Third World property that are currently "extra-legal" or outside the sphere of capitalist property relations. Given the unequal levels of power that exist in the marketplace, the result of such incorporation would most likely be the massive shift of that property from the poor to the rich.

De Soto aims to bring individually owned property that lies outside the market place into a system of capitalist property rights. A parallel argument can be seen in the laws and international agreements in areas such as intellectual property rights, trades, and services. These laws aim at preventing the unrestricted utilization of freely accessible goods, a process that has been described by Harvey as a new phase of "enclosing the commons."[49]

Order no. 81, passed in April 2004 by the U.S. occupying forces in Iraq, provides a perfect illustration of this overlaying of imperialist power, commodification, and property rights. According to its preamble, Order no. 81 aimed to "develop a free market economy characterized by sustainable economic growth through the establishment of a dynamic private sector."[50] It sought "to bring about significant change to the Iraqi intellectual property system as necessary to improve the economic condition of the people of Iraq." In particular, it recognized that "companies, lenders and entrepreneurs require a fair, efficient, and predictable environment for protection of their intellectual property."

Among other things, Order no. 81 makes it illegal for farmers to save seeds bought in the seed market from one crop to the next. Plant varieties will become private property (owned by large agricultural corporations) and it will be illegal for farmers to freely plant or save the seeds of plants registered under the new law.[51] In Iraq, the birthplace of human agriculture, the age-old custom of farmers saving seeds from one planting to the next has been made illegal as plant life itself becomes the private property of transnational agricultural companies.

The example of water commodification is also pertinent, given the fact that one billion people lack potable water around the world. Nevertheless, according to the World Bank, "work is still needed with political leaders in some national governments to move away from the concept of free water for all."[52] In other words, if water is to be made profitable, then its use must be restricted to those who can purchase it.

International agreements are designed to codify these restrictions on use by threatening governments with sanctions if they hinder the profit-making abilities of multinational companies. Under the 1995 General Agreement on Trade in Services (G.A.T.S.), for example, governments can face sanctions if they implement standards aimed at regulating the quality of water or undertake water conservation measures because these might impact the ability of companies to turn a profit.[53] In the case of Bolivian water privatization mentioned above, law no. 2029 made it illegal for residents in Cochabamba to use water from wells and natural springs in the area. Peasants who for centuries had been accustomed to using the water freely provided by nature were suddenly required to obtain permits if they wished to gather rainwater on their properties.[54]

ENDING BARRIERS TO CAPITAL FLOW

A third element to the neoliberal economic program is the abolition of impediments to the free flow of capital. This can be seen in the calls for "free trade" through the reduction of tariffs and any other barriers to the movement of commodities and capital. As a variant on the thesis that exchange is mutually beneficial, neoclassical trade theory argues that as long as countries trade without restriction then all will benefit. According to the World Trade Organization, standard trade theory is "the single most powerful insight into economics."[55] The policy prescriptions flowing from such an approach include ending import quotas, reducing or eliminating tariffs on imported goods, no state subsidization to "non-competitive" sectors or goods destined for export, and minimizing regulatory restrictions on trade and investment.

Neoliberal theory follows a "factor endowment" approach to the question of foreign trade. This model argues that nations should specialize in those commodities that utilize the inputs they can supply most cheaply. Due to the different endowment of natural resources, skill levels, technological abilities, and labor costs, countries have different prices for each of these inputs. According to the standard approach, if each country exports what it can offer most cheaply, then over time the different prices in each country will tend to equalize. Those countries with an abundance of capital will find that capital costs begin to rise and labor costs drop, and vice versa for those countries which have unfortunately been dealt the curse of a plentiful supply of cheap labor but no capital.

Many critics have pointed out that this approach is essentially a justification for the status quo. Without investigating the reasons that have led some countries to become "capital intensive" and others "labor intensive," standard trade theory essentially dehistoricizes the process by which the current form of global hierarchy evolved. To mention only one example, the massive transfer of wealth through slavery and theft of natural resources that led to the pauperization of much of the colonial world simply has no relevance to the current distribution of factors within standard trade theory.[56]

Anwar Shaikh has pointed out, however, that most radical criticisms of free trade accept the basic postulates of the neoclassical paradigm as correct on their own grounds, preferring to offer criticisms of the basic assumptions necessary to prove the theory.[57] In contrast, Shaikh has presented a convincing argument that free trade would lead to an increased poverty gap precisely *because of* free competition between nations not because of problems with the basic assumptions. The central feature of his argument is a theory of money that is divergent from the standard neoclassical approach.

According to standard trade theory, the reason that trade is mutually beneficial is based upon the movement of prices. If two countries trade with each other and one can produce goods more cheaply than the other it will have a trade surplus and therefore a net inflow of funds into the country as it is selling more than it is buying. Over time, this inflow of funds will cause export prices to rise and cheapen imports in the more productive economy either through upward movement in the exchange rate or by raising the general price level through inflation.[58]

Shaikh points out that this standard view of trade theory is based upon a version of the neoclassical quantity theory of money where the amount of money automatically adjusts the price level in the country. The neoclassical approach treats money as simply a way of facilitating barter between two commodities. Shaikh contrasts this with a Marxian theory of money, in which, money is seen as a form of capital (money-capital). As such, the exchange of commodities between nations cannot simply be treated as the exchange of objects. This process must be understood as inseparably linked within a broader circuit of capital. It includes, therefore, other flows of capital, whether in the form of finance capital through international borrowing and lending, or value-producing capital in the sense of investment in factories and so on.[59]

The primary effect of an increase in the amount of money-capital (caused, for example, through a persistent trade surplus) will not be an increase in prices as predicted by the quantity theory of money but rather an increase in the amount of loanable money capital. This will lead to a drop in the rate of interest and an expansion of production in the country with the trade surplus. Alternatively, profit-seeking capitalists may choose to lend readily available money-capital overseas in search of higher profits. The country with a trade deficit, however, will be faced with a higher interest rate as money-capital leaves the country and therefore becomes scarcer. Because of the interest-rate differential between the two countries, money-capital will be lent from the more productive country to the less productive country, which will therefore become chronically indebted.[60] Precisely because money is a form of capital, the consequence of the free-trade policies advocated by the neoliberals will be to accelerate the indebtedness of Third World countries to the advanced capitalist core. The stranglehold of debt on the majority of the world's population confirms this prediction, unlike empirical tests of neoliberal trade theory.[61] The calls for an end to tariffs, and the justification given in the form of standard trade theory, serve to facilitate the ability of money-capital and commodity-capital to move quickly between different geographical spaces, thereby increasing the quantity and rate of wealth transfer from the poorer countries to the rich.

ENFORCING NEOLIBERAL "REFORMS"

One of the myths about "globalization" is that the nation-state is no longer important. The capitalist world order, however, is based upon exploitation and extraction of profit. Its inability to meet real human needs means that the existing social order always generates opposition and therefore must be maintained by force. At the level of the global system this is manifested in Lal's call for the U.S.A. to "shoulder the imperial burden of maintaining the global Pax."[62]

At the level of the nation-state, a state apparatus is required to micro-manage the contradictions of the system in the interests of that imperium. As Leo Panitch and Sam Gindin have stressed in their work on imperialism, the process of neoliberal restructuring is "authored" by individual states, under the particular influence of the U.S. state.[63] The state is critical in ensuring that the conditions are right for capital accumulation.

The role of financial flows and floating exchange rates becomes increasingly important to maintaining a hierarchical world order as the unimpeded movement of capital plays a disciplinary role vis-à-vis the domestic state apparatus. Governmental monetary and fiscal policies become subject to continual "votes of confidence" by the international money markets. With no restrictions on short-term capital flows it becomes increasingly difficult for states to pursue domestic policies aimed at fostering national accumulation through monetary or exchange controls. Instead, states are required to fulfill the function assigned to them as part of the international circuit of capital. If they don't, they face the risk of capital flight and currency collapse.

The internationalization of state functions has accompanied this internationalization of capital.[64] In the era of neoliberalism the domestic state is more integrated into the maintenance of the international circulation of capital, a process that shapes its domestic economic policies. Those sectors of the domestic state apparatus that are concerned with internationalization have become increasingly autonomous in their decision-making ability and further removed from any national democratic control.[65]

In current debates around imperialism and empire, the relationship between states is often reduced conceptually to competing viewpoints emphasizing either interdependence or rivalry. Such a dichotomy, however, does not adequately capture the contradictory forces at play within the global system, and it is more accurate to understand the presence of dual tendencies towards unity and rivalry between imperialist powers.[66] Capital is organized territorially at the level of the nation-state (and through regional trading blocs), yet simultaneously its reach is global and there is a common interest between different capital blocs in maintaining the stability of the system as a whole.

The rhetoric of "failed states" is thus the natural political corollary of neoliberalism. In this regard, Deepak Lal presents a striking example of how the logic of the system generates an irrational, ahistorical ideology. Following the standard approach to free trade and the notion of factor-endowment as being the prime determinant of a country's trade specialization, Lal argues that the reason regions such as Africa and the Middle East have so many "failed states" is because they have been endowed with natural resources that provide an irresistible urge to the "predatory" instincts of state elites. In other words, the reason for the mass\immiseration of the population of these regions is the vast resources of free wealth with which they have been blessed.

At one level, Lal's argument is partially correct. Mass pauperization of the Third World *is* the result of predatory instincts, not from the Third World itself, however, but rather their colonial masters. His solution to the problem provides a clear example of how he sees the role of the imperium in an era of failed states. Firstly, he proposes that ownership of the "mines and wells" be transferred to an international body, which he terms the International Resource Fund (perhaps constituted by an amalgamation of the I.M.F. and World Bank). The political form of the country could then be structured around the use of the natural resources. In the case of Iraq, he argues:

> there is no reason to hold this artificial state together. It is not a nation. The only conceivable reason to keep it united is its oil wealth, concentrated in the north, controlled by the Kurds, and in the South, by the Shia . . . One solution would be to put the revenue from Iraq's oil wealth into [an] International Resources Fund (I.N.R.F.) . . . and for three autonomous self-governing regions to be created.[67]

Lal recognizes that nations whose natural resources have been expropriated in such a manner may retain a desire to regain their wealth. In 2004, while speaking to a Cato Institute conference in Russia on the role of international organizations, Lal asked: how could "predators" be prevented from attacking and capturing the "mines and wells" generating the rents? His answer:

> Here the military prowess of an Imperial power or a coalition of such powers is crucial. Such a power could follow the example of China during the inter-war period. Foreign companies could be leased territory which they could protect with their own police forces, in return for royalties to the I.N.R.F. But even this privatized solution would require the imperial power to maintain "gunboats and Gurkhas" at the ready, in case some local predator decided to mount a challenge to the private controllers of these mines.[68]

In other words, there are some countries in the current world order whose states lack the requisite disciplinary mechanisms to facilitate imperial plunder. These so-called "failed states" should have their functions privatized by international corporations – backed up by the might of the imperial army if necessary.

CONTRADICTIONS OF THE SYSTEM

The economic program of neoliberalism can thus be understood in light of the circuit of capital and the different moments driving the accumulation of profit. It is not simply an obfuscating ideology designed to weaken the poor or transfer wealth to the rich. Rather, it expresses the immanent drive of capital to increase spatial reach, speed up its movement, and establish a disciplinary system that maximizes the extraction of wealth from those who produce it. Specifically, countries should pursue "free" markets and "free" trade. State intervention in the market should be minimized and largely restricted to ensuring the maintenance of a system of property rights and contracts. With the increasing internationalization of capital, the individual nation-state becomes central to securing the economic space for the accumulation needs of internationalized capital. This understanding of neoliberalism captures, however, only one side of the movement of capital. Specifically, it ignores a point continually stressed by Marx, namely that the movement of capital creates its own barriers and thus always holds the potential for crisis.

The spatial expansion of capital and its increasing penetration into different spheres of human activity throws up its own barriers precisely because capitalism is concerned with the accumulation of profit, not the satisfaction of human needs. We can see this tendency at work in the world economy today. In the neoliberal era, wage cut-backs and impoverishment occur alongside the maximization of profits. As part of the drive to accumulate wealth, capitalism automatically creates immiseration and widespread poverty. On one hand capitalism attempts to drive down the living conditions (and hence purchasing power) of its working class, but on the other it requires these very same workers to purchase its commodities.

Thus while capitalism attempts to maximize profit at one end it also tends to maximize poverty at the other, inevitably creating the possibility of crisis as over-accumulation and uneven development runs into its own barriers.[69] This is manifested in increasing levels of debt, large-scale unemployment, and stagnating profit rates across the globe. It also creates a particular form of crisis peculiar to the capitalist system: the phenomenon of massive quantities of unsold commodities unable to find a buyer in a world of widespread want. The problem of satisfying needs becomes – unlike any other point in human history – a problem of too much production, not too little.

The huge capital outlays required for production and technological innovation, combined with the relatively speedy obsolescence of technology in an environment of over-accumulation, increase the risks involved in capitalist production. Neoliberals have attempted to circumvent this spatial fixity of the productive moment in the circuit of capital by distributing the burdens of relocation across a network of suppliers located across the globe. In this way, competitive pressures operate across different nation-states, leading to a process of "competitive austerity" as states and firms become embroiled in encouraging investment to settle within their borders.[70] The burdens of the spatial fixity of productive capital are thus carried by smaller suppliers, the state, and workers rather than internationally mobile capital. As Harvey and others have stressed, the human social geography is shaped by the waves of valorization/devalorization around these spatial structures as well as the social struggles that inevitably coalesce around them.

The accelerating velocity with which capital moves throughout its circuit brings forth a number of important contradictions. As Marx pointed out, while "circulation time in itself is a barrier to realization," it is, at the same time, "the circulation of capital [that] realizes value."[71] These pressures are all too evident today. The recurrent financial crises caused by speculative capital moving rapidly in and out of regions has led some economists to warn of the dangers of floating exchange rates and no capital controls. At the level of the individual, the increased speed with which capital moves through its circuit produces effects such as an ever-present reinforcement of consumerism through the relentless frenzy of advertising, a fast-food culture, a shrinking of product lifecycles with continual innovation, the ubiquitous nature of disposable commodities, the phenomena of a permanent sales culture, speed ups at work, and a general malaise of "not having enough time."

One of the mechanisms through which capitalism has historically attempted to mediate these tendencies towards crisis has been through the use of credit. Credit is a means of bridging the barriers presented by weak demand and over-accumulation through obtaining an advance on value that has not yet been realized.[72] The increasing cost of outlays for labor-saving machinery and new technology also provides an impetus for the growth in credit. For this reason, finance takes on an important role in the circuit of capital, a phenomenon that early theorists of imperialism such as Hilferding, Lenin, and Bukharin identified as indicative of the increasing centralization and concentration of capital on a world scale. It is for this reason that neoliberalism is often understood as an attempt by finance capital to reestablish its dominance following the structural crisis and downturn in the profit rate of the 1970s.[73]

In today's world, credit is critical to the continued functioning of the global economy, with the U.S. consumer acting as virtually the only source of effective demand. This demand must be maintained through increasing levels of debt engineered through low interest rates and enticement of U.S. consumers to continue their consumption via home mortgages, easy access to credit, and zero-down-payment options. The question of when the natural limits to this process will be reached and the ensuing ramifications is an issue that is increasingly finding its way into mainstream economic debate.[74]

CONCLUSION

Neoliberalism is an economic program centered around privatization, minimal state intervention in the market, a reduction of all barriers to trade and capital flows, floating exchange rates, and maximizing the spread of the market. Echoing classical arguments such as those found in the work of Adam Smith, neoliberalism is simply an assertion that the unintended consequences obtained from the selfish acts of maximizing individuals in the marketplace will produce the best outcome. All that is required is a system that will maintain the freedom of exchange – that is, ensure property rights and the sanctity of contracts.

The basic assumptions of neoliberalism, however, are fundamentally wrong. The individual is not a completely isolated, self-contained unit. Our individual desires do not spring fully formed from a pristine, hidden well inside of us, but are – as the huge amounts of resources spent on advertising indicate – shaped and determined by our interactions with other people and the broader society. The market is not concerned with meeting human needs. Its primary goal is the accumulation of profit. By pursuing the maximization of profit it actually distorts, twists, and denies our real needs as human beings.

Neoliberalism, however, is not simply a false ideology based upon wrong assumptions that do not conform to the real world. While the empirical results of neoliberal policy may have been demonstrably disastrous for the globe, neoliberalism is *not* an arbitrary set of policy decisions. Rather, it is the imperative of profit accumulation that provides the material substratum for this ideology. The capitalist mode of production is itself driven incessantly towards a global, borderless, frictionless ideal by the pressure, as Marx put it, to "accumulate and accumulate." Neoliberalism can be seen, therefore, as the ideological reflection of that pressure. As the dominant economic program, neoliberalism has its origins in the material and social forces underlying the system's own reproduction. In the current imperialist phase, neoliberalism, as an expression of the internationalization of this circuit of capital, is aimed at eradicating spatial and temporal barriers to these international flows of capital.

From this analysis a very important conclusion follows. Our consumption patterns are dependent upon the way we organize production. It becomes possible to imagine altering the way our society is structured in order really to meet human needs. The immense stores of wealth, and technological and scientific knowledge that are available to humanity today makes that vision completely possible. The reality of the environmental crisis makes this an imperative.

Standing in the way of a society that democratically plans the satisfaction of human needs are the vested interests of those who profit from this circuit of capital. Only a few years into the twenty-first century we can see the dire consequences of a world order structured around the untrammeled pursuit of private profit. Nevertheless, the system itself always generates opposition. The social devastation that accompanies the spread of neoliberal imperialism faces mounting resistance across the planet. It is precisely this contradiction that underpins the resurgence of the U.S. imperium and leads to calls such as that made by Lal for the United States to shoulder the "imperial burden."[75] If the world will not willingly accept the unrestricted operation of capital, then it must be imposed by force. The necessary partners of economic "freedom" are the guns of the U.S. military precisely because crisis and resistance are the constant shadows of neoliberalism's "successes." To paraphrase Bertold Brecht: it is this contradiction that provides us with hope.

NOTES

1. Deepak Lal, *In Praise of Empires: Globalization and Order* (New York: Palgrave, Macmillan, 2004).

2. Ibid., p. 212.

3. Ibid., p. 207.

4. Deepak Lal and H. Myint, *The Political Economy of Poverty, Equity and Growth* (Oxford: Clarendon Press, 1996), p. 49.

5. Ibid., p. 38.

6. Lal, *In Praise of Empires*, p. 206. Lal's understanding of globalization as the creation of a common economic space is an important counterpoint to other approaches that link the question of globalization solely to the extent of national sovereignty. As Freeman and Kagarlitsky have pointed out, the myth that the era of globalization can be sequestered by a measurement of sovereignty has long been questioned by Third World activists who understand that the power of imperialist capital does not stop at the borders of the nation state. See A. Freeman and B. Kagarlitsky, *The Politics of Empire: Globalisation in Crisis* (London: Pluto Press, 2004).

7. Lal, *In Praise of Empires*, p. 205.

8. Ibid., p. 205. Italics added.

9. Ibid., p. 210.

10. Ibid., p. 211.

11. Ibid., p. 201.

12. Ibid., p. 26.

13. J. Bellamy-Foster, "The New Age of Imperialism," in *Pox Americana: Exposing the American Empire*, ed. J. Bellamy-Foster and R. McChesney (New York: Monthly Review Press, 2004), p. 169.

14. Christian Palloix, "The Internationalization of Capital and the Circuit of Social Capital," in *International Firms and Modern Imperialism: Selected Readings*, ed. Hugo Radice (Harmondsworth: Penguin, 1975).

15. T. Palley, "From Keynesianism to Neoliberalism: Shifting Paradigms in Economics," in *Neoliberalism: A Critical Reader*, ed. A. Saad-Filho and D. Johnston (London: Pluto Press, 2005).

16. Deepak Lal, *Culture, Democracy and Development* (New Delhi: National Council of Applied Economic Research, 1999), p. 7.

17. E. Hunt, *Property and Prophets: The Evolution of Economic Institutions and Ideologies* (New York: Harper & Row, 1976), p. 148.

18. Austrian economists overlook the objection that this perspective is itself an ethical judgment, one based on acceptance of the normative preferability of the status quo.

19. Lal and Myint, *Political Economy of Poverty, Equity and Growth*, p. 27.

20. Ibid., p. 28.

21. Lal, *In Praise of Empires*, p. 147.

22. Deepak Lal, "A Liberal International Economic Order: The International Monetary System and Economic Development," *Princeton Essays in International Finance*, 139, 1980, p. 28.

23. Karl Marx, *Grundrisse* (Harmondsworth: Penguin Books, 1973).

24. Ibid., p. 539.

25. This is a schematic representation of a single capital with the arbitrary beginning point M (presuming, therefore, the existence of money and hence capitalist social relations prior to the beginning of the circuit). It could be expanded to include credit, and value flows between different spaces.

26. A more detailed analysis would need to include other factors such as the role of money (and currency seigniorage), credit, and finance in maintaining the circuit as well as the impact of exchanges between different geographic spaces.

27. D. Harvey, *The Limits to Capital* (London: Verso, 1999), p. 418.

28. Ibid. See also, D. Harvey, "The 'New' Imperialism: Accumulation by Dispossession," in *Socialist Register 2004: The New Imperial Challenge*, ed. C. Leys and L. Panitch (London: Merlin, 2004).

29. Palloix, "Internationalization of Capital."

30. Ibid., p. 74.

31. For information on concentration in the food and agricultural sector see ActionAid International, *Power Hungry: Six Reasons to Regulate Global Food Companies* (Johannesburg, 2005); B. Vorley, "Food Inc.: Corporate Concentration from Farm to Consumer" (UK Food Group, 2003); for media and entertainment see R. McChesney, *Rich Media Poor Democracy: Communication Politics in Dubious Times* (Chicago, Ill.: University of Illinois Press, 1999) and http://www.mediachannel.org.

32. See E. Mandel, *Late Capitalism* (London: Verso, 1983); N. Smith, *Uneven Development: Nature, Capital and the Production of Space* (Oxford: Basil Blackwell, 1990).

33. G. Albo, "Contesting the New Capitalism," in *Varieties of Capitalism, Varieties of Approaches*, ed. David Coates (London: Palgrave, 2005), pp. 63–83.

34. In addition to the profit-seeking opportunities that privatization presents, this neoliberal policy also brings important political benefits as part of the reshaping of the class struggle and patterns of state rule in the advanced capitalist core. Privatization weakens the power of public sector unions which have been traditionally strong during the Keynesian era. It is also aimed at fostering a sense of "share-holder" capitalism and worker internalization of competitive norms, where identification with the company is predicated on financial returns from stock holdings and the ability of the company to compete internationally. For case studies that explore these concepts, see P. Arestis and M. Sawyer, "The Neoliberal Experience of the United Kingdom," in *Neoliberalism: A Critical Reader*, ed. A. Saad-Filho and D. Johnston (London: Pluto Press, 2005), pp. 199–207 for the U.K. experience; Wally Seccombe, "Contradictions of Shareholder Capitalism Downsizing Jobs, Enlisting Savings, Destabilizing Families," in *Socialist Register 1999: Global Capitalism vs. Democracy*, ed. C. Leys and L. Panitch

(London: Merlin Press, 1999), pp. 193–216 for the U.S.A.; G. Albo and J. Jensen, "Remapping Canada: The State in the Era of Globalization," in *Understanding Canada: Building of the New Canadian Political Economy*, ed. W. Clement (Montreal: McGill University Press, 1997), pp. 215–239 for Canada.

35. M. Barlow and T. Clarke, *The World Bank's Latest Market Fantasy* (Polaris Institute, January 2004), http://www.globalpolicy.org (accessed March 2005).

36. The American Association of Jurists and the Europe – Third World Center, 1 March 2005, "The Water War Continues in Bolivia," www.aidc.org (accessed March 2005).

37. Center for Public Integrity, "Windfalls of War – Bearing Point Inc.," http://www.publicintegrity.org (accessed January 2005).

38. T. Christian Miller, "Under Fire: The Rebuilding of Iraq," *Los Angeles Times*, 10 April 2005, p. A1.

39. Michael Dobbs, "Halliburton's Deals Greater Than Thought," *Washington Post*, 28 August 2003, p. A01.

40. "About Halliburton," http://www.halliburtonwatch.org/about_hal/logcap.html (accessed January 2005).

41. J. Rodengen, *The Legend of Halliburton* (Fort Lauderdale, Fla.: Write Stuff Syndicate, 1996), p. 20.

42. Hernando De Soto, *The Mystery of Capital* (New York: Basic Books, 2000), pp. 46–47.

43. Ibid., p. 6.

44. Ibid., p. 7.

45. Ibid., p. 16.

46. Ibid., p. 33.

47. Ibid., p. 111.

48. Ibid., p. 150.

49. Harvey, "The 'New' Imperialism." In reference to the enclosure movement in Britain in the eighteenth and early nineteenth centuries in which communal land was made off-limits to peasants and farmers, forcing them out of agriculture and into the newly created factories.

50. Coalition Provisional Authority, "Patent, Industrial Design, Undisclosed Information, Integrated Circuits and Plant Variety," CPA Order no. 81, 26 April 2004, http://www.iraqcoalition.org/ (accessed November 2004).

51. Focus on the Global South and GRAIN, "Iraq's New Patent Law: A Declaration of War against Farmers," October 2004, http://www.grain.org (accessed February 2005).

52. P. Bond, "Principles, Strategies and Tactics of Decommodification in South Africa," *Links Journal*, 22, 2002, pp. 32–41.

53. S. Shrybman, "Thirst for Control – New Rules in the International Water Grab," *The Blue Planet Project* (Canada: Council of Canadians, 2002).

54. M. Barlow, "Desperate Bolivians Fought Street Battles to Halt a Water-for-Profit Scheme. The World Bank Must Realize Water Is a Basic Human Right," *Globe and Mail* (Toronto), 9 May 2000.

55. World Trade Organization, "Understanding the WTO: The Case for Open Trade," http://www.wto.org/english/thewto_e/whatis_e/tif_e/fact3_e.htm (accessed January 2005).

56. See Walter Rodney, *How Europe Underdeveloped Africa* (Washington, D.C: Howard University Press, 1982).

57. Anwar Shaikh, "Foreign Trade and the Law of Value – Part One," *Science and Society*, 43, 1979, pp. 281–302; "Foreign Trade and the Law of Value – Part Two," *Science and Society*, 44, 1980, pp. 27–57; "Economic Mythology of Neoliberalism," in *Neoliberalism: A Critical Reader*, ed. A. Saad-Filho and D. Johnston (London: Pluto Press, 2004), pp. 41–49.

58. B. Ohlin, "The Theory of Trade," in *Heckscher–Ohlin Trade Theory*, ed. H. Flam and M. J. Flanders (Cambridge, Mass.: M.I.T. Press, 1991), pp. 146–152.

59. Shaikh, "Foreign Trade – Two," p. 301.

60. Shaikh, "Foreign Trade – One."

61. For example, W. Leontief, "Domestic Production and Foreign Trade: The American Capital Position Reexamined," *Proceedings of the American Philosophical Society*, XCVII, 1953, pp. 3–39.

62. Lal, *In Praise of Empires*, p. 215.

63. L. Panitch, "Globalization and the State," in *The Socialist Register 1994: Between Globalism and Nationalism*, ed. R. Miliband and L. Panitch (London: Merlin, 1994), pp. 60–93. L. Panitch and S. Gindin, "Global Capitalism and American Empire," *in Socialist Register 2004: The New Imperial Challenge*, ed. C. Leys and L. Panitch (London: Merlin, 2003), pp. 1–42.

64. R. Cox, *Production, Power and World Order: Social Forces in the Making of History* (New York: Columbia University Press, 1987).

65. Albo, "Contesting."

66. See G. Albo, "The Old and New Economics of Imperialism," in *Socialist Register 2004: The New Imperial Challenge*, ed. C. Leys and L. Panitch (London: Merlin, 2003), pp. 88–113, and S. Savran, "Globalisation and the New World Order: The New Dynamics of Imperialism and War," in *The Politics of Empire: Globalisation in Crisis*, ed. A. Freeman and B. Kagarlitsky (London: Pluto Press/T.N.I., 2004), pp. 140–163.

67. Lal, *In Praise of Empires*, p. 202.

68. Deepak Lal, "The Threat from International Organizations to Economic Liberty," prepared for "A Liberal Agenda for the New Century: A Global Perspective Conference," Cato Institute, The Institute of Economic Analysis and the Russian Union of Industrialists and Entrepreneurs, 8–9 April 2004, Moscow, p. 20. Available at http://www.ice.ru/liberalconf/149982 (accessed January 2005).

69. S. Clarke, "Class Struggle and the Global Overaccumulation of Capital," in *Phases of Capitalist Development*, ed. R. Albritton et al. (New York: Palgrave, 2001), p. 80.

70. G. Albo and J. Jenson, "Remapping Canada: The State in the Era of Globalization," in

Understanding Canada: Building of the New Canadian Political Economy, ed. W. Clement (Montreal: McGill University Press, 1997), pp. 215–239.

71. Marx, *Grundrisse*, p. 543.

72. Marx, *Grundrisse*.

73. A. Saad-Filho, "Introduction," in *Neoliberalism: A Critical Reader*, ed. A. Saad-Filho and D. Johnston (London: Pluto Press, 2005), pp. 9–10.

74. Debates between Nouriel Roubini, Brad Setser, and others provide a good example of these concerns among mainstream economists. A useful selection is available at http://www.stern.nyu.edu/globalmacro/.

75. Lal, *In Praise of Empires*, p. 215.

9

AMERICAN SOFT POWER, OR, AMERICAN CULTURAL IMPERIALISM?

Tanner Mirrlees

THE LEFT AGAINST AMERICAN CULTURAL IMPERIALISM

Twenty-five years ago, the processes denoted by the phrase "American cultural imperialism" were criticized by anti-imperialists rather than celebrated by American neoconservatives, were thought to exist as part of the real world rather than as an impoverished theory, and were not subsumed by a neoliberal discourse called American soft power.

In the 1970s, U.S. multinational corporations dominated the capacities to produce and distribute media-culture and information on an international scale. The American state, with its ideological free flow of information doctrine – a doctrine that extolled the free and democratic qualities of a global media market ruled by corporations – sought to consolidate a global U.S. corporate media monopoly by opening up the national telecommunication systems of postcolonial states to American techno-capital and commercial programming. Backed by the American state, U.S. corporations pressured (with help from the local elite) the privatization of national telecommunication infrastructures, dumped their commercial media on the emerging markets of postcolonial states, and transmitted American values, ideologies, and images around the world.

At this time, many anti-imperialists, scholars, and postcolonial bureaucrats were concerned about the consequences of a global communication system that was being developed to serve the economic interests of U.S. media corporations and the Cold War foreign policies of the American state. In 1971, prior to the C.I.A.-sponsored coup in Chile that installed the dictator General Pinochet, Ariel Dorfman and Armand Mattelart, two Chilean communication scholars inspired by the socialist goals of Allende's Popular Unity government, wrote *How to Read Donald Duck: Imperialist Ideology in the Disney Comic.*[1] They read Disney comics as vehicles of U.S. cultural imperialism. Disney comics, Dorfmann and Mattelart argued, touted the possessive individualism of the American way of life, implied excessive consumerism was the path to happiness, and (like so many colonial texts) constructed non-Americans as culturally savage and primitive.

A more rigorous discussion of U.S. cultural imperialism came from the political economist Herbert Schiller, who was situated within the universities of the imperial core. Schiller described the struggle of U.S. media firms and the American state to shape the global communication system according to their economic and political interests as U.S. cultural imperialism: "the sum processes by which a society is brought into the modern world system and how its dominating stratum is attracted, pressured, forced, and sometimes bribed into shaping social institutions to correspond to, or even promote, the values and structures of the dominating centres of the system."[2] For Schiller, the American empire incorporated different nation-states as peripheries by establishing a technological infrastructure conducive to U.S. political and economic control. On the terrain of ideology and culture, the U.S. media reinforced this process by transmitting, "in their imagery and messages, the beliefs and perspectives that create and reinforce their audiences' attachments to the way things are in the system overall."[3]

For Dorfman, Mattelart, Schiller, and many other critics, U.S. cultural imperialism eventually came to mean the global export of the capitalist/ commercial form of the U.S. media system, the economic and ideological domination of the global communication system by U.S. corporations, and the homogenization and integration of the world with the social relations and cultural values of a globally expanding yet American-led capitalism. U.S. cultural imperialism was said to have many effects. Globally dispersed populations were transformed into new audience commodities for American advertising firms and new consumers for U.S. media corporations. The capacities of newly "liberated" postcolonial states and populations to autonomously produce media and represent themselves through this media to the rest of the world were diminished. Struggles for cultural autonomy, central to anti-colonial struggles for political and economic sovereignty that sought to move beyond the historical remnants of British colonialism and the emerging dynamics of capitalist neo-imperialism were, without a sovereign communication and cultural system, quickly undermined.

The unequal, imbalanced, and asymmetrical international production, distribution, and consumption of media and information, which largely flowed from North to South, from the American imperial core to the rest of the world, was also said to result in a condition of cultural dependency. Without the financial and technological means to represent their cultural identities and communicate their aspirations for political-economic independence to the world, postcolonial states became dependent on the technology transfers, informational networks, and professional know-how emanating from the American empire. At the same time, cultural differences, traditions, and languages were assimilated by an electronically produced tide of Anglo-American consumerist media.

The miscellaneous criticisms of U.S. cultural imperialism, coming from within and from without the imperial core, turned into a radical chorus at a number of international summits by the late 1970s. This provided the moral support for declarations of a New World Information and Communication Order (N.I.W.C.O.) by the Non-Aligned Movement. Through the United Nations Educational, Scientific and Cultural Organization (U.N.E.S.C.O.), the Non-Aligned Movement's N.W.I.C.O. envisaged and struggled to establish a pluralistic, equitable, and balanced mode of internationally producing and distributing information. Seeking an alternative to the American empire's free-market ideology and global media monopoly, intellectuals, socialists, and policy-makers aligned with or sympathetic to the struggles of the Non-Aligned Movement wielded the political slogan of cultural imperialism nationally, to inspire struggles for cultural sovereignty, and internationally, to make arguments for a democratic and culturally diverse global communication system.

In the historical context of its production and use, the phrase "American cultural imperialism" was thus political and critical: it revealed the real inequities that were concealed by America's ideological free-flow-of-information doctrine and was wielded as a political tool by anti-imperialists. In the early 1980s, the political slogan of U.S. cultural imperialism came under fire. At a time when the Thatcher and Reagan administrations dropped out of U.N.E.S.C.O., waged a corporate-supported propaganda war against postcolonial proposals for a N.W.I.C.O., and aggressively pushed for the globalization of neoliberal communications policy, the idea of cultural imperialism was problematized by many Anglo-American cultural studies scholars and communication theorists.

By the 1990s, the anti-imperial concept of cultural imperialism was being widely resisted and criticized. Published at the so-called end-of-history, when America emerged as the world's only superpower, John Tomlinson's *Cultural Imperialism: A Critical Introduction*, subjected the concept of cultural imperialism to a systematic deconstruction. Tomlinson declared: "the idea of cultural imperialism has been heavily criticized and, as a result, is far less fashionable a critical position in academic circles in the 1990s than it was during the 1970s and 1980s."[4] For Tomlinson, the idea of U.S. cultural imperialism mistook economic control for cultural domination, ignored the hybrid complexities of cultures, and painted a disparaging picture of Third World consumers. Tomlinson implied that the concept of cultural imperialism was in itself essentially connected to some imperialist or Western colonialist project. "The discourse we're concerned with," argued Tomlinson, "is inescapably lodged in the culture of the developed West. . . . Cultural imperialism is a critical discourse which operates by representing the cultures whose autonomy it defends in its own (dominant) Western cultural terms."[5]

Criticisms such as these often relied on reductive conceptual caricatures of U.S. cultural imperialism and lacked adequate historical and political understanding of the subject. They nonetheless provided the basis for a thoroughgoing delegitimization of the critical concept of U.S. cultural imperialism, which was eventually replaced by more positive accounts of cultural globalization in the 1990s. The Clinton administration too declared the emergence of a post-imperial, post-national, and global cultural order of things. In the same year that Tomlinson's book rebranded the anti-imperial political slogan of U.S. cultural imperialism as a conceptual problematic for Anglo-American academics, a well-organized and well-financed group of U.S. neoconservative intellectuals began referring to themselves openly as American cultural imperialists. While the idea of a centreless and deterritorialized cultural globalization began to supplant the reality described by discourses of American cultural imperialism, neoconservative intellectuals were recommending cultural imperialism as American foreign policy.

THE RIGHT FOR AMERICAN CULTURAL IMPERIALISM

In 1991 the neoconservative Ben Wattenberg's *The First Universal Nation* was published. Wattenberg argued that the collapse of the Soviet Union gave the American empire a golden opportunity to aggressively universalize the American way of life: "Only Americans have the sense of mission and gall to engage in benign, but energetic, global cultural advocacy. We are the most potent cultural imperialists in history."[6] In "The Emerging American Imperium," published six years later, Irving Kristol stated: "Without clearly intending it or fully realizing it, the United States has come to dominate the world militarily and culturally. One of these days the American people are going to awaken to the fact that we have become an imperial nation."[7] For Kristol, the world wanted and needed the American empire to happen. There would be challenges, as the American empire's lack of an authentic Christian missionary spirit made its global moral leadership vulnerable to attack. Nevertheless, Kristol was cognizant of the global cultural influence of America's postmodern society of the spectacle. He perceptively remarked: "Our missionaries live in Hollywood."[8]

In an article published in 1997 audaciously titled "In Praise of Cultural Imperialism?," David Rothkop declared that the American empire was indispensable to the management of global affairs. As such, it was necessary for the American empire actively to globalize U.S.-style liberal capitalist democracy. To achieve this goal, the U.S. state and U.S. media corporations needed to "win the battle of the world's information flows, dominating the airwaves as Great Britain once ruled the seas."[9] Rothkop continued:

> It is in the interests of the United States to ensure that if the world is moving toward a common language, it be English. If the world is moving toward common telecommunications, safety, and quality standards, they be American; that if the world is becoming linked by television, radio, and music, the programming be American; and that if common values are being developed, they be values with which Americans are comfortable. These are not simple idle aspirations. English is linking the world. American information

technologies and services are at the cutting edge of those that are enabling globalization. Access to the largest economy in the world is the primary carrot leading other nations to open their markets. Indeed, just as the United States is the world's sole remaining military superpower, so is it the world's only information super-power.[10]

To universalize U.S.-style liberal capitalist democracy, then, the American state and American corporations needed to dominate the global commu-nication, information, and media infrastructure. This would ensure American dominance in the future and assist the integration of other nation-states into global capitalism. Thus, for some imperialist neo-conservatives, U.S. imperial dominance should be (and was being) assisted by U.S. cultural imperialism.

Neoconservatives regularly rationalized U.S. cultural imperialism by appealing to two ideological beliefs. First, a belief in America's exception-alism (the idea that America's institutions and values are the best in the world) rationalized the export of these institutions and values to the rest of the world as America's moral responsibility, its global gift. Second, a belief in America's universality (the idea that America's institutions and values reflect the true and collective interests of the planet) rationalized the export of these institutions and values to the rest of the world as a progressive force of global modernization. Beneath the smokescreen cast by the twin ideologies of American exceptionalism and American univer-salism, however, was a realist desire to sustain U.S. political and economic dominance – and global capitalism – in the twenty-first century. Two French intellectuals, Bourdieu and Wacquant, argued that cultural imperialism requires "the power to universalize particularisms linked to a singular historical tradition by causing them to be mis-recognized as such."[11] The universalization of a particularly totalizing image of U.S. culture by neoconservatives throughout the 1990s identifies them as cultural imperialists.[12]

But though neoconservatives are proud U.S. cultural imperialists, for them, the practice of cultural imperialism as a foreign policy tactic comes second to the unilateral use of military force.[13] The Bush adminis-tration's national security strategy[14] and foreign policy in the post-9/11 context reflected the imperial underpinning of neoconservative ideol-ogy. Iraq became the geopolitical theatre in which the core tenets of neoconservative doctrine were performed for the world: unilateral military pre-emption, strategic regime change and state-building, the attempted export of U.S.-made liberal capitalist democracy, and the global promotion of America as a benevolent imperialist power.

Such unabashed imperialism, however, jeopardized America's image as an anti-imperialist force. While the Bush administration's unilateral foreign policy pleased neoconservative ideologes,[15] it was openly despised and publicly challenged by much of the enlightened world. Considering the global transformation of America's image, Immanuel Wallerstein stated: "Over the last 200 years, the United States acquired a considerable amount of ideological credit. But these days, the United States is running through its credit even faster than it ran through its gold surplus in the 1960s."[16] Thomas Friedman, the globalization cheerleader and pro-American imperialist even sadly admitted: "I have never known a time in my life when America and its president were more hated around the world than today."[17]

The swelling global anti-American sentiment signalled a crisis of America's world hegemony, or, its moral leadership. The U.S. empire's struggle for world hegemony involves a delicate balancing act of strategies of coercion with those that attempt to organize consent. The U.S. empire's occupation of Iraq not only failed to spread democracy and freedom throughout the Middle East, but also was undertaken without sufficiently organizing global consent to this coercion. As a result, the U.S. empire's moral credibility was demolished. The propaganda of weapons of mass destruction and the con of pre-emptive regime change may have duped half of the U.S. population, but it did not fool the world. Nor did the imperialism-lite of human rights discourse with its belated attempt to organize global consent to a political leadership that had already been identified as fraudulent.

Some neoconservatives recognized America's global hegemonic crisis in the years following the invasion of Iraq. Robert Kagan argued that the United States, for the first time since World War Two, had suffered a crisis of international legitimacy.[18] Some explanations were provided. Joshua Muravchik, for example, argued that anti-Americanism was on the rise because the U.S. state had disarmed the ideological weapons it used to fight the Cold War: "U.S.I[nformation].A[gency]. funding was slashed repeatedly as conservative isolationists and budget hawks teamed up with liberal relativists averse to American propaganda."[19] For Muravchik, a reloading of the U.S. empire's propaganda apparatuses was needed to win back international consent to America's world leadership: "We must carry out a campaign of explanation aimed at Europe and the rest of the world about our view of the uses of American power."[20]

ENTER THE DISCOURSE OF AMERICAN SOFT POWER

On this political and historical terrain, the discourse of U.S. cultural imperialism shifts political hands from left to right, the militarism of the neoconservative-inspired Bush administration results in a crisis for U.S. imperial hegemony, and this hegemonic crisis seeks an imaginary resolution in the form of new weapons of ideological suasion. On this terrain, one might suppose that the neoconservatives, given their Wilsonian faith in the supremacy of the American way of life, would make more explicit arguments for U.S. cultural imperialism – the instrumental use of America's unrivalled communicational and cultural resources to strengthen and fulfil U.S. foreign policy objectives. And one might presume that left-leaning scholars, given their radical critiques of the various dimensions of U.S. imperialism, would, following older attacks on U.S. cultural imperialism, attempt to account critically for the ways by which the U.S. empire's propaganda apparatuses have been reloaded.

Despite the abundance of affirmative and critical discourses on U.S. imperialism at the present time, affirmative and critical discourses of U.S. cultural imperialism have not reappeared per se. Yet, since 2001, a number of neoliberal intellectuals have made arguments that praise America's communicational and cultural dominance. Joseph F. Nye's *Soft Power: The Means to Success in World Politics*,[21] Leigh Armistead's *Information Operations: Warfare and the Hard Reality of Soft Power*,[22] and Mathew Fraser's *Weapons of Mass Distraction: Soft Power and American Empire*[23] are exemplary. These authors are responsible for a new discourse called American soft power, which, as this chapter will reveal, is an apologia for U.S. cultural imperialism.

Apologia is usually defined in three ways: first, as words of regret for an offence; second, as a systematic defence of a doctrine or explanation of the truth or justice of something; and third, as a poor substitute.[24] Nye, Armistead, and Fraser are apologists in the second and third usages. The discourse of American soft power advocates the use of government communication agencies and corporate media industries to re-establish and extend America's global hegemony through the export of American cultural values. Each author appeals to dubious moral, universalist, and contextual criteria to rationalize the process and effects of American soft power. The discourse of soft power also acts as an impoverished neoliberal substitute for the critical discourse of U.S. cultural imperialism. By advocating what the theory of U.S. cultural imperialism once criticized in the name of left and socialist political alternatives, the discourse of American soft power acts as an imaginary resolution to the U.S. empire's crisis of legitimacy.

JOSEPH NYE: AMERICAN SOFT POWER AS AMERICAN WORLD HEGEMONY

Joseph Nye was once Deputy Under Secretary of State in the Carter administration and more recently, worked as an Assistant Secretary of Defense for the Clinton administration. For the past fifteen years, Nye has challenged arguments that U.S. power was in decline. Nye has asserted that America, despite the new realities of globalization, continues to be the world's superpower. Dean of Harvard University's Kennedy School of Government, Nye no longer participates as frequently in official state politics. But from the margins, in magazines, journals, and policy-consulting networks, Nye has consistently encouraged the use of soft power as a means of sustaining America's superpower position. Nye's most recent text, *Soft Power: The Means to Success in World Politics*, is the most detailed discussion of and political argument for American soft power.

Nye describes soft power in three interrelated ways. First, Nye construes soft power as America's national identity, the aggregate of America's particular political, social, economic, and cultural values: soft power "arises from the attractiveness of a country's culture, political ideals, and policies";[25] soft power represents America's "attractive personality, culture, political values and institutions, and policies";[26] "soft power grows out of our [America's] culture, out of our [America's] domestic values and policies, and out of our [America's] foreign policy."[27] American national identity, as constructed by Nye, includes freedom, democracy, human rights, individual opportunity, wealth, and free trade.[28]

Second, Nye describes soft power as the noncoercive means through which the U.S. state struggles to organize the consent of non-American states, organizations, and populations to the values associated with American national identity (soft power in the first instance). Soft power "is the ability [of the American state] to get what it want[s] through attraction rather than coercion or payments,"[29] "co-opts people rather than coerces,"[30] and has "the ability to attract."[31] The U.S. state's central instruments of soft power are government communication and cultural agencies and corporate media industries. Government soft power apparatuses include: the State Department's Office of Public Diplomacy, the radio station Voice of America, the universities, the military (including psychological warfare operations), and the Central Intelligence Agency (C.I.A.). Corporate industries of American soft power include: Hollywood and television, news media, nongovernmental organizations (N.G.O.'s), U.S. corporations and their commodities, and the art market.

In Nye's third description, soft power refers to something akin to U.S. ideological dominance or global hegemony. Soft power describes the extent to which America is perceived as a morally legitimate global leader by non-American states, organizations, and populations: "The soft power of a country rests primarily on three resources: its culture (in places where it is attractive to others), its political values (when it lives up to them at home and abroad), and its domestic and foreign policies (when they are seen as legitimate and having moral authority)."[32] Here, soft power (as consent to America's morally legitimate global leadership) appears as the desired effect or outcome of soft power in the second sense: the U.S. state's strategies and means of ideological suasion, its struggle on the terrain of communication and media culture to manufacture and organize international consent to the values of America's national identity.

Nye rationalizes American soft power by investing it with two moral functions. American soft power's first moral obligation is to rid the world of the evils of terrorist networks,[33] and thus is aligned with the Bush administration's national and global security imperatives. Soft power's second moral duty is to help the Middle East to modernize more efficiently,[34] and thus bestows America with a new white man's burden, a civilizing mission. Nye's political solution to the apparent problem of Middle Eastern anti-modernity is soft power, which must educate people there about the just and benevolent intentions of America. Nye recommends that the public diplomacy missionaries of American soft power work with Al Jazeera and Al Arabiya to respond to what he feels is distorted coverage of U.S. intervention, explain U.S. foreign policies more effectively, and "develop a long term strategy of cultural and educational exchanges that develop a richer and more open civil society in Middle Eastern countries."[35] Like the colonialist intelligentsia of the British Empire that rationalized cultural imperialism as part of a civilizing mission to bring a backward Other into modernity, Nye imagines America and American soft power as bringing enlightenment to the Middle East.

The process and effect to which Nye's soft power discourse refers resembles the process and effect once described by the critical discourse of U.S. cultural imperialism. Government communication apparatuses and corporate media globally export and legitimize American values to international audiences. The ideal effect of this process is the organization of international consent to American values, the establishment of America's moral legitimacy as a global superpower, and the realization of U.S. foreign policy objectives (which entails the remaking of different social formations in America's image). However, by denying the existence of an American empire and universalizing American multiculturalism as reflective of an emergent global culture, Nye attempts to differentiate his soft power discourse from the discourse of U.S. cultural imperialism.

"The United States," argues Nye, "is certainly not an empire in the way we think of European overseas empires of the nineteenth and twentieth centuries because the core feature of such imperialism was direct political control."[36] Nye prefers congenial terms such as American primacy, American leadership, and American superpower to the menacing notion of American empire. But though Nye does not like the idea of American empire, he does not seem to have a problem with America's unrivalled global dominance: "the American military has a global reach with bases around the world," "the American economy is the largest in the world,"[37] "nearly half of the top 500 global companies are American,"[38] and "The United States may be more powerful than any other polity since the Roman Empire."[39]

By denying the existence of an American empire, Nye erodes the conceptual foundations of U.S. cultural imperialism and attempts to escape the critical gaze of those that might align him with the neoconservatives.

Yet, Nye succinctly outlines America's extraordinary global cultural dominance: American "English is a lingua franca like Latin";[40] America is "the world's number one exporter of films and television programs";[41] "America publishes more books than any other country";[42] America "has twice as many music sales as next-rated Japan";[43] America "publishes nearly four times as many scientific and journal articles as the next runner-up Japan";[44] and America houses 28 percent of the "1.6 million students enrolled in universities outside their own countries."[45]

Empirical evidence such as this clearly illustrates the global power and reach of the American cultural industry. But U.S. cultural dominance should not be confused with a belligerent U.S. cultural imperialism that threatens to Americanize or destroy local cultures. Why? Nye, like so many U.S. modernization thinkers that judge world-historic progress, development, and reality according to American definitions, ideals, and standards, implies that America possesses an exceptional and universal culture that already reflects the diversity of the globe. "When a country's culture includes universal values and policies and interests that others share," argues Nye, "it increases the probability of obtaining its desired outcomes because of the relationships of attraction and duty that it creates. . . . The United States benefits from a universalistic culture."[46] "America," exclaims Nye, "has always been a land of immigration and its culture and multi-ethnic society reflect many different parts of the world. America has borrowed freely from a variety of traditions and immigration keeps it open to the rest of the world."[47]

Nye's universalization of American multicultural society is ideologically useful: it pre-emptively neutralizes arguments for national or regional cultural sovereignty (often made by critics of U.S. cultural imperialism) and undermines the principle of cultural difference by taking American multiculturalism to be the original template of an emerging world culture. Nye feels that American multicultural society includes, absorbs, and presently stands for everything, everyone, and everywhere else. Global culture is reflected by American multicultural society and American multicultural society already reflects global culture. Following Nye's universalizing logic (the world was, is, and is becoming American, so why bother to change it?), the idea of U.S. cultural imperialism and its potentially deleterious effects (the denial or erasure of non-American cultures) is untenable.

Nye's denial of American empire and his universalization of American multicultural society help him to distinguish his slogan of American soft power from the critical discourse of U.S. cultural imperialism. Through the discourse of American soft power, Nye rationalizes America's global superpower status and the U.S. state's global promotion and extension of American cultural values while attempting to distinguish his politics and foreign policy prescriptions from the Bush administration's neo-conservatives. By the conclusion of Nye's text, the line between Nye and neocons begins to blur:

> We have been more successful in the domain of hard power, where we have invested more, trained more, and have a clearer idea of what we are doing. We have been less successful in the areas of soft power, where our public diplomacy has been woefully inadequate and our neglect of allies and institutions has created a sense of illegitimacy that has squandered our attractiveness. . . . America's success will depend upon our developing a better balance of hard and soft power in our foreign policy.[48]

This statement reveals the *realpolitik* that, throughout Nye's text, is diluted by multilateralist and diplomatic posturing. Nye, like so many neoliberal Democrats who distinguish their foreign policy tactics and goals from the explicit power projections of the neoconservatives with glossy diplomatic phrases such as "soft power" and "American leadership," does not do a good job of it at the end of his text. Nye supports America's global rule and issues a way to strengthen the imperial state's hegemonic goal of balancing strategies of coercion with strategies of ideological suasion (or cultural imperialism).

LEIGH ARMISTEAD: AMERICAN SOFT POWER AS AMERICAN INFORMATION OPERATIONS

Imperial powers have used propaganda (the deliberate effort to persuade people to think and behave in a specific way) and a class of propagandists (people that conduct propaganda campaigns) to achieve strategic goals.[49] Leigh Armistead was a former instructor of information warfare at the Joint Forces Staff College. He thus worked as a military propagandist for the U.S. empire. Currently, Armistead is a doctoral candidate at Edith Cowan University, Perth, Australia, writing a dissertation on U.S. information operations as American soft power. This is also the subject of an instruction manual that he recently edited entitled *Information Opera-tions: The Hard Reality of Soft Power.*

Armistead's text was originally conceived to educate the U.S. empire's next generation of military propagandists.[50] It was also conceived to coordinate the conduct of the short-lived Office of Strategic Influence, a Pentagon agency initially intended to produce and globally disseminate black propaganda (official lies) to counter critical accounts of America in foreign news organizations. Although widespread public criticism resulted in the Office of Strategic Influence's official dismantling (or perhaps, its renaming as another office that has yet to be disclosed to the public), which invalidated *Information Operations'* raison d'être,[51] this text describes how the U.S. military conceptualizes and rationalizes American soft power, the military communication agencies that are responsible for waging soft power warfare against non-American popu-lations, and the strategies and tactics of American soft power warfare in the terror-war context.

Armistead defines soft power as "the ability of A to get B to do something B would not otherwise do."[52] For Armistead, soft power (or strategic information operations) is the most effective instrument of international politics.[53] The emergence of the global information infra-structure, time-and-space compressive communications technology, and digitized media has made information operations a weapon in the arsenal of the U.S. state.

The origin of the concept of information operations resides in two recently declassified U.S. military documents. *Joint Vision 2010*[54] pub-lished in 1996, and *Joint Vision 2020*,[55] published in 2000, describe information operations as the total actions employed by the U.S. state to affect an adversary's information and information systems while defending and enhancing its own information and information systems. The stated goal of information operations is to achieve full spectrum dominance over the deterritorialized and territorial battle-space of the global information infrastructure. Armistead agrees: "the global infor-mation environment has become a battle-space in which the technology of the information age . . . is used to deliver critical and influential content in order to shape perceptions, influence opinions, and control behaviour."[56] The purpose and ideal effect of the U.S. control of global perceptions, opinions, and behaviour is to win global "information superiority," which is defined as the U.S. state's ability to "collect, shape, process, and disseminate an uninterrupted flow of information while exploiting or destroying an adversary's ability to do the same."[57]

Information operations are thus conceived as an ideological instrument of American foreign policy. "Informational capability," contends Armistead, "more than any other component of power, is truly crucial to effective [American] foreign policy in this new era";[58] "information is rapidly assuming a place of primacy in the conduction of [American] foreign policy . . . and it must be understood for what it truly is: a weapon."[59] Armistead believes that the sooner the U.S. state develops information weapons to control and manipulate the flow of information (as military intelligence, propaganda, electronic wavelengths, and computer data streams) the more successful it will be in winning future international struggles and achieving global information superiority.

Armistead provides a detailed overview of the U.S. government agencies, offices, and councils that can play a role in the American state's offensive and defensive information operations. In addition to recommending better intra-agency and government coordination of information operations, Armistead outlines a number of defensive and offensive informational operations strategies. Defensive information operations involve intelligence gathering, counter-intelligence, and surveillance, so that the American state can know, monitor, and debilitate the actions and informational strategies of its adversaries.[60] Offensive information operations are more complicated, and involve five strategies.

Armistead recommends a computer network attack (C.N.A.) as the first offensive information strategy. C.N.A. is "any information strategy that disrupts, denies, degrades, or destroys information that is resident in the computer networks of an adversary, or the computers and networks themselves."[61] After addressing how "space plays an integral role in all aspects of [American] military operations,"[62] Armistead discusses the second strategy of offensive information operations: the deepened militarization of space by the U.S. state and the continued commodification of space by U.S.-based transnational media, surveillance, and technology corporations. The goal of this project is to "develop a better strategy for handling the availability of space technology overseas while maintaining the nation's domination in space."[63] The third offensive information strategy proposed by Armistead is electronic warfare, or, the U.S. state's direction or use of electromagnetic energy to control or attack the electromagnetic field of an adversarial entity.[64]

The fourth strategy of offensive information operations discussed by Armistead is "international perception management," or what is officially referred to as international public information (I.P.I.). I.P.I. includes a combination of public affairs and public diplomacy efforts coordinated by the U.S. State Department. I.P.I. seeks to educate foreign populations about American culture, persuade non-American audiences to identify their interests with U.S. foreign policy, and counteract international media coverage that is critical of America. Armistead discusses international military information (I.M.I.) as the final strategy of information operations. I.M.I., argues Armistead, "is a useful acronym for psychological operations (PSYOPS) or perception management."[65] I.M.I. is used by the U.S. military "to shape the perceptions of people, especially the adversary's minds."[66] For Armistead, these five information operations or military soft power strategies complement or provide an alternative to direct kinetic assaults and military coercion.

Armistead's rationalization of American soft power as military information operations is not mediated by the universalizing claims of American exceptionalism. Armistead uncritically outlines a doctrine to guide the conduct of American informational warfare. The instrumental use of communication technology and information by a government to shape perceptions, influence opinions, and control behaviour is not the stuff of 1970s science-fiction paperbacks or conspiracy theory films, but the lesson of Armistead's pedagogy of propaganda. Armistead does not appeal to universal criteria to rationalize American soft power. American soft power is construed as a necessary response to America's national and international security crisis in the post-9/11 context.

In response to America's post-9/11 crisis of national security, Armistead argues that the U.S. state must counteract the information strategies of "cyber-terrorists, rogue states, foreign militias, and the enemies within America's borders as well as to showcase the opportunities available from a properly orchestrated information campaign."[67] The U.S. state must "develop a comprehensive national Information Operations strategy for the global war on terrorism and continue its efforts to develop an effective strategic communications policy that clearly states U.S. actions and clearly conveys U.S. intentions to friends and enemies alike."[68] All "components of national power,"[69] exclaims Armistead, "should now be integrated into a satisfactorily planned, designed, and executed soft power information strategy."[70] Hence, Armistead appeals to the context of America's post-9/11 national security crisis and the war on global terrorism to rationalize American soft power.

Through his rationalization of American soft power (as military information operations), Armistead contradicts America's purported principles of a free, pluralistic, and democratic commercial media system. The ideal of a free-market media system that is not subject to state regulation, under partisan political control, or susceptible to propagandistic intervention by the military is laid to waste with Armistead's recommendations. Dismissing the erosion of American civil liberties and advocating the military recruitment of the commercial media for government propaganda purposes, Armistead worries:

> The openness and freedom that make life in America so precious to its citizens also make it vulnerable to informational warfare by its adversaries. . . . The very laws that protect our civil liberties make it possible for our adversaries to operate in relative obscurity, right under our noses. . . . [T]here is now serious debate about curbing civil liberties in exchange for security. . . . Though, to an extent, this sense of anxiety has settled down with the American populace, still the nation has obviously forgotten about the necessity for cooperation between military and media during national emergencies, a practice that was so common during World War II. It can be easy to blame the news media's lack of discretion today, and we as a nation have to do better.[71]

"Doing better" appears to be an acceptance of military and state propaganda as a necessary function of U.S. national security. Forget about the free-market ideology espoused by the proponents of the U.S. commercial media system, which used the threat of big government to demonize all public struggles for media reform and regulation. "In contemporary information operations," argues Armistead, "the full integration across government agencies with private industry must occur."[72] This "means horizontal as well as vertical integration and cooperation, and includes not only United States Government Agencies and departments, but also non-government units and private industry as well";[73] information operations "must also be led from the top-down, with full White House and National Security Council leadership to ensure full inter-agency participation."[74]

Armistead's desire to temper the supposed freedom of the American commercial press with a totalitarian propaganda structure has dire implications for non-American news media as well. Qatar-based Al Jazeera, perhaps the only broadcasting network in the region that exemplifies the pluralistic and open ideals of the U.S. commercial media, is, in Armistead's mind, "a market competitor for U.S. psychological operations and public affairs broadcasting in the Middle East."[75] Al Jazeera's critical coverage of the U.S. occupation of Iraq and critical commentary on U.S. foreign policy is a problem for Armistead. As if to make Al Jazeera the next target of American information operations, Armistead states, "the United States Government's response to Al Jazeera thus far has been rather clumsy. The government has yet to display a coordinated communications strategy to deal with Al Jazeera and similar Middle Eastern media outlets. Until this happens, the United States will continue to lose ground in global media confrontations."[76]

Following Armistead's recommendations, a C.N.A. on Al Jazeera's information database or a well-crafted psychological operations campaign to indoctrinate its journalists with pro-U.S. values might be an adequate strategy for dealing with this pesky competitor. Armistead's perception of Al Jazeera (with its U.S.-style commercialism and purported commitment to a balanced reportage of events) as a threat to U.S. foreign policy in the Middle East contradicts America's purported goals: if the point is to spread liberal capitalist democracy and its associated institutions, then why must the media that looks most like America's be dealt with so sternly? Global media market openness, a diversity of perspectives, and objective reporting is allowed to flourish, but only when openness, diversity, and objective news media respect the worldview of Washington. For unapologetic military strategists like Armistead, the soft power of the U.S. state may encourage freedom of the press at home and abroad, but only when liberated media transmit the cultural codes of imperial America.

MATTHEW FRASER: AMERICAN SOFT POWER AS THE GLOBAL AMERICAN CULTURAL INDUSTRY

Most empires rule by collaborating with the local elite of their subject territories, which help the empire to foster and manage more effectively the political, economic, and cultural conditions that are amenable to its dominance. The local elite aligns itself with the ruling-class interests of the imperial power and usually reaps significant economic and cultural benefits by doing so.

Mathew Fraser, former editor-in-chief at Canada's right-leaning newspaper, the *National Post*, is, like local imperial elites of the past, a sympathetic ally and proponent of the U.S. empire. In his most recent publication, *Weapons of Mass Distraction: Soft Power and American Empire*, Fraser lends his rhetorical skills to the interests and worldview of the Bush administration by historicizing and advocating for American soft power.

Fraser appropriates Nye's definition of soft power as "the ability to achieve desired outcomes in international affairs through attraction rather than coercion."[77] Like Nye, Fraser asserts that though American hard power (or military and economic coercion) should be used by the state when necessary, "American leadership in the world must [also] depend on the assertion of soft power – namely, the global appeal of American lifestyles, culture, forms of distraction, norms, and values."[78] But while Nye discusses government and corporate soft power, Fraser focuses solely on the American cultural industry and its commodities as America's core soft power instrument and resource. Indeed, "American soft power – movies, pop music, television, fast food, fashions, theme parks – spreads, validates, and reinforces common [American] norms, values, beliefs, and lifestyles."[79]

By elevating "Hollywood, Disneyland, C.N.N., M.T.V., Madonna, Big Macs, and Coca-Cola to a higher status in the complex dynamics of global geopolitics,"[80] Fraser's text seeks to historicize and illustrate "*the instrumental role of American pop culture in US foreign policy*".[81] Fraser's hypothesis is that the American cultural industry and its commodities are functional to the U.S. empire's political-economic dominance. They "spread America's underlying [cultural] values and its commitment to free markets and liberal democracy"[82] and legitimize these American neoliberal values to non-American others. "Make no mistake," exclaims Fraser, "America's global domination is based mainly on the superiority of U.S. hard power. But the influence, prestige, and legitimacy of the emerging American Empire will depend on the effectiveness of its soft power."[83]

Fraser substantiates his thesis about the ideological and economic functionality of American soft power by providing a historical overview of how the American cultural industries (Hollywood and television, popular music, Coca-Cola, and McDonald's) and their commodity-output (films and television shows, popular music and concerts, beverages and burgers) secured America's rise to global dominance throughout the twentieth century. "Hollywood," argues Fraser, "has been a powerful instrument of U.S. foreign policy from the birth of the motion picture,"[84] and presently "Hollywood's historical alliance with Washington is stronger than ever,"[85] along with its "commitment to a core set of [American] values and beliefs: individualism, capitalism, liberalism, and democracy."[86]

During the Cold War, the American music industry was recruited as an instrument of U.S. foreign policy, with jazz icons such as Dizzie Gillespie and pop rock being used by the United States Information Agency to sonically globalize American values; today, American-Anglo pop continues to be the engine of the global music industry.[87] The Coca-Cola Corporation and its sugar-liquid, along with the McDonald's Corporation and its junk food, also acted as cultural instruments of U.S. foreign policy. The products and experiences packaged by the Coca-Cola Corporation (which worked as a mini-state department for Jimmy Carter) and by the McDonald's Corporation (with its productive and consumptive cult of efficiency, calculability, and predictability) appealed to wealthy foreigners and provided them with another way to distinguish their cultural identities from the poor. And today, "McDonald's and Coke are interchangeable with America itself."[88]

Fraser is convinced that the globalization of the American cultural industry and the commodity export of American values have undoubtedly made the world a much better and safer place. In the conclusion to his text, he asks: "[D]o things really go better with Coca-Cola? Would the world be a better place if Disneyland theme parks were constructed in Baghdad and Damascus? Would global stability be less precarious if Big Macs were sold with a smile in Pyonygang and Tehran?"[89] The answer is predictable:

> Supported by historical analysis presented in the preceding chapters, *we persist in the affirmation that American soft power (movies, television, pop music, fast food) promotes values and beliefs that, while contentious, are ultimately good for the world.* American entertainment – Hollywood, Disneyland, C.N.N., M.T.V., and Madonna – convey values that have made America great, such as

an abiding belief in democracy, free enterprise, and individual liberties. What's more, much of the world's population has embraced America as a model society that has championed these values.[90]

Fraser's assertion rationalizes American soft power by appealing to a moral justification that reproduces a neoconservative faith in America's moral mission to spread America's exceptional values. Following Fraser's argument, American culture is simply the best, and because American culture is the best, it should be universalized. Fraser's tautological rationalization of the cultural Americanization of the world as an essentially good thing, and his belief that America provides the cultural model that the rest of the world should and could follow, is morally repugnant, unsympathetic to non-American paths to cultural and economic development, and biased to principles of the U.S. empire's neoliberal ideology.

First, America, which fights the most wars, overconsumes world resources more than any other country, and requires the underdevelopment of other nations to sustain its growth, is not a sustainable model for global cultural development. Fraser's argument that the rest of the world could one day be just like American culture, and that America could allow this to happen, is naïve. Second, Fraser ridicules all paths to global development that provide an alternative to America's neoliberal prescriptions for culture. Struggles for national cultural sovereignty and the decolonization of culture undertaken by many non-Americans in postcolonial countries through the late twentieth century are reduced to the economic opportunism of bloated union bureaucracies and the political interests of corrupt party elites. Multilateral approaches to global communicational and cultural development are also unacceptable. The cultural aspirations of the Non-Aligned Movement in the 1970s at U.N.E.S.C.O. are reduced to irrational anti-Americanism and Marxist diatribe. In sum, Fraser reductively dismisses alternative paths to global cultural development that fail to abide by the principles of his neoliberal ideology.

But Fraser's praise for the universalization of American culture does not stop here. He advocates the aggressive use of soft power to assimilate cultures that are hostile to American and Western values.[91] American soft power must be strategically deployed to pre-empt the end of Western civilization, save the world from the possibility of global anarchy, and defend the U.S. empire and global capitalism from attacks by terrorists.[92] The final paragraph of Fraser's text typifies the America-centrism that guides his moralistic rationalization of American soft power: "America's weapons of mass distraction are not only necessary for global stability, but also *should be built up and deployed more assertively* throughout the world. The world needs more M.T.V., McDonald's, Microsoft, Madonna, and Mickey Mouse. Yes, things really do go better with Coke."[93]

Let us review Fraser's argument. America is an empire, a "uni-polar superpower with no likely rival in the foreseeable future."[94] Although American empire rests on military and economic power, American empire is also an "essentially cultural construction"[95] that represents an American way of life, a set of ideological values, and a system of belief (rugged individualism, laissez-faire free-market capitalism, competition, consumerism, "democracy," and so on). American soft power (a code word for America's global cultural industry and its commodities) transmits and legitimizes – though not without contradiction – American cultural values to non-American populations.[96] By globally popularizing American cultural values, soft power, in turn, assists the foreign policy imperatives of the U.S. imperial state. Soft power establishes economic and ideological conditions that correspond with and strengthen the political interests of the American nation-state and the economic interests of America's internationalizing capitalist classes.[97] In sum, American soft power has historically "led to the emergence of an American Empire."[98] And at present, American soft power is an instrument of a U.S. foreign policy that seeks the "extension and mainte-nance of American imperial power."[99]

As we see, there is nothing conceptually original in Fraser's discourse on American soft power; it simply regurgitates and then affirms the processes and effects that Marxist critics of U.S. cultural imperialism have attempted to understand and challenge for the past thirty years. Paradoxically, though Fraser goes to great lengths to illustrate and celebrate the economic and ideological instrumentality of America's global cultural industry to American imperial domination, he simulta-neously attempts to deny the reality of U.S. cultural imperialism by debunking the claims made by its original Marxist authors.

Fraser argues that Marxist critics of U.S. cultural imperialism "believe, falsely, that merely because America exports massive amounts of tele-vision programs, the automatic result is cultural homogenization. The observable reality, however, is manifestly different."[100] Fraser contends that the manifestly different observable reality that Marxian discourses of U.S. cultural imperialism apparently mystify is, for the most part, rooted in the unpredictable ways by which global consumers may interpret and use U.S. media. "The term cultural imperialism as it pertains to television," argues Fraser, "fails on a number of levels":

> Cultural imperialism theory assumes that television audiences are passive receptors of foreign television messages. But as numerous studies have demonstrated, television viewers actually tend to be active negotiators of meaning when they watch foreign television programs. . . . To be sure, American commercial domination in the global television market is indisputable. But this is precisely the trap into which cultural imperialism proponents have fallen: they mistakenly equate commercial success with cultural domination. Yet there is no solid evidence about allegedly negative effects of American television exports.[101]

Any reader of Marxist discourses of cultural imperialism will note that Fraser's clichéd criticism debunks a straw man. Like so many postmodern cultural ethnographers who highlight how non-American consumers actively interpret American television programmes within their local cultural contexts, Fraser punches holes through Marxian discourses of U.S. cultural imperialism by scolding their authors for failing to substantiate their theoretical claims about the deleterious effects of this cultural imperialism with solid evidence.

Yet in the same chapter, Fraser contradicts his delegitimization of his Marxist straw man by presenting solid evidence to illustrate the culturally homogenizing and potentially negative effects of American television exports on non-American cultural audiences:

> In Fiji, female plumpness was traditionally a sign of beauty: "You've gained weight" was a flattering compliment to a Fijian. But after teenaged Fijian girls began watching American television soap operas, constant exposure to images of attractive, blonde, rich – and thin – female characters introduced new canons of beauty on the tropical island. Following American television's invasion of Fiji, local health officials began observing troubling levels of bulimia and low self-esteem among young women.[102]

Thus, when the globalization of American commodity culture is labelled by critical Marxists as U.S. cultural imperialism, Fraser attempts to debunk and scrutinize their assertions: non-Americans aren't being persuaded, the world isn't being culturally Americanized, and American commodity culture is ineffective as an instrument of American foreign policy. But when the globalization of American commodity culture is labeled by Fraser as American soft power, this process serves the interests of American empire very well: non-Americans are beginning to desire and identify themselves with American cultural values, the world is becoming a global American empire, and American commodity culture is, and has been, an effective instrument of U.S. foreign policy.

In sum, Fraser affirms the functionality of American commodity culture to American empire (when this process and its effects are described as American soft power) and denies the functionality of American commodity culture to American empire (when this process and its effects are described critically as U.S. cultural imperialism). He happily accepts the existence and the good effects of American soft power while paradoxically denying the existence and the bad effects of U.S. cultural imperialism. This double standard in Fraser's rhetoric is revealed in the following slippage which illustrates a semantic drift of U.S. cultural imperialism into American soft power and the contradictory essence of Fraser's apologia for American empire: "The attraction of American culture has been analyzed and debated for many decades. Many have been highly critical of the effect of so-called American cultural imperialism. . . . Hostility towards American soft power is frequently a negative symptom of its effectiveness."[103]

AMERICAN SOFT POWER, OR, AMERICAN CULTURAL IMPERIALISM

Writing from prison, Antonio Gramsci considered the relation between intellectuals and their concepts and politics and political struggles.[104] Organic intellectuals fought for and attempted to represent the struggles and experiences of oppressed groups while bourgeois intellectuals worked on behalf of and represented the struggles and world-view of dominant groups. Intellectuals, organic or bourgeois, articulated the ideological terrain on which struggles for political hegemony between social groups were organized.

With the discourse of American soft power, bourgeois intellectuals like Nye, Armistead, and Fraser represent the beliefs, values, and ideas that are functional or intrinsic to U.S. imperial hegemony. Their discourse on soft power defends and advocates the instrumentality of government communication apparatuses and corporate media to U.S. foreign policy. Soft power serves U.S. foreign policy interests, which Nye, Armistead, and Fraser construe as universally applicable, morally right- eous, and contextually necessary. The ideal effect of soft power is the extension of U.S. imperial hegemony, the universalization of American culture, and the establishment of infrastructures and cultural ideologies that are amenable to a U.S.-led global capitalist system. Thus, the bourgeois discourse of American soft power normalizes the processes that were once criticized by organic Marxist intellectuals as cultural imperialism.

As much as the discourse on soft power can be understood as an intel- lectual contribution to U.S. imperial hegemony, it should also be read as an imaginary political solution to the crisis and contradictions of U.S. imperial hegemony at the present time. The very historical existence of the discourse of American soft power, which seeks to redress the violent excesses of neoconservative power politics with better propaganda, which seeks resolve the global failure of neoliberalism with more ideological fixes, and which seeks to remedy American conceit with a contemporary dosage of public diplomacy, is a reminder that U.S. imperial hegemony is not complete. This symptom, which points to and attempts to resolve the cultural contradictions of the U.S. empire today, gives the world's organic media alliances and networks good reason to challenge American soft power as U.S. cultural imperialism.

NOTES

1. A. Dorfman and A. Mattelart, *How to Read Donald Duck: Imperialist Ideology in the Disney Comic* (New York: International General Editions, 1971).

2. H. Schiller, *Communication and Cultural Domination* (Armonk, NY: M. E. Sharpe, 1976), p. 9.

3. Ibid., p. 30.

4. J. Tomlinson, *Cultural Imperialism* (Baltimore, Md.: The Johns Hopkins University Press, 1991), p. 79.

5. Ibid., p. 2.

6. B. Wattenberg, *The First Universal Nation: Leading Indicators and Ideas about the Surge of America in the 1990s* (New York: Free Press, 1991), p. 20.

7. I. Kristol, "The Emerging American Imperium," *Wall Street Journal*, 18 August 1997, p. 1.

8. Ibid., p. 2.

9. D. Rothkop, "In Praise of Cultural Imperialism?," *Foreign Policy*, 22 June 1997, p. 1.

10. Ibid., p. 5.

11. P. Bourdieu and L. Wacquant, "On the Cunning of Imperialist Reason," *Theory, Culture and Society*, 16, 1999, p. 41.

12. Dorrian reflects upon the neoconservative's embrace of the imperialist label: "Bill Kristol says that neo-imperialism, neo-conservative, pan Americanist, unipolarist, and neo-reaganite apply equally well to him; Charles Krauthammer coined the term unipolarism and also goes by neo-imperialist; Joshua Muravchik prefers neoconservative or Pax Americanist and is a chief proponent of democratic globalism; Ben Wattenberg calls himself a neo-Manifest Destinarian and unipolarist; Max boot describes himself as a liberal imperialist and also claims neoconservative; Stanley Kurtz prefers liberal imperialist" (G. Dorrian, *Imperial Designs: Neoconservatism and the New Pax Americana* [New York: Routledge, 2004], pp. 5–6).

13. Halper and Clarke state: "neoconservatives focus on the unipolar power of the United States, seeing the use of military forces as the first, not the last option of foreign policy. They repudiate the lessons of Vietnam which they interpret as undermining American will toward the use of force, and embrace the lessons of Munich, interpreted as establishing the virtues of pre-emptive military action" (S. Halper and J. Clarke, *America Alone: The Neo-Conservatives and the Global Order* [Cambridge: Cambridge University Press, 2004], p. 11).

14. Guyatt, scrutinizing the National Security Strategy (N.S.S.) of the United States, states: "its initial overview of America's international strategy offered a two-paragraph summary of twentieth century world history, which amounted to the victory of 'freedom and equality over destructive totalitarian visions.' . . . the N.S.S. suggested that the past hundred years had seen a great struggle between the American system of capitalism and the militant visions of class, nation and race which promised a utopia and delivered misery. The struggle had ended triumphantly with the collapse of the Soviet Union, but America still faced a threat from failing states which remained in denial of this mighty victory. The prefatory letter to the N.S.S., under Bush's own signature, confirmed that the decisive victory for the forces of freedom had left a single sustainable model for national success: freedom, democracy, and free enterprise. . . .

   Elsewhere, the N.S.S. outlined the American right of self-defence, confirming that the United States would take pre-emptive action against terrorists and rogue states. The document pointed out that the United States has long maintained the option of pre-emptive actions to counter a sufficient threat to national security" (N. Guyatt,

Another American Century? The United States and the World Since 9/11 [London: Zed Books, 2003], pp. 246–247).

15. Dorrian argues that the neoconservatives "cheered Bush's unapologetic unilateralism. The early Bush administration disavowed the ABM Treaty, rejected the Kyoto Protocol and the Biological Weapons Convention, abrogated the Land Mine Treaty and the Comprehensive Test Ban Treaty, and denounced the International Criminal Court" (Dorrian, *Imperial Designs*, p. 100).

16. I. Wallerstein, *The Decline of American Power* (New York: The New Press, 2002), p. 26.

17. T. Friedman, "Restoring Our Honour," *New York Times*, 6 May 2004, p. A31.

18. R. Kagan, "A Tougher War for the U.S. is one of Legitimacy," *New York Times*, 24 January 2004, p. A17.

19. J. Muravchik, "America Loses its Voice," *AEI Online*, 9 June 2003, p. 2.

20. Ibid., p. 3.

21. J. Nye, *Soft Power: The Means to Success in World Politics* (New York: Public Affairs, 2004).

22. L. Armistead, *Information Operations: Warfare and the Hard Reality of Soft Power* (Washington, D.C.: Brassey's Inc., 2004).

23. M. Fraser, *Weapons of Mass Distraction: American Empire and Soft Power* (Toronto: Key Porter Books, 2003).

24. W. Avis, P. Dysdale, R. Gregg, V. Neufeldt, and M. Scargill, *Gage Canadian Dictionary* (Toronto: Gage Educational, 1983).

25. Nye, *Soft Power*, p. x.

26. Ibid., p. 6.

27. Ibid., p. 142.

28. Ibid., pp. 55–62.

29. Ibid., p. x.

30. Ibid., p. 5.

31. Ibid., p. 6.

32. Ibid., p. 11.

33. Ibid., p. xiii.

34. Ibid., p. 120.

35. Ibid., p. 122.

36. Ibid., p. 135.

37. Ibid.

38. Ibid., p. 32.

39. Ibid., p. ix.

40. Ibid., 135.

41. Ibid., p. 33.

42. Ibid.

43. Ibid.

44. Ibid.

45. Ibid.

46. Ibid., p. 11.

47. Ibid., p. 41.

48. Ibid., p. 147.

49. See P. M. Taylor, *Munitions of the Mind: A History of Propaganda* (Manchester: Manchester University Press, 2003), for example, on the history of propaganda.

50. Armistead, *Information Operations*, p. 8.

51. Ibid., p. xiii.

52. Ibid., p. 10.

53. Ibid., p. 13.

54. Joint Publication, *Joint Vision 2010* (Washington, D.C.: Government Printing Press, 1996).

55. Joint Publication, *Joint Vision 2020* (Washington, D.C.: Government Printing Press, 2000).

56. Armistead, *Information Operations*, p. xvii.

57. Ibid., p. 19.

58. Ibid., p. 9.

59. Ibid., p. 231.

60. Ibid., p. 59.

61. Ibid., p. 114.

62. Ibid., p. 118.

63. Ibid., p. 122.

64. Ibid., p. 123.

65. Ibid., p. 128.

66. Ibid.

67. Ibid., p. 3.

68. Ibid., p. 161.

69. Ibid., p. 19.

70. Ibid.

71. Ibid., p. 5.

72. Ibid., p. 19.

73. Ibid., p. 42.

74. Ibid., p. 137.

75. Ibid., p. 148.

76. Ibid., p. 155.

77. Fraser, *Weapons of Mass Distraction*, p. 18.

78. Ibid.

79. Ibid., p. 1.

80. Ibid., p. 9.

81. Ibid., italics mine.

82. Ibid., p. 11.

83. Ibid., p. 13.

84. Ibid., p. 35.

85. Ibid., p. 108.

86. Ibid., p. 111.

87. Ibid., p. 219.

88. Ibid., p. 223.

89. Ibid., p. 260.

90. Ibid., italics mine.

91. Ibid., p. 33.

92. Ibid., p. 265.

93. Ibid., p. 266, italics mine.

94. Ibid., p. 262.

95. Ibid.

96. Ibid., pp. 261–262.

97. Ibid., p. 261.

98. Ibid., p. 262.

99. Ibid.

100. Ibid., p. 166.

101. Ibid., pp. 167–168.

102. Ibid., p. 112.

103. Ibid., p. 19.

104. D. Forgacs, *The Antonio Gramsci Reader: Selected Writings 1916–1938* (New York: New York University Press, 2000).

10

U.N. IMPERIALISM:

UNLEASHING ENTREPRENEURSHIP IN THE

DEVELOPING WORLD

Paul Cammack

INTRODUCTION

Over the first five years of the present century, a new imperialist project took shape where one might have least expected it – at the New York headquarters of the United Nations. It was orchestrated around the Millennium Development Goals (M.D.G.'s) adopted by the General Assembly in September 2000, and installed at the heart of the U.N. system with the adoption of Secretary-General Kofi Annan's report, *In Larger Freedom*, at the World Summit convened in September 2005 to review progress towards the Goals after five years.

The Millennium Goals may not have looked at first glance like the new face of imperialism for a new century. They seemed, on the contrary, to promise a new spirit of North–South cooperation aimed at alleviating ills and promoting human welfare across the globe: eradicating extreme poverty and hunger; achieving universal primary education; promoting gender equality and empowering women; reducing child mortality; improving maternal health; combating H.I.V./A.I.D.S., malaria, and other diseases; ensuring environmental sustainability; and developing a global partnership for development. However, they came not as a new start but as the focal point of a project devised and implemented during the 1990s, intended to make capitalism global. Integral to this was the systematic institutional reform pursued by Kofi Annan after he became

U.N. Secretary-General at the beginning of 1997 – one that effected a shift from security through peace-keeping (Annan's previous remit) to security through capitalist hegemony, and succeeded by 2005 in transforming the U.N. into the lead agency for the global dissemination of capitalist values and imperatives.

Although it bears a family resemblance to the imperialism identified by Lenin and others as centred on the export of capital, the new imperialist project differs from it in two respects. First, it is defined not by the export of capital, but by the export of *capitalism*: the social relations of production that define it and institutions devised to promote and sustain them. Second, as the central role of the U.N. suggests, it is led not by states but by international organizations committed to capitalism *as a global project*. The World Bank, in increasingly close partnership with the International Monetary Fund (I.M.F.), laid the basis for it in its reformulation of its mission over the 1990s in its Heavily Indebted Poor Countries (H.I.P.C.) initiative (1996) and its Comprehensive Development Framework and Poverty Reduction Strategy Papers (1999). The E.U., the European Bank for Reconstruction and Development (E.B.R.D.), the Organization for Economic Co-operation and Development (O.E.C.D.) and the World Trade Organization (W.T.O.) have also been significant contributors to the enterprise, which has engaged the advanced countries, in the main, through their development and donor agencies and through multilateral groupings (the G8, the G20) rather than through their executives. It is not a project controlled by one or even a few leading states – its leading architects have generally come from *outside* the United States, and from across the developed and developing world: among them are Gordon Brown (U.K.), Trevor Manuel (South Africa), Paul Martin (Canada), and Ernesto Zedillo (Mexico); and in so far as there has been U.S. involvement, it has come much more from the successive Clinton administrations than from the Republicans under Bush. Furthermore, the leaders of the project, in their efforts to embed and legitimize it, have worked as much through N.G.O.'s and 'civil society' as through governments. Against this general background, the assumption of leadership of the project by the central U.N. organizations in the wake of growing global protests against the I.M.F. and the World Bank, themselves somewhat semi-detached members of the larger U.N. family, represented a significant institutional development, a calculated transfer of authority from institutions whose legitimacy was perceived to be fragile. The reform of the U.N.'s Economic and Social Council over the last decade, leading to the floating at the 2005 World Summit of the proposal for an Economic Security Council, reflects this development.

Advance notice of the new imperialist project was given when Secretary-General Kofi Annan travelled to Davos within a month of his assumption of the post to outline it to the World Economic Forum, and it was spelled out in detail in a report in his name to the Economic and Social Council six months later. Two years of intensive institutional and programmatic reform followed, making it possible for the project to be 'rolled out' with impressive speed after the adoption by the General Assembly of the Millennium Declaration and the M.D.G.'s. Among the key steps in the realization of the project thereafter were, in chronological order, the Brussels Declaration and Programme of Action agreed at the Third U.N. Conference on the Least Developed Countries in May 2001; the adoption by the U.N. General Assembly of the Secretary-General's "Road Map towards the Implementation of the United Nations' Millennium Declaration" of 6 September 2001; and the adoption of the "Monterrey Consensus" in March 2002 at the first International Conference on Financing for Development. The central elements of the project – country "ownership" and the promotion of an "enabling environment for business" – were built in to the conclusions of the September 2002 Johannesberg World Summit on Sustainable Development and the São Paulo Consensus agreed at the June 2004 meeting of the U.N. Conference on Trade and Development (U.N.C.T.A.D.).

In the lead-up to the 2005 World Summit, the publication under the auspices of the U.N. Development Programme (U.N.D.P.) of *Unleashing Entrepreneurship: Making Business Work for the Poor* and *Investing in Development: A Practical Plan to Achieve the Millennium Development Goals* revealed just how unashamedly pro-capitalist the U.N. as an organization had become. The story of their commissioning, publication, and later insertion within the U.N. system provides in microcosm an insight into the manner in which the new imperialist project was orchestrated. *Unleashing Entrepreneurship*, the report of the Commission on the Private Sector and Development established by Annan in July 2003 at the instigation of U.N.D.P. Administrator Mark Malloch Brown, was published in March 2004 with an advisory note that it did not "necessarily reflect the views of the United Nations Development Programme, its Executive Board, or the United Nations Member States." In the run-up to the September 2005 World Summit, however, Kofi Annan issued his own report, "Strengthening the Role of the Private Sector and Entrepreneurship in Financing for Development," in response to Economic and Social Council Resolution 2004/64 of 16 September 2004, which helpfully "requested the Secretary-General to submit a report to the General Assembly on financing for development pertaining to the role of the private sector, taking into consideration the report entitled *Unleashing Entrepreneurship: Making Business Work for the Poor*, to be considered at its fifty-ninth session."[1] Similarly, *Investing in Development* was the product of the U.N. Millennium Project, an "independent advisory body commissioned by the U.N. Secretary-General to propose the best strategies for meeting the Millennium Development Goals." It was set up in July 2002 in close consultation with U.N.D.P. Administrator Mark Malloch Brown, and directed by Jeffrey Sachs, appointed as Special Advisor to the Secretary-General. The report was published in January 2005 (in the U.K., under the imprint of Earthscan), and in March 2005 Annan remitted its photocopied Executive Summary for consideration at the September 2005 World Summit.[2]

All this came about in the context of significant enabling changes in the way the U.N. is organized as an institution. In October 2000 the long-standing Administrative Committee on Coordination (A.C.C.) was converted into the Chief Executives Board for Coordination (C.E.B.), and its various subsidiary bodies were replaced by two High-Level Committees, on Management and Programmes respectively. The High-Level Committee on Programmes, which met for the first time in February 2001, operated from the start as the project board for the new imperialism, as the minutes of its twice-yearly meetings make clear. Since its inception it has brought together representatives of all the major international organizations in order to coordinate their activities around a small number of strategic themes unified around the M.D.G.'s. The most prominent of these have been the creation of a single policy framework which integrates the World Bank's Poverty Reduction Strategy Papers with the U.N.D.P.'s Common Country Assessments and the U.N. Development Assistance Framework (U.N.D.A.F.), the establishment of the U.N. Resident Coordinator at country level as the key link between the U.N. system and the national government, and the promotion of "country ownership" of integrated poverty-reduction strategies revolving around private investment, entrepreneurship, and competition. At the same time, it has taken a leading role in the preparation of key policy documents, most notably the Secretary-General's report to the September 2005 "World Summit" in New York.[3] As a consequence of this closely coordinated activity, the "World Summit" saw the consummation of the parallel processes of institutional reform and the reorientation of the U.N. towards the promotion of capitalism on a global scale, with the M.D.G.'s as ever the focal point: the endorsement of the proposals for reform set out under Annan's name in *In Larger Freedom* set the seal on both the new imperialist project and U.N.'s claims to leadership of it.

The novel form of contemporary imperialism – the promotion of capitalism on a global scale by international organizations – reflects the fact that the phase of monopoly capitalism within which Lenin and others situated their analysis is long behind us. The "neoliberal revolution" of the late 1970s, with its objective of restoring the social efficacy of the law of value, and the phase of "completion of the world market" which culminated in the incorporation of the former Soviet Union and Eastern Europe into the global capitalist system, have combined to propel capitalism into a new age of competition on a global scale. This is the context within which the new imperialist project has emerged at the heart of the U.N., and it embraces rather than resists the logic of competitiveness. Entrepreneurship is to be unleashed everywhere, in developed and developing countries alike, among the rich and among the poor, as poverty reduction requires economic growth which in turn requires private investment, and "[g]overnments and intergovernmental agencies can facilitate private sector development only by fostering properly functioning competitive markets."[4] This chapter sketches the emergence of the project, analyses its content and identifies its characteristic discursive strategies, with extensive direct reference to the official documents in which it is set out. Its central argument is that the M.D.G.'s, far from representing a rejection or attenuation of the "neoliberal revolution" of the late twentieth century, have been envisaged and deployed from the outset as a vehicle for its realization and legitimation on a global scale.

IMPERIALISM IN THE CONTEXT OF GLOBAL CAPITALISM

My argument is not just that this project is imperialist, but that it represents imperialism in the most advanced form currently conceivable. To grasp its imperialist character it is pertinent to recall Lenin's insistence that imperialism emerges as the "development and direct continuation of the fundamental characteristics of capitalism in general,"[5] and to identify at the heart of the project precisely the commitment to the promotion of those "fundamental characteristics of capitalism in general." To capture what makes it new, however, it is necessary to identify the double shift that has taken place since Lenin himself noted the emergence of a new form of imperialism a century ago. Lenin's "new twentieth-century imperialism" displaced its earlier manifestation, which aimed at the export of *goods* to markets in colonized territories, with a single empire in which industrial capital was dominant. In contrast, it featured the export of *capital* to sometimes colonized and sometimes "quasi-colonial" territories by competing empires in which finance capital was dominant. The new imperialism of the twenty-first century features the export of *capitalism* to politically independent states within a comprehensive regulatory framework governed by cooperating international organizations and aimed at imposing the "fundamental characteristics of capitalism in general" across developed and developing states alike.

I have described elsewhere how the World Bank developed systematically through the 1990s the project of turning the world's poor into a proletariat – with headlines that promised the abolition of poverty, but with the bottom line that it was to be "abolished" by producing hundreds of millions of "free workers" available across the world for exploitation at the bargain global wage of $1–2 a day.[6] It is easy to demonstrate that the World Bank's "poverty reduction" strategy was precisely what Marx had described over a century before as "primitive accumulation": the production of a class of individuals with no option but to sell their capacity to work (labour power) in a competitive labour market, and "empowered" to do so by the provision of basic education and primary healthcare in an environment in which the state was charged with the duty of "supporting the market."[7] In increasingly close cooperation with the I.M.F., the World Bank had produced by the turn of the century the intellectual and institutional framework through which the new imperialists would seek to impose their designs on the developing world.[8]

It might have been the case that the sole aim of this project was to renew and reinforce the scope for the export of capital from the advanced capitalist states, or by largely Western multinational and transnational corporations. If so, whatever might be said about the manner in which the "new imperialism" was promoted, its content would not be so new. However, it soon became clear that its goal was more ambitious: to transform the economies, societies, and institutions of developing countries in such a way as to propel them into capitalism, and thereby to create the basis for sustainable indigenous capitalist accumulation across all states. What is more, this was not to be done as an act of benevolence, but *as a matter of necessity*. Of course, this did not exclude the prospect of profit for either finance capital or transnational corporations. What was new was the insistence that a necessary condition for such a prospect was the commitment of the international organizations to the full development of capitalism in the developing world. In terms that hark directly back to the words of the *Manifesto of the Communist Party*, written by Marx and Engels a little over 150 years earlier, their project "compels all nations, on pain of extinction, to adopt the bourgeois mode of production."[9] The "new new imperialism," then, echoes the "old new imperialism" in its interventionism, and its reflection of the fundamental characteristics of capitalism in general; but it is new in its endeavour to install the social relations of capitalist production and thereby the foundations for sustainable capitalist accumulation in the developing countries themselves through a project led not by imperialist states but by institutions oriented to the logic of global capitalism. Its ideology – its representation of itself as benevolent and inclusive, and oriented towards the elimination of poverty – is also new. Again, the vision conjured up in the *Communist Manifesto* points towards the meaning of the proposed transformation. Marx and Engels proclaimed that the bourgeoisies of the industrial nations of the day would compel other nations "to become bourgeois themselves," and thereby create "a world in their own image."[10] In fact, this project goes further. The transformation of the U.N. system and the international organizations into the custodians of the "interests of capital in general" goes hand in hand with and is premised upon the neoliberal revolution through which the advanced capitalist states seek to make capitalism work *in their own countries*: to restore to dominance there the disciplines and social relations of capitalist reproduction and the hegemony of the bourgeoisie. With the so-called "end of the Cold

War" (the reclaiming for capital of spaces for a period beyond its reach, mystifyingly represented as a question of *security*), the call has gone out, from the U.N. of all places, for hegemonic domestic bourgeoisies to be installed everywhere.

The universal project attached to the M.D.G.'s has as its objective, then, the creation in the developing world not only of markets and economies open to penetration, or even of new proletarians exploitable by foreign capital, but also of hegemonic domestic bourgeoisies, capable both of accumulating through capitalist production (in Marxist terms, through the increasing extraction of relative surplus value from "free" workers), and of securing the legitimacy to govern by democratic means. It is these aspects of the project which open the way for such characteristic ideologues of the new imperialism as Jeffrey Sachs, Nicholas Stern, and Joseph Stiglitz to present it as progressive. To gauge the limits of its progressive character, though, it is only necessary to recall the terms in which Lenin reminded Kautsky that capitalism is still capitalism: "the *forms* of the struggle may and do constantly change in accordance with varying, relatively specific and temporary causes, but the *substance* of the struggle, its class *content*, positively *cannot* change while classes exist"; and therefore denounced "that profoundly mistaken idea which only brings grist to the mill of the apologists of imperialism, i.e., that the rule of finance capital *lessens* the unevenness and contradictions inherent in the world economy, whereas in reality it increases them."[11]

The Millennium Declaration and the M.D.G.'s are, then, the public face of a broader project embedded at the heart of a range of global institutions subscribing to a common purpose which can be summarized as the promotion of capitalism and competition on a truly global scale. Its ultimate logic, as capitalism becomes truly global in scope, is that the effort to restore the imperatives of capitalist reproduction to full efficacy in the advanced capitalist countries themselves requires it.

LAUNCHING THE PROJECT: KOFI ANNAN AT THE WORLD ECONOMIC FORUM

Kofi Annan's address to the World Economic Forum in Davos on 1 February 1997 gave advance notice of the new imperialist project that was about to unfold. It committed the institution under his leadership to the promotion of economic and political liberalization and the development of dynamic private sectors as the best strategy for effective peace-keeping across the world. First, he declared, the U.N. was unequivocally supportive of private enterprise: "the programmes, funds and specialized agencies that make up the United Nations family are working with Member States, as never before, to foster policies that encourage further growth of the private sector and the free market."[12] Second, these initiatives reflected three connected "realities of a changing world":

> First, there is the new universal understanding that market forces are essential for sustainable development. Second, the role of the State is changing in most of the developing world, from one that seeks to dominate economic life, to one which creates the conditions through which sustainable development is possible. Third, there is growing and compelling evidence that the poor can solve their own problems if only they are given fair access to financial and business development services.[13]

Third, these changes were to be secured by means of a reinforced partnership between the U.N., governments, and the international corporate community; and fourth, changed circumstances required a new understanding of peace-keeping and security and a new approach to it:

> In the post-cold-war era, peace and security can no longer be defined simply in terms of military might or the balance of terror. The world has changed. Lasting peace requires more than intervention of Blue Helmets on the ground. Effective peace-building demands a broader notion of human security. We cannot be secure amidst starvation. We cannot build peace without alleviating poverty. We cannot build freedom on foundations of injustice. In today's world, the private sector is the dominant engine of growth; the principal creator of value and wealth; the source of the largest financial, technological, and managerial resources. If the private sector does not deliver economic growth and economic opportunity – equitably and sustainably – around the world, then peace will remain fragile and social justice a distant dream.[14]

Here, then, were the cardinal points of the new imperialist project: it proposed capitalism, on a global scale, as the lasting solution to insecurity; it put the private sector at the centre, and identified the state as an active force in support of it; it depicted the poor as agents, in the market, of their own security; and it deployed a legitimizing and mystifying rhetoric, shrouding the explicit class content of the project, which revolved around partnership, equity, security, and justice, and centred on the alleviation of poverty. As noted above, none of this argument was new, nor was the U.N. the only site of its dissemination. Nevertheless, even with the limited hindsight of less than a decade, the capture of the U.N. as the lead agency for taking the project forward can be seen as a fundamental turning point.

Kofi Annan's argument was simple. The explosion in trade and capital flows linking people and markets in a new global economy was welcome, but it was essential that the world's poorest nations should not be marginalized. Hence the need for a new partnership amongst governments, the private sector, and the international community, in which the U.N. could play a key role. Whereas rapidly growing flows of private investment went selectively to just a few countries, U.N. assistance went predominantly to low-income countries, where it could pave the way for private sector development. In an unprecedented redefinition of the role of the U.N., its new Secretary-General then told the corporate leaders gathered at Davos that "[t]he United Nations and the private sector can and must work together to bring 60 per cent of the world's population into the market," and assured them that "[o]ur job is to help create the conditions that make your job successful."[15] His brief summary of U.N. work in pursuit of this ambition announced the Four Point programme of the new imperialist project: U.N. leadership; the reshaping of states in the developing world as agents of global capitalism; the provision of international regimes through which that global capitalism could be governed; and the creation of local bourgeoisies:

> The United Nations has a vital role to play in supporting and preparing the ground for domestic and foreign private investment. Our detailed work in this area has included assistance for public administration reform, for economic restructuring, for privatization programmes and for essential infrastructure, as well as the strengthening of legal and regulatory frameworks. We set the international norms and standards that make progress possible. The United Nations has played its part in creating special economic zones, removing trade barriers, supporting entrepreneurs, and in the development of small and medium-sized enterprises. In all of these areas, we have a proud record.[16]

Having begun by suggesting that the age of security and the balance of power in its most recent manifestation in the Cold War and the "balance of terror" was over, Annan closed with a succinct statement of the new imperialist project: "For both the United Nations system and the private sector, our goal for the twenty-first century is nothing less than the creation of a true global economy, genuinely open to all of the world's peoples."[17] This rhetorical flourish, echoing the vision of the *Communist Manifesto* but at the same time stripping it entirely of its critical insight, registered a crucial shift from security to political economy as the focus of international politics and international relations, and did so in a way that sought to embed it immediately in a new legitimizing framework neatly adapted from the old.

Of course, the delivery of this speech, significant though it was, did not in itself represent the hegemony of the new project. It was as much an attempt, by no means assured of success then or now, to win global corporate capital and the governments of the leading capitalist states away from the pursuit of self-interest narrowly conceived to a broadly inclusive project in which a regulatory and legitimizing role would be played by international organizations in an effort to minimize and manage the contradictions that capitalism inevitably involves. At the same time, the key to the project in world-historical terms, or at least in comparison to the reformist projects with which the U.N. and many of its central agencies had been associated since their inception, was that the objective was now to entrench the logic and the social relations of competitive capitalism on a global scale, rather than to block and resist them. This was a project erected not only upon the collapse of "socialism" in eastern Europe and the former Soviet Union, but also, unmistakably, upon the "triumph of neoliberalism" in the West, and the series of class defeats associated with it. It spelled the conversion of the U.N. from a site of admittedly partial and equivocal opposition to the global sway of capitalism to its leading advocate and architect.

REFORMING THE U.N. SYSTEM

The U.N. system is bewilderingly complex. Connections between its various agencies are multiple, and the sheer volume of activity in which they engage, and the amount of documentation their activity generates, threaten to defy comprehension. The following sketch of organizational reform relevant to the emergence of the new imperialist project is necessarily selective, and subject to correction on the basis of future research. However, the broad thrust of what has been happening since Kofi Annan became Secretary-General is clear. The key bodies of the U.N., and especially those that in the past have been institutional resources for national developmentalism and resistance to global neoliberal reform, have been or are in the process of being subjected to a new logic and a new programme which had its origins in the Bretton Woods institutions, themselves formally part of the U.N. system but relatively autonomous in their operation. The process of reform overseen by Kofi Annan and engineered through the Central Executives Board and its two committees has tied a range of U.N. bodies and initiatives closely to what was initially the World Bank/I.M.F. agenda. After inaugurating an annual high-level meeting (first held in April 1998) between the U.N. Economic and Social Council (ECOSOC), U.N.C.T.A.D., and the Bretton Woods organizations (I.M.F., World Bank), Annan has reformed the central administration of the U.N., reshaped ECOSOC, and coordinated its activities with those of U.N.C.T.A.D. and the five regional commissions; and given the U.N.D.P. under Mark Malloch Brown a central promotional role. This process builds on developments already under way before he became Secretary-General, dating back to the Paris Declaration of the Second U.N. Conference on the Least Developed Countries in 1990. They culminated in General Assembly resolution 50/227, adopted in 1996 prior to his appointment,[18] and the decision of ECOSOC in late 1996 that the Secretary-General should submit to the high-level segment of its substantive session of 1997 a report on the theme of "fostering an enabling environment for development," prepared in collaboration with the Bretton Woods institutions and the W.T.O.

It fell to Annan to present the resulting report to ECOSOC in June 1997 for its consideration. This marked the beginning of increasingly close formal cooperation between ECOSOC, U.N.C.T.A.D., and the Bretton Woods organizations led by the World Bank, and laid out an agenda not merely for global neoliberal macroeconomic reform, but for the active promotion of local capitalist development. The highly orchestrated Spring Meetings of ECOSOC with the Bretton Woods institutions and the W.T.O. that have taken place annually from 1998 onwards have provided a forum for this increasingly close cooperation behind the scenes, principally through the agenda-setting reports made by the Secretary-General to each meeting.

Much of the 1997 report was concerned with the need for international cooperation on policy coherence and new regimes on trade, aid, and debt, strongly endorsing initiatives under way at the I.M.F. and the W.T.O. in particular. Before turning to such issues, however, it spelled out what it termed a "new consensus" regarding the character and objectives of domestic policy in developing countries. It noted that a majority of developing countries now accepted and pursued the macroeconomic and outward-oriented policies required to foster rapid economic growth, including structural adjustment and economic reforms, and that entrepreneurship and the private sector were widely recognized as dynamic factors of growth. This reflected the emergence of "a general consensus on the policies required to foster an enabling environment for development at the national level," and agreement that "these policies are also the ones most conducive to investment (domestic and foreign), capital inflows and successful integration into the world economy through trade."[19]

The central message of this section of the report was that while international cooperation and partnership had a vital role in creating a favourable climate for capital flows, investment, and trade to flourish, *each country had the primary responsibility for its own development.*[20] Central to this was government action, in cooperation with N.G.O.'s and the private sector, in support of entrepreneurship and investment:

Non-governmental actors and, in particular, the private sector are playing an increasingly important and dynamic role in promoting development, with the result that Governments are re-examining and adjusting the extent and scope of public sector involvement in the economic sphere. However, Governments have a definite economic role: they must ensure an appropriate policy environment, encourage entrepreneurship, create favourable conditions for the business sector and for attracting foreign direct investment, provide basic infrastructures and develop human resources.[21]

Four principal recommendations were made to the Council, all uncompromising in their support for the active promotion of capitalist development across the global economy. The first reiterated the need for strengthened economic cooperation. The other three read as follows:

The Council may stress the importance of sound and stable macroeconomic policies for accelerated growth through better integration in the world economy. Equally important is the need for the rule of law, a stable and transparent legal framework and public administration, and policies that promote entrepreneurship, savings and investment. The establishment of realistic exchange and interest rates, reform of the trade and payments system, as well as the liberalization of other domestic prices should continue as they provide an appropriate incentive structure for producers and encourage outward-oriented growth strategies.

The Council may urge that structural reforms aimed at establishing a competitive domestic financial system, privatization and/or restructuring of public enterprises continue to be implemented in order to enhance the efficient allocation of resources and support private sector development; such reforms are also expected to boost domestic savings and investment and thereby contribute to higher economic growth.

The Council may emphasize that the availability and proper maintenance of adequate economic infrastructure, in particular a trained workforce and telecommunications and transportation facilities, affect the pace of integration of countries in the world economy and should be of high priority. High-quality communications are essential for countries that aim to participate in the globalized production structures established by multinational corporations, to respond promptly to rapidly changing market conditions in industrialized countries or to participate in new export markets. The Council may wish to call for innovative policies designed to promote public–private partnerships and opening up the social and infrastructure sectors to private investment to meet the enormous needs in these areas.[22]

By this point in mid-1997, then, the U.N. system was seeking to develop a new project that actively endorsed the promotion of local and global capitalism, and placed the "enabling" state as defined by the World Bank at much the same time at the centre of the project. The authority of the Secretary-General was placed behind the explicit proposal that the U.N. agencies concerned with social and economic issues should become active agents of intervention across the developing world in order to create and sustain the conditions for bourgeois hegemony and capitalist development. At the same time, the report endorsed the new disciplinary regimes being developed by the Bretton Woods institutions, inviting the Council to call on the I.M.F. to work with the World Bank to develop "a more comprehensive international regulatory and supervisory regime" for banking and financial markets and to "encourage the I.M.F. to fully exercise its role of overseeing the international monetary system to ensure its effective operation, inter alia, through symmetric surveillance of the macroeconomic policies of each of its members."[23] It urged U.N.C.T.A.D. to cooperate with the W.T.O. and the other organizations to devise and promote rule-based investment regimes, called for continued concerted action to remove all remaining obstacles to free and open trade, and concluded with a final recommendation that linked trade and competition:

> The Council may wish to note that work is under way in W.T.O. and U.N.C.T.A.D. in the areas of trade, investment and competition, and invite these organizations to cooperate in studying all the implications of the relationship between trade and investment to lay the basis for developing sound and equitable rules in this area. In addition, U.N.C.T.A.D. could be invited to pursue and advance its work on the linkages between trade and competition policies.[24]

Close coordination between the newly oriented ECOSOC and U.N.C.T.A.D. on the one hand, and the I.M.F., World Bank, and W.T.O. on the other, was systematically pursued over the following three years, with a significant link forged in the chain by the recruitment of World Bank Vice-President and Director of External Relations Mark Malloch Brown, as U.N.D.P. Administrator (Chief Executive) in 1999. Brown had worked for the London-based *Economist* as its political correspondent in the 1970s before making his way via the U.N.H.C.R. to the World Bank. There he served as its chief propagandist (Vice-President and Director of External Relations).

Mark Malloch Brown gave an early indication of his orientation in the post of U.N.D.P. Administrator, and of his vision for the U.N.'s potential to act as an instrument for legitimizing global capitalism, when he addressed the New York Chapter of the Society for International Development in January 2000. Speaking in the immediate aftermath of the Seattle meeting of the W.T.O. and the protests that surrounded it, he identified a "crisis of legitimacy" facing the I.M.F. and the W.T.O., offered the opinion that the U.N.D.P. had lost ground over recent years to the World Bank, and defined a new role for the U.N.D.P.:

> If we can use our development assistance to create the environment of laws, physical infrastructure and education which will attract private capital, there is a potentially powerful partnership between public development assistance and private capital which can leverage our reserve way the heck beyond what has been possible in the past.[25]

Agencies such as U.N.D.P. were no longer to be seen as "instruments of transfer of development assistance from North to South, but as a catalytic force for helping the South seize the opportunities available to it in this changing world"; and the present moment, despite the widespread sense of crisis, could be "a really historic moment for development": a moment where, even with modest means, an organization like U.N.D.P., which enjoys an extraordinary global platform and convening power, a bully in the pulpit from which to argue for change in the world, that the possibilities of driving change "have never been better." Identifying himself at this point as "a completely self-confessed liberal free trader" (and attributing his convictions to Barbara Ward and *The Economist*), he set out the agenda that he had promoted at the World Bank under Wolfensohn: free trade will promote growth only if government provides the right environment and management; the U.N.D.P., now, should therefore help countries "develop the right policies and the right institutions that will allow them to manage their successful integration into the global economy"; this required it "to help them with the national institutions of political governance that they want to see strengthened when they ask it of us," and "to help them develop the institutions of managed market economies." This is the authentic voice of the new imperialist project: interventionist in the extreme, and committed to engineering fully fledged market economies in the developing world at the request of the leaderships of those countries themselves; intended to create states capable of leading a process of integration into the global capitalist economy; and led by the international institutions in accordance with a universal model. By the time that the M.D.G.'s were proposed and agreed, an enabling framework for achieving them was fully in place, promoted by the Secretary-General, overseen by the High-Level Committee on

Programmes (H.L.C.P.), and involving the concerted action of the principal development arms of the U.N. (ECOSOC, U.N.C.T.A.D., and U.N.D.P.), closely coordinated with the Bretton Woods institutions and the W.T.O., with the explicit purpose of building the capacity for capitalist development around the world.

THE HIGH-LEVEL ROAD TO MONTERREY

The terms of reference of the H.L.C.P. approved by the U.N.'s Administrative Committee on Coordination in October 2000 make explicit the broader strategic context in which the M.D.G.'s were set from the start. The H.L.C.P. was made responsible to the A.C.C./C.E.B. for "fostering system-wide cooperation and coordination as well as knowledge and information sharing in policy, programme and operational areas"; it was to "foster and support the integrated and coordinated preparation of and follow-up to major U.N. conferences and summits, *including in particular the Millennium Summit*" (emphasis mine); its focus would be on emerging issues and challenges around globalization and poverty; and it would address effective programme implementation at country level.[26] Its character as the nerve centre of the new imperialism emerged clearly from the delineation of the manner in which this was to be achieved. It would "share experiences on policy development, programming and monitoring modalities, such as results-based approaches and the integration of statistics and indicators into policy formulation," with special attention to "enhancing the capacity of the system and member countries to assess and measure progress in the pursuit of agreed international goals, and to streamlining requirements for national reporting"; it would "foster dialogue and propose ways in which the collaboration and interaction with the private sector, N.G.O.'s and other parts of civil society can be enhanced, and can contribute to the achievement of agreed system-wide goals"; it would "facilitate dialogue on the implications of the reform processes within the system for programme and operational activities, and identify best practices; and adopt innovative, timely and cost effective working mechanisms, including the consideration of policy themes and clusters, the establishment of time-bound task forces and other ad-hoc machinery, and the related designation of lead agency or agencies"; and it would "review existing subsidiary structures with a view to their streamlining and . . . keep any new arrangements under review."

At its first meeting, the H.L.C.P. took as the first substantive point on its agenda the follow-up to the Millennium Declaration, considering in turn three strategic topics: poverty eradication and development, Africa, and the global agenda and global public goods. On poverty eradication and development it agreed that the "comprehensive and authoritative policy framework provided by the Millennium Declaration" created the opportunity for the Committee to become "a key agent of system-wide change and progress", and for the M.D.G.'s themselves to be "the driving force of the work of the system as a whole." It was essential, for this to be achieved, that "each organization should 'internalize' the poverty eradication goals embodied in the Millennium Declaration and for all organizations to join in a major advocacy effort in support of those goals." Each one should assess the analytical contribution it could make, and "the analyses should provide the basis for the development of a comprehensive framework within which relevant initiatives and activities would be introduced and placed in relation to each other."[27] On Africa, it identified "strong imperatives for working towards a unified framework of action by the United Nations system," in which the guiding principle should be "realism, urgency, efficiency, and, most of all, African leadership and ownership of programmes"; and it noted the "recent initiative of three African Presidents (Presidents Bouteflika, Mbeki, and Obasanjo) for an African recovery and renaissance plan" as a promising point of departure – the plan that would eventually become the New Partnership for Africa's Development (N.E.P.A.D).[28] On the global agenda and global public goods, it considered a note prepared for the World Bank, and agreed to initiate a discussion with outside experts in order to identify priority public goods related to the poverty eradication agenda.[29] The record of this and subsequent meetings of the H.L.C.P. provide rich evidence of the systematic development of the new imperialist project outlined here, and the effort to infuse the same comprehensive logic through the strategic initiatives leading to the 2005 Summit.

If the adoption of the M.D.G.'s laid the institutional framework for the new imperialist project and for selling it as a humanitarian venture, the decisive steps in developing its content and generating the environment in which the governments of developing states would be led to embrace it, came with a series of other initiatives: the Brussels Declaration and Programme of Action adopted at the third U.N. Conference on Least Developed Countries in May 2001; the Secretary-General's "Road Map

Towards the Implementation of the United Nations' Millennium Declaration" adopted by the U.N. General Assembly in September 2001; and the report of the High-Level Panel on Financing for Development appointed by Kofi Annan in December 2000, leading to the landmark "Monterrey Consensus" in March 2002. While it is not possible, or necessary, to detail every aspect of the coordination of the new imperialist project across U.N. agencies and other international organizations in the immediate aftermath of the adoption of the M.D.G.'s, these initiatives require specific attention, not only because they confirmed the commitment of the U.N. system to capitalist development worldwide, but also because they put in place and endorsed a system of U.N. monitoring and review explicitly aimed at constructing bourgeois hegemony in least-developed and developing states.

The Brussels Declaration agreed at the Conference on Least Developed Countries began by endorsing the new imperialist project in what was already its standard form. The conference participants pledged, in the "first years of the new millennium, to free our fellow women, men and children from the abject and dehumanising conditions of extreme poverty," drawing on the Millennium Declaration to commit themselves to "working for the beneficial integration of the least developed countries into the global economy."[30] There followed a ten-point declaration which stated that "the eradication of poverty and the improvement of the quality of lives of people in L.D.C.'s" would be achieved "by strengthening their abilities to build a better future for themselves and develop their countries"; and that this could only be achieved "through equitable and sustained economic growth and sustainable development based on *nationally owned and people-centred poverty reduction strategies*" (emphasis mine):

> Good governance at the national and international level; the rule of law; respect for all internationally recognised human rights, including the right to development; promotion of democracy; security through preventive diplomacy and the peaceful resolution of armed conflicts; gender equality; investment in health, education and social infrastructure; strengthening of productive capacities and institution building are all essential in order to realise the vast and untapped human and economic potential in L.D.C.'s.[31]

The declaration then went on to insist that the primary responsibility for development in the least-developed countries rested with these countries themselves, although they required "concrete and substantial international support from Governments and international organisations in a spirit of shared responsibility through genuine partnerships, including with the civil society and private sector."[32] After endorsing measures to combat the H.I.V./A.I.D.S. pandemic, and other communicable diseases, and to address desertification, the preservation of biological diversity, the supply of safe drinking water, and climate change, it then itemized one by one the elements of the new imperialist consensus and the means by which they were to be achieved: *increased trade*, to be pursued on the basis of a "transparent, non-discriminatory and rules-based multilateral trading system" and the accession of the least-developed countries to the W.T.O. through the fourth W.T.O. Ministerial Meeting in Doha in November 2001, and through the recognition of trade and growth issues in (World Bank) poverty reduction strategies; *increased domestic and foreign financing*, to be pursued on the basis of the creation of "an enabling environment for savings and investment, which includes strong and reliable financial, legal and administrative institutions, sound macro-economic policies and the transparent and effective management of public resources" through the Conference on Financing for Development in March 2002 in Monterrey, Mexico; *increased official development assistance; improved aid effectiveness;* and *debt reform and relief*, to be pursued through the H.I.P.C. framework and the enhanced H.I.P.C. initiative.[33]

The last of the ten points stressed the critical importance of "effective follow-up to the Conference at the national, regional and global level," and placed responsibility for it in the hands of the Secretary-General.[34] What this meant was spelled out in the much more detailed Programme of Action that accompanied the Declaration. It detailed, as was by now to be expected, the entrepreneurial-, productivity-, and competition-oriented character of the strategy to be pursued at national level, but also devoted a section to "Arrangements for Implementation, Follow-up and Monitoring and Review."[35] As the title suggests, it proposed a comprehensive framework for the close surveillance of the development programmes of the least-developed countries, linking the U.N.'s own Common Country Assessments (C.C.A.'s) and the United Nations Development Assistance Framework (U.N.D.A.F.) to the World Bank's Poverty

Reduction Strategy Papers (P.R.S.P.'s), and adding regional and global layers of surveillance to the scrutiny of programmes at the national level, topped off by peer review:

> The goals and targets set out in the Programme of Action will be used to review and evaluate performance of L.D.C.'s and their development partners in implementing the various commitments. Besides follow-up mechanisms identified below, such performance reviews could be facilitated by independent peer reviews of the application of commitments by individual L.D.C.'s and their partners as part of the follow-up at national, sectoral, subregional, regional and global levels.[36]

Such schemes, characteristic of meta-regulatory frameworks at all levels of contemporary neoliberalism, are common enough in the Bretton Woods institutions. The point of interest here is that the U.N. system proposed for *itself* a new role as midwife of capitalist development and promoter of global bourgeois hegemony. The Secretary-General was requested "to ensure at the secretariat level the full mobilization and coordination of all parts of the United Nations system to facilitate coordinated implementation as well as coherence in the follow-up and monitoring of the Programme of Action at the national, regional, sub-regional and global levels," and governments were instructed to ensure "the involvement of civil society, including the private sector, on the basis of a broad-based inclusive dialogue." The following paragraph disclosed the logic of the framework of surveillance and mutual emulation:

> In some L.D.C.'s, national arrangements are already in place for broad-based and inclusive dialogue on development issues and policies. These forums are critical to ensuring genuine consensus and national ownership of national programmes of action and need to be fully supported. Other L.D.C.'s should follow this example by developing such national forums.[37]

What was to be imposed and monitored was not simply the adoption of an appropriate set of macroeconomic policies, but a process of building the national hegemony of a government committed to capitalist development. As part of the process, "model" apprentices were to be accorded the honour of reviewing their peers and spreading "good practice" – precisely the strategy adopted, inter alia, for the promotion of competition policy in Latin America, and, through N.E.P.A.D., for the dissemination of neoliberal reform in Africa.[38]

Kofi Annan's September 2001 Road Map towards the implementation of the U.N. Millennium Declaration took the same line, stating at the outset that "States need to demonstrate the political will to carry out commitments already given and to implement strategies already worked out."[39] Section III of the Road Map, "Development and Poverty Eradication: the Millennium Development Goals," not only set out once again the elements of the programme, but also insisted at the outset that "It is crucial that the millennium development goals become national goals and serve to increase the coherence and consistency of national policies and programmes."[40] Buried in the middle of the document were two paragraphs that encapsulated the whole of the new imperialist project and the leading role proposed for the U.N. system in its implementation and monitoring:

> The Third United Nations Conference on the Least Developed Countries, held in May 2001, adopted a programme of action that provides a framework for a global partnership to accelerate sustained economic growth and sustainable development in least developed countries. The least developed countries and their partners are committed to fostering a people-centred policy framework; good governance at the national and international levels; building productive capacities to make globalization work for least developed countries; enhancing the role of trade in development; reducing vulnerability and protecting the environment; and mobilizing financial resources.
>
> The programme of action recognizes the important role that Governments, civil society and the private sector have to play in its implementation and follow-up, through stronger public–private partnerships. There is a critical need for an effective mechanism to support intergovernmental review and follow-up of the implementation of the programme of action; to mobilize the United Nations system, as well as other relevant multilateral organizations; and to facilitate substantive participation of least developed countries in appropriate multilateral forums.[41]

The High-Level Panel on Financing for Development, chaired by ex-President of Mexico Ernesto Zedillo, was a key component of the mobilization of the U.N. system behind the proposed programme to which Annan's Road Map referred. It illustrates further the core strategy in the development and legitimization of the new imperialist project noted above in relation to *Unleashing Development* and *Investing in Development* – the production by a carefully assembled team of "experts" of an arm's length "independent" commissioned report pre-set to deliver a message scripted in advance. As stated in the press release that announced the formation of the panel, it was a response to the U.N. Millennium Declaration and its development and poverty eradication goals. It was noted that the 2002 Financing for Development meeting to which it would make its recommendations was "mandated by the U.N. General Assembly to involve the active collaboration of the International Monetary Fund, the World Bank and the World Trade Organization, as well as representatives of civil society and the private sector," and endorsed in the Millennium Declaration, and within these tightly defined parameters the panel was charged with advising the Secretary-General on "measures he can recommend to fulfill the finance needs of the world's developing countries."[42] Its membership, also announced in the press release, reflected the strategy of engaging developed and developing countries, "civil society" (business), and N.G.O.'s: it comprised Abdulatif Al-Hammad, the President of the Arab Fund for Economic Development; David Bryer, the Director of Oxfam; Mary Chinery-Hess, former Deputy Director-General of the International Labour Organization (I.L.O.); Jacques Delors, former Finance Minister of France and President of the European Commission; Rebeca Grynspan, former Vice-President of Costa Rica; Majid Osman, former Finance Minister of Mozambique, turned commercial banker; Robert Rubin, former Secretary of the U.S. Treasury under Clinton and architect of the "rescue" of Mexico in 1994; and Manmohan Singh, former Indian Minister of Finance, and architect then and since of India's neoliberal reforms.

The March 2002 conference to which it duly reported, the First International Conference on Financing for Development, culminated in the adoption of the "Monterrey Consensus," the founding public document of the new imperialist project. The proponents of the conference were absolutely clear about the character of this intervention in the global political economy, the innovation which it represented, and the key actors involved. It is still advertised on the home page of the Conference as the "first United Nations-hosted conference to address key financial and development issues," and "the first quadripartite exchange of views between governments, civil society, the business community, and the institutional stakeholders on global economic issues"; and the presence of the leaders of the I.M.F., World Bank, and W.T.O. – Horst Kohler, James Wolfensohn, and Michael Moore, respectively – identified as "institutional stakeholders," is noted.[43] They were there to give their blessing to what was unequivocally the culmination of a process of colonizing the core U.N. institutions, including, as it happens, such one-time strongholds of national developmentalism as the Economic and Social Council, U.N.C.T.A.D. and the regional agencies E.C.L.A.C. (the Economic Commission for Latin America and the Caribbean) and E.C.A. (the Economic Commission for Africa), and remaking them as the promoters of global capitalist development.

Right at the outset, the Monterrey Consensus, prepared in advance of the meeting and adopted by acclamation, made the fundamental connection between the headline commitment to poverty reduction and the bottom-line commitment to the all-out promotion of capitalism on a global scale which is the key to the ideology of the new imperialism. Its first article declared roundly: "Our goal is to eradicate poverty, achieve sustained economic growth and promote sustainable development as we advance to a fully inclusive and equitable global economic system"; and this key document went on to call for "a new partnership between developed and developing countries, committed to sound policies, good governance at all levels and the rule of law."[44] It acknowledged that "each country has primary responsibility for its own economic and social development, and the role of national policies and development strategies cannot be overemphasized," then spelled out precisely what those policies should be:

> An enabling domestic environment is vital for mobilizing domestic resources, increasing productivity, reducing capital flight, encouraging the private sector, and attracting and making effective use of international investment and assistance. . . . We will pursue appropriate policy and regulatory frameworks at our respective national levels and in a manner consistent with national laws to encourage public and private initiatives, including at the local level, and foster a dynamic and well functioning business sector, while improving income growth and distribution, raising productivity,

empowering women and protecting labour rights and the environment.[45]

As the following paragraphs made clear, the "enabling domestic environment" was to facilitate foreign and domestic investment on equal terms, and to expose each to an environment made competitive by regulatory intervention:

> Private international capital flows, particularly foreign direct investment, along with international financial stability, are vital complements to national and international development efforts. Foreign direct investment contributes toward financing sustained economic growth over the long term. It is especially important for its potential to transfer knowledge and technology, create jobs, boost overall productivity, enhance competitiveness and entrepreneurship, and ultimately eradicate poverty through economic growth and development. . . . To attract and enhance inflows of productive capital, countries need to continue their efforts to achieve a transparent, stable and predictable investment climate, with proper contract enforcement and respect for property rights, embedded in sound macroeconomic policies and institutions that allow businesses, both domestic and international, to operate efficiently and profitably and with maximum development impact. Special efforts are required in such priority areas as economic policy and regulatory frameworks for promoting and protecting investments, including the areas of human resource development, avoidance of double taxation, corporate governance, accounting standards, and the promotion of a competitive environment.[46]

If the M.D.G.'s had become the obligatory points of reference for the intended *outcomes* of development, the Monterrey Consensus has become the obligatory point of reference for the policy framework adopted by the developing countries themselves as the means of achieving them. But as we have seen, it was the product of long and careful preparation within the U.N. system itself. Its adoption signalled the success of the new imperialist project within the U.N. system and across its membership, and established the entrepreneur, preferably indigenous and ideally female, as its emblematic figure. From this point on, it was the specific content of the Monterrey Consensus that drove the development of the U.N.'s imperialist project forward, rather than the means-neutral M.D.G.'s.

Towards the end of July 2003, U.N. Secretary-General Kofi Annan called a press conference to announce the setting up of a high-level Commission on the Private Sector and Development. According to the press briefing issued at the time, its task was "to develop strategic recommendations on how to promote strong indigenous private sectors" in the developing world.[47] The Commission had been proposed by U.N.D.P. administrator Mark Malloch Brown, who told the press conference that "the issue of building a private sector in developing countries was the critical next development challenge," adding later that "while Africa was a challenge to all involved in development, the report would not be limited to Africa. The issue of private sector development was common to the whole developing world." One of the two co-chairs of the Committee, former Chief Executive of Canada Steamship Lines and Canadian Finance Minister Paul Martin, would become leader of his country's Liberal Party and then Prime Minister later in the year. The other was ex-President of Mexico Ernesto Zedillo, of the High-Level Panel on Financing for Development which had prepared the way for the Monterrey Consensus.

The report of the Commission, cited at the beginning of the chapter, proposed to "unleash entrepreneurship" across the world. With its publication, the new imperialist project moved into the sphere of public relations, packaging the Monterrey message in a glossy brochure full of pictures, figures, and lyrical prose, courtesy of the make-over given to it by Bruce Ross-Larson, President of Communications Development Incorporated, and author of such guides to effective writing as *Stunning Sentences*, *Powerful Paragraphs*, and *Riveting Reports*:

> This report is about walking into the poorest village on market day and seeing entrepreneurs at work. It is about realizing that the poor entrepreneur is as important a part of the private sector as the multinational corporation. It is about acknowledging that the private sector is already central to the lives of the poor and has the power to make those lives better. It is about using the managerial, organizational and technological innovation that resides in the private sector to improve the lives of the poor. It is about unleashing the power of local entrepreneurs to reduce poverty in their communities and nations.[48]

THE 2005 WORLD SUMMIT: THE IMPERIALIST PROJECT UNLEASHED

As noted at the outset, the analysis and recommendations of *Unleashing Entrepreneurship*, and its more comprehensive companion-piece, *Investing in Development*, were fed directly into the September 2005 World Summit by the Secretary-General. His report, *In Larger Freedom*, placed security and human rights in the context of development, and interpreted development precisely in the terms of the Monterrey Consensus and its subsequent elaboration:

> Each developing country has primary responsibility for its own development – strengthening governance, combating corruption and putting in place the policies and investments to drive private sector-led growth and maximize domestic resources available to fund national development strategies. Developed countries, on their side, undertake that developing countries which adopt transparent, credible and properly costed development strategies will receive the full support they need, in the form of increased development assistance, a more development-oriented trade system and wider and deeper debt relief.[49]

However, with everything apparently in place for the consecration of the U.N.'s ambitious imperialist project at the World Summit in September 2005, intense conflict broke out over the wording of the document to be agreed by heads of state at the Summit. The draft outcome document was first circulated in June 2005, and by the time the second revised version was produced in August, it strongly endorsed both the M.D.G.'s and the Monterrey Consensus, along with a range of specific commitments on the part of the developed countries. It also included numerous references to the need to strengthen and extend the authority of the U.N. itself and its Secretary-General.[50] At this point the U.S. government, in the person of newly appointed Ambassador to the U.N. John Bolton, proposed extensive revisions to the text, with a clear logic: they removed all explicit commitments binding upon the U.S. government, and all references to the output targets enshrined in the M.D.G.'s, and removed or watered down all references to enhancing the authority of the U.N. At the same time, however, they left in place the policy commitments of the Monterrey Consensus, and the multiple references to the need to improve the climate for investment and support entrepreneurship in the developing world.[51]

The proposed U.S. amendments had the merit of revealing the two rival imperialist projects that were now in contention. The first was the "old" U.S. imperialism focused narrowly on national interest which refused to be bound by supranational authority; the second was the "new" U.N. imperialism which sought to place supranational authority behind a project aimed at stabilizing and legitimizing capitalism on a global scale, and demanded that *all* states commit themselves to the project. Significantly, despite their differences, both supported the export of the social relations of capitalist production and of institutions to promote and sustain them. In the end, the U.S.A. backed away from its attempt to remove all references to the M.D.G.'s, but maintained its refusal to commit to an increase in U.S. aid towards the target of 0.7 percent of GDP. However, to return to the central point, the document fully reflected the strategy of promotion of an enabling environment for both domestic accumulation and foreign investment, as spelled out in the Monterrey Consensus.[52] What is more, President Bush's address to the General Assembly underlined U.S. support for this aspect of the project. His one tepid reference to U.S. commitment to the M.D.G.'s contrasted with his enthusiasm for the Monterrey Consensus:

At Monterrey in 2002, we agreed to a new vision for the way we fight poverty, and curb corruption, and provide aid in this new millennium. Developing countries agreed to take responsibility for their own economic progress through good governance and sound policies and the rule of law. Developed countries agreed to support those efforts, including increased aid to nations that undertake necessary reforms. . . . I call on all the world's nations to implement the Monterrey Consensus. Implementing the Monterrey Consensus means continuing on the long, hard road to reform. Implementing the Monterrey Consensus means creating a genuine partnership between developed and developing countries to replace the donor–client relationship of the past. And implementing the Monterrey Consensus means welcoming all developing countries as full participants to the global economy, with all the requisite benefits and responsibilities.[53]

Bush may have had his fingers crossed behind his back when he went on to support the Doha Round and pledge that "The United States is ready to eliminate all tariffs, subsidies and other barriers to free flow of goods and services as other nations do the same,"[54] but the pledge was given all the same. Nevertheless, the commitment to the Monterrey Consensus, the Doha Round, and the elimination by all states of barriers to trade reflected acceptance by the U.S.A. of the inevitable logic of a genuinely global capitalist system, and to a broader imperialist project than it could possibly control. Whatever else had fallen by the wayside, the uncompromisingly pro-capitalist project developed by the U.N. over a decade had won universal acceptance. What is more, the endorsement of the U.N.'s global imperialist mission passed without comment.

NOTES

1. U.N. General Assembly, "Strengthening the Role of the Private Sector and Entrepreneurship in Financing for Development," Report of the Secretary-General, A/59/800, 19 May 2005, Section I, para. 1, p. 3.

2. U.N. Millennium Project, *Investing in Development: A Practical Plan to Achieve the Millennium Development Goals* (New York and London, 2005); U.N. General Assembly, "Follow-up to the outcome of the Millennium Summit", Note by the Secretary-General, A/59/727, 7 March 2005.

3. See in particular C.E.B. High-Level Committee on Programmes, "Report of the High-Level Committee on Programmes (H.L.C.P.) at its Ninth Session, Rome, Italy, 23–25 February 2005," CEB/2005/4, 21 March 2005, pp. 3–6.

4. Commission on the Private Sector and Development, *Unleashing Entrepreneurship: Making Business Work for the Poor*, Report to the Secretary-General of the United Nations, U.N.D.P., 2004, p. 23.

5. V. I. Lenin, *Imperialism, the Highest Stage of Capitalism* [1916] (Moscow: Progress Publishers, 1982), ch. 7, p. 83.

6. P. Cammack, "Making Poverty Work," in *A World of Contradictions: Socialist Register 2002*, ed. L. Panitch and C. Leys (London: Merlin, 2001), pp. 193–210.

7. P. Cammack, "Attacking the Poor," *New Left Review*, Second Series, no. 13, January–February 2003, pp. 125–134.

8. P. Cammack, "What the World Bank Means by Poverty Reduction and Why it Matters," *New Political Economy*, 9(2), 2004, pp. 89–211.

9. K. Marx and F. Engels, "Manifesto of the Communist Party" [1850], in K. Marx, *Political Writings*, vol. 1: *The Revolutions of 1848*, ed. David Fernbach (London: Penguin/New Left Review, 1973), pp. 67–98, see p. 71.

10. Ibid.

11. Lenin, *Imperialism*, ch. 5, p. 71, and ch. 7, p. 89.

12. "Secretary-General, in Address to World Economic Forum, Stresses Strengthened Partnership between United Nations, Private Sector," press release SG/SM/6153, at http://www.un.org/news/press/docs/1997/19970131.sgsm6153.html (accessed 8 September 2005), p. 1.

13. Ibid., p. 2.

14. Ibid.

15. Ibid., p. 3.

16. Ibid.

17. Ibid., p. 4.

18. U.N. General Assembly, Resolution 50/227, 24 May 1996.

19. "Fostering and Enabling Environment for Development: Financial Flows, Including Capital Flows; Investment; Trade," Report of the Secretary-General, 5 June 1997, at http://www.un.org/documents/ecosoc/docs/1997/e1997-67.htm (accessed 8 September 2005), section I, para. 14.

20. Ibid., section I, para. 11 (my emphasis).

21. Ibid., section I, para. 18.

22. Ibid., section I, recommendations 2–4.

23. Ibid., section II, para. 61, recommendations 1 and 2.

24. Ibid., section II, para. 69, recommendation 9.

25. Mark Malloch Brown, "Development and Globalization: U.N.D.P. in the 21st Century," keynote address to the New York Chapter of the Society for International Development, 16 February 2000 (no page numbers) at http://www.undp.org/dpa/statements/administ/2000/february/29afeb00.htm (accessed 8 September 2005). All quotations in this paragraph are from the same source.

26. United Nations, Administrative Committee on Coordination (A.C.C.), "Terms of Reference of the High-Level Committee on Programmes," ACC/2001/CP/INF.2, at http://ceb.unsystem.org/hlcp/documents/hlcp_tor.pdf (accessed 8 September 2005). All quotations in this paragraph are from the same source.

27. A.C.C., "Report of the High-Level Committee on Programmes on its First Regular Session of 2001," ACC/2001/6, 13 August 2001, paras. 4, 7, 8 and 10, pp. 2–3.

28. Ibid., paras. 15 and 17, p. 4.

29. Ibid., paras. 19–22, p. 5.

30. U.N. General Assembly, "Brussels Declaration," A/Conf.191/12, 2 July 2001, at http://www.unctad.org/en/docs/aconf191d12.en.pdf (accessed 8 September 2005), p. 1.

31. Ibid., paras. 1 and 2, p. 2.

32. Ibid., para. 3, p. 2.

33. Ibid., paras. 6–9, pp. 2–3.

34. Ibid., para. 10, p. 3.

35. U.N. General Assembly, "Programme of Action for the Least Developed Countries for the Decade 2001–2010," A/Conf.191/11, 8 June 2001, Section III, pp. 57–64.

36. Ibid., para. 94, p. 57.

37. Ibid., paras. 98–100, pp. 58–9.

38. On the first of these, see Paul Cammack, "'Signs of the Times': Capitalism, Competitiveness, and the New Face of Empire in Latin America," in *The Empire Reloaded: Socialist Register 2005*, ed. L. Panitch and C. Leys, (London: Merlin, 2004), pp. 256–270.

39. U.N. General Assembly, "Road Map Towards the Implementation of the United Nations Millennium Declaration: Report of the Secretary-General," A/56/326, 6 September 2001, para. 7, p. 7.

40. Ibid., para. 81, p. 19.

41. Ibid., paras. 139, 140, pp. 27–28.

42. U.N., International Conference on Financing for Development, "High Level Panel on Financing for Development," press release, 15 December 2000, at http://www.un.org/esa/ffd/przedillo1200.htm (accessed 8 September 2005).

43. U.N., International Conference on Financing for Development, home web page, at http://www.un.org/esa/ffd/ffdconf/ (accessed 8 September 2005).

44. U.N., International Conference on Financing for Development, "Final Outcome of the International Conference on Financing for Development," A/Conf/198, 1 March 2002, paras. 1 and 4, p. 2.

45. Ibid., paras. 10, 12, pp. 3–4.

46. Ibid., paras. 20–21, pp. 5–6.

47. United Nations, Press Briefing, "Secretary-General Launches Commission on Private Sector and Development at Headquarters," press briefing, New York, 25 July 2003, at http://www.un.org/news/briefings/docs/2003/UNDPbrf.doc.htm, no page numbers (accessed 8 September 2005). Subsequent quotations in this paragraph are from the same source.

48. Commission on the Private Sector and Development, *Unleashing Entrepreneurship*, p. 5.

49. U.N. General Assembly, "In Larger Freedom: Towards Development, Security and Human Rights for All," Report of the Secretary-General, A/59/2005, 21 March 2005, para. 32, p. 12 (this passage is bold in the original).

50. "Revised Draft Outcome Document of the High-Level Plenary Meeting of the General Assembly of September 2005 Submitted by the President of the General Assembly," future document, A/59/HLPM/CRP.1/Rev. 2, released at 9:30 P.M., 5 August 2005, at http://www.un.org/summit2005/documents.html (accessed 8 September 2005). Representative references to the need to enhance the authority of the U.N. appeared in paragraphs 55, 124, and 129.

51. At the time of writing (8 September 2000), a facsimile of the document as amended by the U.S.A. was available on the website of the Global Policy Forum at http://www.globalpolicy.org/msummit/millenni/m5outcomedocindex.htm.

52. U.N. General Assembly, "2005 World Summit Outcome," A/60/L1, 15 September 2005, especially paras. 24 and 25, pp. 6–8.

53. "President Addresses United-Nations High Level Plenary Meeting," 14 September 2005, at http://www.whitehouse.gov/news/releases/2005/09/20050914.html, no page numbers (accessed 16 September 2005).

54. Ibid.

INDEX

Locators in brackets refer to notes

A.B.M. Treaty 29
Abu Ghraib torture 48, 49, 50, 58, 73, 91, 99–103
academic freedom, curtailment of 62
Acharnians, The (Aristophanes) 149–50, 158
Achcar, Gilbert 130
Acheson, Dean 33
Adam Smith Institute 168
Aeschylus 150
Afary, Janet 75
Afghanistan 48
    Amanullah 57
    constitution (2004 draft) 71
    and democracy 9, 10, 11
    political Islam 73, 77
    secularism 70
    torture by Americans 98–9
    U.S. policy 36, 39
Africa 128–9, 246, 250, 254
Ahmed, Aijaz 127–8
Ahrensdorf, Peter 143
Al Arabiya 209
Alcibiades 157
Algeria 1–2, 36
Al Jazeera 209, 216
Allawi, Iyad 46
al-Qaeda 49, 58, 118
Amanullah Khan 57
American Civil Liberties Union 100
American Council for Cultural Policy 40
American cultural imperialism 220–3

the left against 199–203
the right for 203–6
see also American soft power
American Enterprise Institute (A.E.I.) 34, 168, 169, 172
American Heritage Institute 35
American Islamic Congress 70
American soft power 199, 206–7, 222–3
    Armistead 211–16
    Fraser 216–22
    Nye 207–11
Amery, Jean 102
Amnesty International 71, 96–7, 103
Anderson, Kevin 75
Annan, Kofi 229–33, 236–40, 247, 250–1, 254–5
Anti-Ballistic Missile (A.B.M.) Treaty 29
Al Arabiya 209
Aristophanes 150
    The Acharnians 149–50, 158
Aristotle 150, 164 (58, 64)
Armistead, Leigh 206–7, 211–16, 223
Ashcroft, John 48
"Athenian thesis" 143, 144, 157, 159
Austrian school of economics 168, 175

Baghdad 181
Ballistic Missile Defense (B.M.D., "Son of Star Wars) 103, 109 (62)
Battalion 316 (Honduras) 97–8
Battle of Algiers, The 7 (3)
Bayly, C. A. 120–1

BearingPoint 181
Bechtel 181
Bedford, David 163 (41)
Beirut 82 (3)
Bell, Daniel 41
Bellah, Robert 32
Ben Bella, Ahmed 7 (2)
Bentham, Jeremy 122
Berlusconi, Silvio 28
Bhutto, Zulfikar Ali 56
binarism 65–8, 80
bin Laden, Osama 27, 31, 118
bipolarity 138–9
Blair, Tony 47, 90
Bloom, Professor 26
Bobbit, Philip 114
Bolivia 180, 185
Bolton, John 255
Boot, Max 116, 224 (12)
Bourdieu, Pierre 204
Brecht, Bertold 193
Bremer, Paul 21, 37, 167
British Empire 13, 46, 170, 209
    nostalgia for 116, 117, 118–30, 131 (2),
        132 (23)
Brown, Gordon 230
Brown, Mark Malloch 231, 232, 240, 243,
    254
Brown, Wendy 92
Bryer, David 251
Brzezinski, Zbigniew 26, 41
Bukharin, Nikolai 172, 179, 192
Bush, George W.
    Arab world 35
    Ballistic Missile Defense plan 103
    democracy 9, 21, 22
    imperial aspirations 47
    Iraq 38, 41, 45, 47, 58, 90
    and Tocqueville 26, 42
    U.N. imperialism 256–7
    war on terror 50, 58
Bush, Laura 48
Bush administration
    democracy 10–11, 17, 18, 21
    Iraq 3, 103, 118, 204–5
    Islamic fundamentalism 61–2
    National Security Strategy 115, 204–5
    neoconservatism 81, 172, 204–5, 211

neoliberalism 171
pre-emptive doctrine 114, 137, 138
soft power 208, 211, 217
Straussian influence 137, 138
U.N. imperialism 230

Cairo 82 (3)
Camus, Albert 7 (2)
capital flow, ending barriers to 185–7
capitalism 51–2
    American cultural imperialism 200,
        204
    and democracy 11–17, 18, 20, 22
    and essentialism 67
    "frictionless" 113
    "gangster" 51
    "gentlemanly" 122
    neoliberalism 169, 171, 177–80, 182,
        184, 187, 190–1, 193
    nostalgia for empire 111, 112, 122, 130
    and secularism 76
    structural shifts in 4–5, 6
    U.N. imperialism 230–6, 239, 241–2,
        249–50, 252, 257
Carter, Jimmy 218
Carter administration 138
Castro, Fidel 50
Center for Public Integrity 41
Central Intelligence Agency (C.I.A.) 36,
    99, 100, 200, 208
Chalabi, Ahmed 45, 57, 58
Cheney, Dick 182
Chibber, Vivek 115
Chicago School 50
Chile 200
China 19–20, 31, 54
Chinery-Hess, Mary 251
Chomsky, Noam 33
Churchill, Winston 118
C.I.A. 36, 99, 100, 200, 208
circuit of capital 177–8, 186, 190–2, 193
civilization 52–3
Clarke, J. 224 (13)
class relations 11–12, 14, 17–19, 112
Cleon 144, 146, 153–4, 157
Clinton, Hillary 48
Clinton administration 113, 172, 202, 230
"Clinton Doctrine" 113

Coca-Cola Corporation 218
Cochrane, C. N. 145, 162 (31)
Code, Lorraine 66
Committee on Un-American Activities 30
commodification 180
computer network attack (C.N.A.) 213
Congo 31
Conrad, Joseph, *Heart of Darkness* 87–9, 103–4
consumerism 191, 200, 201
consumer sovereignty 174
Cornford, F. M. 145, 163 (41, 51)
Cox, Robert 139
credit 191–2
Croix, G. E. M. de Ste. 162 (31)
Crucible, The (Miller) 29
cultural imperialism, American 220–3
the left against 199–203
the right for 203–6
see also soft power, American
cultural relativism 63
Curzon, Lord 123, 124, 125

Davis, Mike 122, 123, 124–5
Delors, Jacques 251
democracy 9–11, 19–23
and capitalism 11–17, 18–19, 20, 22
and colonial legacy 129
and Islam 57
neoconservatism 114–15
Spengler 52
U.S. 9–11, 13–14, 17–23
and Tocqueville 25, 26, 27, 28, 29, 31, 36
Democritus 145, 161 (24)
De Soto, Hernando 182–4
dialectics 68, 72, 73, 78, 79
dichotomization, critique of 65–6, 78
difference feminism 74–5
Diodotus 154, 156
dirigisme 170
Djerejian, Edward P. 27
Dorfman, Ariel 200
Dorrian, G. 224 (12), 225 (15)

East India Company 120, 121
Ebadi, Shirin 73, 74
Egypt 21, 36, 57, 77, 129–30

electronic warfare 213
Elgin, Lord 124
Elkins, Caroline 135 (90)
El Salvador 96–7
Engels, Friedrich 235
English capitalism 5, 12, 13
English language 203, 210
entrepreneurship, and U.N. imperialism 233, 238, 241, 253–4, 256
Esposito, John 84 (22)
essentialism 65–8
ethical issues, and Ignatieff 91–3, 95, 100–1
eugenics 30, 63
Euripides 150
The Women of Troy 149
European Bank for Reconstruction and Development (E.B.R.D.) 230
European Union 28, 73, 230
executions 31

"failed states" rhetoric 188–9
Faisal 129
Fay, Major General George 100
Feinstein, Diane 41
feminism 65–7, 76–7, 80–1
Islamic 77–8
Ferguson, Niall 111, 116–22, 124–31, 132 (19), 135 (90, 91)
fetishism 88–9, 105
feudalism 73
Foster, John Bellamy 172
Foucault, Michel 75
Foundation for the Defense of Democracies 70
France 112
Fraser, Donald 82 (3)
Fraser, Mathew 206–7, 216–22, 223
Freeman, A. 194 (6)
Freud, Sigmund 106 (7), 109 (67)
Friedman, Thomas 205
Fukuyama, Francis 9, 50, 51, 114, 132 (23), 137

Gaddis, John Lewis 117
Gandhi, Mahatma 45
gangster capitalism 51
Gates, Bill 113

gender 61, 64, 69–81
General Agreement on Trade in Services
  (G.A.T.S.) 184–5
Geneva Conventions 49
Giap, Vo Nguyen 50
Gindin, Sam 187
global capital 14–16, 23
global inequality 179–80
globalization 4, 113
  and democracy 15–16, 22
  nation-state's importance 187
  and neoliberalism 113, 170, 187
Gowan, Peter 129
Gramsci, Antonio 222
Great Britain
  and Afghanistan 57
  Atlanticist orientation 29
  empire 13, 46, 170, 209
    nostalgia for 116, 117, 118–30, 131
      (2), 132 (23)
  English capitalism 5, 12, 13
  and Iraq 46, 47
  neoliberalism 168
  public opinion, manipulation of 32
  secularism 70
Grenada invasion 113
Grynspan, Rebeca 251
Guantanamo Bay 49, 103, 108 (49)
guerrilla warfare 50
Guevara, Che 50
Gulf War (1991) 113
Guyatt, N. 224 (14)

Halliburton 40, 182
Halliburton, Earle 182
Halper, S. 224 (13)
Al-Hammad, Abdulatif 251
Hardt, Michael 20
Harvey, David 5, 178–9, 184, 191
Hashemite monarchy 129
Heart of Darkness (Conrad) 87–9, 103–4
Hegel, G. W. F. 51, 68
hegemony and empires, distinction
  between 171
Heraclitus 68
Herodotus 150, 151–2
Hilferding, Rudolf 172, 179, 192
Hobbes, Thomas 147

Homer, *The Iliad* 148–9
Honduras 97–8
Hong Kong 132 (23)
Hudson Institute 35
human rights issues 91–5, 103
  see also torture by Americans
Huntington, Samuel 9, 35, 50–3, 54, 57
Hussein, King 129

Ibn Saud 129
Ignatieff, Michael viii, 26, 87–105
Iliad, The (Homer) 148–9
Independent Women's Forum (I.W.F.) 70
India 13, 120–8, 132 (23)
Indian Mutiny 121, 126
Indonesia 55, 56
information operations, American soft
  power as 211–16
Institute of Economic Affairs 168
International Committee of the Red
  Cross 99
International Court of Justice 29
internationalization
  of capital 173, 179, 188, 190
  of state functions 188
  see also globalization
international military information
  (I.M.I.) 214
International Monetary Fund (I.M.F.)
  Annan's Road Map 251
  capitalism 230, 234–5
  Huntington 53
  Monterrey Consensus 252
  neoliberalism 92, 170, 173
  and U.N. reform 240–1, 243, 244, 245
international public information
  (I.P.I.) 214
Iran
  C.I.A. 36
  clerical regime 58
  gender 71, 76–7
  Nobel peace prize (2003) 73, 74
  political Islam 63, 71, 72, 74, 75, 76–7
  revolution 63, 75, 117–18
Iraq 4
  Constitution (2005 draft) 70–1
  democracy 10–11, 21
  Democrats 138

elections (2005) 37
Ferguson 118
Gulf War (1991) 113
ideologies and lies 2, 3
Ignatieff 89–90, 93
insurgency 2
Islam 45–50, 56, 57–8
military orders 167–8, 181, 184
national culture, confiscation of 40–1
Negroponte 97
neoconservatism 204–5
neoliberalism 168, 180–2, 184, 189
political Islam 72, 73, 77, 80
Provisional Ruling Council 37
and secularism 70
and Tocqueville 25, 27, 35–6, 37–42
Iraq Revenue Watch 41
Ireland, Republic of 12
Islam and Muslims
demonization 35, 54–9, 62–3
political Islam 63–4, 69–81
stereotypes 28
Islamic feminism 77–8
Israel 27, 28, 39
U.S. policy towards 27, 30, 35, 46–7,
57, 63
Istanbul 82 (3)
Italy 28, 32

Jamaat-i-Islami 55
Jay, Nancy 65
Al Jazeera 209, 216
Jefferson, Thomas 26
Joint Vision 2010 and *Joint Vision 2020*
212
Judt, Tony 39

Kagan, Robert 34, 114, 205
Kagarlitsky, B. 194 (6)
Kant, Immanuel 114
Kaplan, Robert D. 132 (22)
Kass, Leon 137
Kellog, Brown & Root (K.B.R.) 182
Kenya 130
Keyes, Alan 137
Keynesianism 173
Khalilzad, Zalmay 39, 58

Khomeini, Ayatollah 63, 75, 77, 118
Kissinger, Henry 34
Kohler, Horst 252
Korean War 133 (35)
Krauthammer, Charles 224 (12)
Kristol, Irving 137, 203
Kristol, William 137, 224 (12)
Kumar, Deepa 81
Kurds 80, 81
Kurtz, Stanley 224 (12)
Kyoto Protocol 29

labor, division of 18, 20, 22
bin Laden, Osama 27, 31, 118
Lal, Deepak 168, 169–72, 175–7, 179, 187,
188–9, 193
Lawrence, T. E. 57
Lebanon 21, 37, 40
Lenin, Vladimir Ilich 68, 172, 179, 192,
230, 233, 234, 236
Lewis, Bernard 51, 56
"liberal" international economic order
(L.I.E.O.) 170–1
Liberty Institute 168
Lipset, Seymour Martin 41
litigiousness, U.S. 32
Livingstone, David 118
Locke, John 13, 122
Luther, Martin 76
Luxemburg, Rosa 172
lynchings 30
Lytton, Earl of 123, 124, 126

MacArthur, General Douglas 133 (35)
Macaulay, Thomas Babington 118, 125
MacMillan, Margaret 109 (66)
Madison, James 18
Malthus, Thomas 122, 123, 124, 126, 164
(64)
Mamdani, Mahmood 128–9
Mann, Thomas 54
Manuel, Trevor 230
Mao Zedong 50
Marcuse, Herbert 33
Martin, Paul 230, 254
Marx, Karl
Aristotle's influence 164 (64)

Marx, Karl – *continued*
  circuit of capital 177–8, 186, 190, 191, 193
  class relations 139
  dialectics 68
  feminism 62
  fetishism 106 (7)
  Manifesto of the Communist Party 235
  primitive accumulation 4–5, 234
  religion 76, 83 (21)
Marxism 71, 72, 75, 168
  American cultural imperialism 220, 221, 223
mass media *see* media
Mattelart, Armand 200
Mau Mau uprising 130
Mayer, Karl E. 111
McDonald's Corporation 218
media
  freedom of the press 82 (3)
  Iraq war 47–8
  Italy 28
  public opinion, manipulation of 32–3
  U.S.A. 32–3
    American cultural imperialism 199–204, 223
    American soft power 209, 215–16, 221
Mesopotamia 129
militarism
  and capitalism 5–6, 16
  and democracy 10, 13, 16, 20
  U.S.A. 3–4, 5, 10, 20, 92, 103, 204–5
Mill, John Stuart 122
Miller, Arthur, *The Crucible* 29
Mills, C. Wright 33
Mitterand, François 7 (2)
Monroe Doctrine 34
Monterrey Consensus 231, 247, 251–7
Moore, Michael 252
More, Thomas, *Utopia* 12
Morgenthau, Hans 34, 143
Morocco 36
Mossadeq, Dr. 63
Mubarak, Haida 79
Muravchik, Joshua 205–6, 224 (12)
Muslim Brotherhood 21

narcissism, imperial 87–105
National Security Act 1947 (U.S.A.) 31
Negri, Antoni 20
Negroponte, John 97–8
neoclassical economics 174–5, 176, 177, 185–7, 192
neoconservatism 3, 4, 34, 54, 62, 113–15
  American cultural imperialism 202–3, 204–5
  American soft power 209, 211, 219, 223
  gender 80–1
  Lal 168, 172
neoliberalism 4
  American soft power 199, 206–7, 211, 219, 223
  belief system 174–7
  circuit of capital 177–8
  contradictions of the system 190–2
  and democracy 16–17, 22
  ending barriers to capital flow 185–7
  enforcing "reforms" 187–9
  ever-expanding market place 178–82
  Ferguson 118
  Fukuyama 114
  and globalization 113, 170
  Ignatieff 92
  material and social roots 172–4
  under Pax Americana 167–93
  "revolution" 233, 235
  right to property 182–5
  U.N. imperialism 239
New Bridge Strategy 41
New World Information and Communication Order (N.W.I.C.O.) 201, 202
Nicaragua 138
Nicias 156–7
Nietzsche, Friedrich 147, 162 (33)
Nineteen Eighty-Four (Orwell) 130–1
Nizan, Paul 1
Nobel peace prize 73, 74
Non-Aligned Movement 201, 219
Norton, Ann 144, 160 (2)
nostalgia for empire 111–31
Nye, Joseph F. 206–11, 217, 223

Office of Public Diplomacy, U.S. State
    Department 208
Office of Strategic Influence 212
oil
    Iraq war 4, 58, 189
    and the U.S. global strategy 54
Open Door policy 19–20
Open Society Institute 41
Organization for Economic Cooperation
    and Development (O.E.C.D.) 230
Organization of the Islamic
    Conference 36
Orientalism 64, 69, 74, 75, 76, 126
Orwell, George, *Nineteen
    Eighty-Four* 130–1
Orwin, Clifford 144, 161 (10), 163 (49)
Osman, Majid 251
Ottoman Empire 129

Pahlavi, Mohammed Reza 63
Pakistan 36, 51, 55–6
Palestine 27, 47, 57, 129
Palley, T. 173
Palloix, Christian 173, 179
Panama invasion 113
Pangle, Thomas 143–4
Panitch, Leo 187
patriarchy 66, 67
    political Islam 73, 74, 75–6, 77, 79,
        80–1
Patriot Act (U.S.A.) 31
Pax Americana, neoliberalism
    under 167–93
Peloponnesian war 141–8, 151, 153–5,
    158–9
penal regime, U.S.A. 31
Pericles 144, 156, 157
Perle, Richard 137, 172
Pinochet, General Augusto 200
Plato 140, 146, 150, 153, 157, 164 (58, 64)
Plutarch 157
Poland 39
political correctness, U.S.A. 32
political history, Straussian
    thought 141–2, 144–5, 146
political Islam 63–4, 69–81
Pontecervo, Gillo 7 (3)
postcolonialism 94

post-structuralism 61–2, 64, 80–1
    critique of binarism and essential-
        ism 65–8
    imperialism, secularism, and gender
        relations 69–80
privatization 4, 5, 21
    Iraq 167, 180–2
    neoliberalism 168, 180–2
Prohibition 30
Project for the New American
    Century 172
propaganda 206, 211, 212, 215–16
property
    right to 182–5
    theory of 12–13

al-Qaeda 49, 58, 118
quantity theory of money 186
Quit India Movement 128
Qur'an 72, 74, 76, 78–9

racism 11, 35, 63, 69, 103
Rand Corporation 34
Reagan, Ronald 101–2, 138
Reagan administration 202
Realism 138, 139, 143–4, 159
Red Cross 38, 99
Regalado, Dr. Hector Antonio
    ("Dr. Death") 97
relativism 67
religious belief
    China 54
    Huntington 52, 53
    India under the Raj 125
    Marx and Marxism 72, 76, 83 (21)
    Russia 54
    secularism 69–80, 81
    U.S.A. 35, 53–4
    see also Islam and Muslims
Roman Empire 171
Romero, Archbishop 97
Ross-Larson, Bruce 254
Rothko, David 203–4
Royai, Yadollah 74
Rubin, Robert 251
Rumsfeld, Donald 3, 29, 45, 101
Russia 54
Ryan, Susan 67

Sachs, Jeffrey 232, 236
Sadat, Anwar 36
Saddam Hussein 37, 38, 45, 70, 89–90, 93
Said, Edward 64, 69, 126
Salem witch trials 29
Saudi Arabia
    democracy 57
    Islam 55, 57
    resistance 48
    secularism 69–70
    and U.S. Afghan engagement 36
    U.S. policy towards 36, 46–7, 57, 63
Sayyid, Bobby 71–2
Scarry, Elaine 100
Schiller, Herbert 200
Schmitt, Carl 34, 50
School of the Americas (S.O.A.) 97, 99
secularism 69–80, 81
September 11 attacks 54, 58
Shaikh, Anwar 186
sharia 72–3, 74, 76, 78
Shorris, Earl 137
Sicilian expedition 151, 156–7
Singapore 132 (23)
Singh, Manmohan 251
Singh, Uday 135 (91)
Sistani, Ayatollah 57
slavery 118–19, 186
Smith, Adam 171, 174, 192
social Darwinism 35
soft power, American 199, 206–7, 222–3
    Armistead 211–16
    Fraser 216–22
    Nye 207–11
Somalia 113
"Son of Star Wars" (Ballistic Missile
    Defense) 103, 109 (62)
Sontag, Susan 102–3
Sophocles 150
space, weaponizing and
    commodifying 103, 213
Spain 29
Spengler, Oswald 35, 52–3
Spivak, Gayatri Chakravorty 67
Stabile, Carol 81
Starr, Kenneth 31
Steele, James 96
Stern, Nicholas 236

Stiglitz, Joseph 236
strategic essentialism 67
"strategic hamlets" scheme 50–1, 135 (90)
Strauss, Leo 50, 137, 140, 143–6, 152, 160
    (3)
Straussian influence 137, 138, 139–48,
    154, 159–60
structuralism 64, 66–7
Suharto, General 55
Syria 57

Taguba Inquiry 48
Taliban 63
taxation, Iraq 167
Tehran 82 (3)
telecommunication system,
    global 199–200
Temple, Sir Richard 123, 124
Thatcher administration 202
Thucydides 139–40, 141–59, 160
Tocqueville, Alexis de 25–42
Tomlinson, John 202
torture by Americans 48–9, 50, 58, 98–9
    Ignatieff 91, 99–103
Truman Doctrine 36
Turkey 63, 72, 77

United Kingdom see Great Britain
United Nations
    Brussels Declaration 246–50
    Commission on the Private Sector and
        Development 254
    Convention Against Torture and Other
        Cruel, Inhuman or Degrading
        Treatment or Punishment 101
    Convention on the Elimination of All
        Forms of Discrimination
        Against Women 83 (15)
    Economic and Social Council
        (ECOSOC) 240, 243, 245, 252
    El Salvador 97
    High-Level Committee on
        Programmes (H.L.C.P.) 244–6
    Huntington 53
    imperialism 229–57
    Iraq 38

Millennium Development Goals
(M.D.G.s) 229, 231–3, 236,
244–7, 253–6
Monterrey Consensus 231, 247, 251–7
reform 232, 239–45
Road Map Towards the Implement-
ation of the Millennium
Declaration 247, 250–1
United Nations Conference on Trade and
Development (U.N.C.T.A.D.) 240,
243, 245, 252
United Nations Development Program
(U.N.D.P.) 240, 243–4, 245
United Nations Education and Scientific
Organization (U.N.E.S.C.O.) 42,
201, 202, 219
United Nations Security Council 29
United States Institute for Peace 42
U.S.S. *Cole* 93
U.S. War Crimes Act 1996: 49
Utopia (More) 12

Veblen, Thornstein 33
Vellacott, Philip 162 (35)
Victoria, Queen 124
Vidal, Gore 42 (1)
"Vietnam syndrome" 113
Vietnam War 50–1, 95–6, 113, 117, 135
(90), 138
Voegelin, Eric 147
Voice of America 208

Wacquant, L. 204
Waltz, Kenneth 138–9
Wallerstein, Immanuel 205
Walzer, Michael 9
Ward, Barbara 244
war on terror

American soft power 214–15
and democracy 10, 22
human rights abuses 103
Islam 54
neoliberalism 171
post-structuralism 61–3
"Washington consensus" 178
water systems 180, 184–5
Wattenberg, Ben 203, 224 (12)
Weber, Max 164 (64)
Wendt, Henry 169
Whitehead, Alfred North 147–8
Wilson, Woodrow 117
Winspear, A. D. 163 (42)
Wolfensohn, James 244, 252
Wolfowitz, Paul 38, 137, 172
Women for Women International 70
Women of Troy, The (Euripides) 149
Workman, Thom 163 (41)
World Bank
Annan's Road Map 251
capitalism 230, 234–5
Heavily Indebted Poor Countries
(H.I.P.C.) initiative 230, 248
Monterrey Consensus 252
neoliberalism 92, 170, 173
poverty reduction strategies 232,
234–5, 248, 249
and U.N. reform 240, 242, 243, 244,
245
water commodification 184
World Trade Organization (W.T.O.) 185,
230, 241–1, 243–5, 248, 251, 252

Zakaria, Fareed 115
Zedillo, Ernesto 230, 251, 254
Zia-ul-Haq, General 36, 51
Zizek, Slavoj 3